Comic Women, Tragic Men

A Study of Gender and Genre in Shakespeare

LINDA BAMBER ──────────────────────────

Comic Women, Tragic Men
A Study of Gender and Genre in Shakespeare

STANFORD UNIVERSITY PRESS   1982
STANFORD, CALIFORNIA

Stanford University Press
Stanford, California

©1982 by the Board of Trustees of the
Leland Stanford Junior University

Printed in the United States of America

ISBN 0-8047-1126-7

LC 81-51903

For Fred

Contents

Acknowledgments

I am deeply grateful for the help I had from friends and relations while I was writing this book. Most particularly I want to acknowledge the contributions of my sister, Patsy Vigderman, who was at various times the manuscript's first and best reader, editor, and agent. One chapter in particular, "After Tragedy: *The Tempest*," has benefited from her work on it.

Many other friends read the manuscript in various forms and have supported my work in important ways: Sylvan Barnet, Marjorie Berger, Marianne De Koven, Eva Hoffman, Elizabeth Mayers, Bernard and Jane McCabe, and Rich Moran. I would also like to thank Jay Cantor, Philip Finkelpearl, Michael Fixler, and Susan Lintott for their encouragement and assistance. I am grateful to my editor at Stanford University Press, Peter Kahn, for his early support of the book, and to Daveda Tenenbaum, who contributed many good ideas. Mary Caldwell typed the manuscript in a spirit of friendship to the book, and Lewis Hyde proofread it. My parents, Edythe and Alfred Vigderman, supported the enterprise all along the way.

The major intellectual debt of the book is to Martin Green, whose work has been meat and drink to me for a decade.

L.B.

Comic Women, Tragic Men

A Study of Gender and Genre in Shakespeare

Comic Women, Tragic Men

Contemporary feminist criticism was born in 1970 with the publication of Kate Millett's *Sexual Politics;*[1] but the critical stance of this book has been notably avoided by the dozens of women who have been writing as feminists since then. Millett's posture is hostile to the authors she interprets; she finds them guilty of male chauvinism and invites our angriest responses to their work. The logical conclusion of such criticism is silence. If these authors offend us, we should refuse to write about them, refuse to teach them, refuse to do our part in keeping them alive in the culture. Obviously *Sexual Politics* creates a problem for literary feminists, most of whom are in the business of teaching, discussing, and writing about literature. Some feminists have chosen to concern themselves exclusively with women authors, but most continue to be interested in male authors as well. How is a feminist to write about literature by men without proposing her own silence? How is a critic to write as a feminist without dismissing her subject, if her subject is writing by men? Everyone who worries about these issues comes up with a different answer. My own subject in this book is Shakespeare, and the book itself must be my best answer to these questions. But perhaps it is worth acknowledging here that my own answers have been partially shaped by my resistance to the ground-breaking work of other people in my field. In this book I am in reaction against a tendency for feminist critics to interpret Shakespeare as if his work directly supports and develops feminist ideas. In *Shakespeare and the Nature of Women,* for instance, Juliet Dusinberre argues that Renaissance feminism is a major influence on Shakespeare's work;[2] in " 'O my most sacred lady': Female Metaphor in *The Winter's Tale,*" Patricia Gourlay finds in *The Winter's Tale* "the triumph of female values over the masculine social order";[3] in "*The Taming of the Shrew:* Shakespeare's Mirror of Marriage," Coppelia Kahn reads *The Taming of the Shrew* as an ironic statement on patriarchal conventions of marriage.[4] And the list could be extended. These critics have solved the problem I describe by assimilating Shakespeare into the system of feminist ideas; my response to their work, important as it has been to my thinking, is to insist on Shakespeare's indifference to, independence of, and distance from this system. My approach locates the feminism in the critic—not in the author or even the work.

My reasons for taking this approach are easy enough to explain. Shakespeare's work, as I understand it, is as likely to defy the effort of assimilation as to yield to it. An article by Myra Glazer Schotz illustrates the problem.[5] Schotz finds a progression in Shakespeare's later plays toward a recognition of the Mother. The reunion of Perdita and Hermione in *The Winter's Tale* is the climax of her story. But then, as Schotz herself points out, Shakespeare goes on to write *The Tempest,* where "the mother again disappears." From Schotz's point of view *The Tempest* is simply a disappointment; she calls it "a retraction." As a value system, therefore, the feminist ideas of this article are in conflict with our evaluation of Shakespeare as a whole. Only some plays can be grouped to illustrate a progression toward the feminist desiderata, however we define the desiderata themselves. Only some plays, or some portions of some plays, can satisfy our desire as feminists to share common ground with this great writer.

The sharpest contradiction of all is between the tragedies and the comedies. In the comedies Shakespeare seems if not a feminist then at least a man who takes the woman's part. Often the women in the comedies are more brilliant than the men, more aware of themselves and their world, saner, livelier, more gay. In the tragedies, however, Shakespeare creates such nightmare female figures as Goneril, Regan, Lady Macbeth, and Volumnia. How are we to account for these terrible portraits, charged as they are with sexual antagonism? For these characters are not just women who happen to be evil; their evil is inseparable from their failures as women. Again and again Shakespeare darkens their cruelty by locating it on the very site of our expectations of a woman's kindness. The classic example is Lady Macbeth's gratuitous fantasy of infanticide:[6]

> I have given suck, and know
> How tender 'tis to love the babe that milks me:
> I would, while it was smiling in my face,
> Have plucked my nipple from his boneless gums,

And dashed the brains out, had I so sworn as you
Have done to this.   (I.vii.54–59)

Lady Macbeth's murderous ambition is more horrible than her
husband's because a woman, as this speech reminds us, should
represent nurture and human connectedness. Lady Macbeth is not
entirely a monster; she does refrain from stabbing Duncan herself,
and her moral feelings ultimately do assert themselves in her madness. But to argue for a redistribution of sympathy in *Macbeth*, as
some feminists have done,[7] is a pretty desperate measure. Although
Lady Macbeth is not altogether evil, she is ugly enough; the
feminist argument in her favor goes against the grain of common
sense.

It is not just the ugly portraits that present difficulties in the
tragedies. We have also to account for the violent misogyny of the
very characters we feel closest to. Lear, Hamlet, Antony, and
Othello all turn on women at some point or other in hatred and
disgust. Leslie Fiedler goes so far as to identify the plays themselves
with their heroes' misogyny; in the tragedies, Shakespeare's
"hatred and fear of female sexuality pass over into hysteria," he
says,[8] citing Lear's mad rant

> Down from the waist they are Centaurs,
> Though women all above:
> But to the girdle do the gods inherit,
> Beneath is all the fiend's.
> There's hell, there's darkness, there's the sulphurous pit,
> Burning, scalding, stench, consumption, fie, fie, fie!
> Pah, pah!   (IV.vi.124–30)

The tragedies, says Fiedler, are obsessed with the dark side of
women's sexuality. The challenge Fiedler offers is sizable. The
tragedies *are* populated by castrating mothers, fiendish daughters,
bearded witches. The question of a woman's sexual constancy *is*
raised with surprising frequency, and the sexuality of an inconstant
woman is imagined in the language of disgust. Unlike the comedies, these plays present serious difficulties to critics who approach
them as feminists. At times it seems that the feminine here is as
Fiedler sees it: threatening, unpleasant, disloyal, ugly.

How then are we to reconcile the author behind the comedies
with the author of the tragedies? Some schools of criticism, of
course, would dispute the necessity of doing so. In post-structuralist

criticism the author disappears, and the contradictions of the text (in this case the entire Shakespeare canon) are its glory. But if we are interested in producing a coherent author for these plays—whether or not this author corresponds to the Shakespeare we construct from the data of his biography—we must admit that we cannot do so by testing the plays with feminist ideas. Some give one answer and some another.

If Shakespeare is not consistently a feminist, however, he is consistently an author whose response to the feminine is central to the general significance of his work. By "the feminine" I mean to imply some general principle of which the individual female characters are partial representations: Woman with a capital W. Sometimes the feminine in Shakespeare is the cultural stereotype of the feminine, the feminine that Jungians refer to. This feminine is associated with the earth, sensuality, personal relationships, imagination, intuition, nature, and so on. In their different ways Cleopatra, Miranda, Rosalind, and Queen Isabel are all versions of the Jungian feminine. But this is not the feminine in Shakespeare that interests me the most. I am interested in the feminine as a principle of Otherness; the feminine in Shakespeare may or may not be associated with nature, but it is always something unlike and external to the Self, who is male. For my purposes the crucial quality of the feminine is simple difference; the feminine here is that which exists on the other side of a barrier, the barrier of sexual differentiation. In Shakespeare the Self is always, as it were, referenced to the Other. What happens on one side of the barrier can be seen as alternately cause or effect of what exists on the other.

Critics like Dusinberre, Gourlay, and Kahn, however, imply that Shakespeare's achievement as an analyst of gender relations is in surmounting that barrier and understanding the feminine from its own point of view. They emphasize those plays or portions of plays that share the feminist vision of relations between men and women, or of women per se. But the powerful misogyny in the tragedies is surely a sign that Shakespeare is dealing with gender relations here from a masculine point of view; and to some plays, like *The Tempest,* the feminine perspective is simply irrelevant. In order to make sense of the plays that do not answer to feminist ideas, it seems more useful to assume that *all* of the plays are governed by a masculine perspective and to discuss them on that basis.

It may seem that I have come full circle, for of course masculine perspective is the issue in *Sexual Politics*. But in *Sexual Politics* masculine perspective is indistinguishable from sexism. My idea of gender perspective, whether masculine or feminine, is different from Millett's. It seems to me, first of all, inevitable. Men must write as men and women as women; male or female chauvinism is a separate issue. Sexual chauvinism assumes the *superiority* of one's own sex; gender-centered writing merely reveals the author's *sense of identification* with his or her own sex. It is natural for a writer to attribute to same-sex characters the privileges of the Self— privileges that, as we shall see, attach in Shakespeare most notably to the tragic hero. But this amounts to sexism only if the writer fails to attribute to opposite-sex characters the privileges of the Other. In Shakespeare the Self is privileged in tragedy, the Other in comedy; it is with these two genres, therefore, that I shall begin.

But Shakespeare's gender-centered relations with women are interesting not merely because the Other is privileged in one of his genres. What is most striking is that in *every* genre the possibilities for the masculine Self and the nature of the feminine are functions of one another. Masculine identity and masculine self-achievement in every genre are systematically related to the nature of the feminine in that particular mode. Each project for the masculine Self, whether the project is to go on holiday, as in the comedies, or to transcend loss, as in the romances, can be understood in terms of the feminine Other as it changes from genre to genre. What does not change is the shaping connection Shakespeare makes between Self and Other, male and female. Whenever Shakespeare comes to imagine a new enterprise for the masculine Self, he must re-imagine the feminine as necessary to resist, challenge, lead, or assist the masculine Self. Or, to reverse the cause and effect relationship, the imagination of the feminine as it changes from genre to genre determines the nature of the enterprise for the male. Neither Shakespeare nor his work, then, can be wholly assimilated to feminism. Feminism is a system in which the feminine is either a form of Self or a form of value; in Shakespeare's work it is never the former and only irregularly the latter. My claims as a feminist are limited. I claim only that the dialectic with the feminine is persistent, various, surprising, and wholehearted—not that Shakespearean drama can be consistently reconciled to feminism. Shakespeare must be a hero for feminists not because he shares the feminist perspective but because in every genre except history he associates the feminine with whatever it is outside himself he takes most seriously. Whatever most significantly challenges the masculine Self—whatever matters most in tragedy, comedy, and romance—Shakespeare associates with the feminine. It is not that he is always sympathetic to his women characters or even to their femininity; it is that after history the two genders are equal within the fiction. They balance each other as the world balances the Self. The possibilities for the masculine Self are referenced point for point in Shakespeare with what is outside that Self, and what is outside the Self is regularly associated with women. It is because women are so important a dialectical element in Shakespeare that I am interested in him—not because he offers any particular assistance in imagining the feminine as Self. Shakespeare's female characters sometimes are and sometimes are not impressive as impersonations of the opposite sex. But the dialogue between Self and Other, between the same-sex center of the world and the world as opposite sex, is always brilliant.

In tragedy the privileges of the Self are attributed to the masculine hero. The hero is to begin with *concerned* with himself; the first privilege of the Self is to have an *extra* Self who comments on or is simply aware of the original one. The tragic hero explains and justifies himself, he finds fault with himself, he insists on himself, he struggles to be true to himself. The most obvious example is Hamlet, but all the heroes have moments of dissatisfied self-scrutiny. Lear on the heath condemns himself for forgetting the poor:

> O, I have ta'en
> Too little care of this! Take physic, pomp;
> Expose thyself to feel what wretches feel,
> That thou mayst shake the superflux to them,
> And show the heavens more just. (III.iv.32–36)

Othello despairs of himself after killing Desdemona:

> I am not valiant neither;
> But every puny whipster gets my sword.
> But why should honor outlive honesty?
> Let it go all. (V.ii.243–46)

Antony accuses himself of cowardice after hearing news of Cleopatra's suicide:

> Since Cleopatra died,
> I have lived in such dishonor that the gods
> Detest my baseness. I, that with my sword
> Quartered the world and o'er green Neptune's back
> With ships made cities, condemn myself to lack
> The courage of a woman; less noble mind
> Than she which by her death our Caesar tells
> "I am conqueror of myself."   (IV.xiv.55–62)

And Macbeth's self-condemnation is saddest of all:

> My way of life
> Is fall'n into the sear, the yellow leaf,
> And that which should accompany old age,
> As honor, love, obedience, troops of friends,
> I must not look to have; but, in their stead,
> Curses not loud but deep, mouth-honor, breath,
> Which the poor heart would fain deny, and dare not.
>   (V.iii.22–28)

Paradoxically, it is because the Self is an object for the tragic hero that the tragic hero seems like a subject to us. The Self is a problem for the tragic hero in a way that it never is for the women characters. The hero cannot lay hold of his Self when he needs it most, or he discovers it to be something other than he thought. Certainly none of the women in the tragedies—Cordelia, Desdemona, Lady Macbeth, Ophelia—worries or changes her mind about who she is. One of these women, Cleopatra, seems protean; but it is not she who worries about her changes—it is Antony, and us.

The tragic heroes, moreover, give the illusion of having an inner life. They have thoughts and feelings which are hidden from the other characters and sometimes even from themselves. If they are aware of their inner thoughts they reveal them to us in soliloquies; if not, they pursue the shadows cast by what is happening inside them. Their inner lives may be revealed by what Maynard Mack has called "umbrella speeches,"⁹ speeches by other characters under which the consciousness of the tragic hero may shelter. The Fool's speeches in *King Lear* are an example: we understand from listening to the Fool what is going on inside Lear. Another umbrella is Enobarbus's description of Cleopatra on her barge. These speeches reflect the unconscious or unexpressed thoughts of the tragic heroes. Their inner life is mirrored for us even when they are silent. No such umbrella speeches shelter the consciousness of the women characters in the tragedies. Nor do they soliloquize; and only rarely do we have glimpses of something behind-the-scenes in their personalities. There are exceptional moments: Cleopatra's brief remarks to Charmian on her own technique as a courtesan; Desdemona's confidences to Emilia in the willow song scene; and, most striking of all, Lady Macbeth's madness, which reveals unsuspected elements of her personality. But even when, as in the case of Lady Macbeth, something hidden is revealed, it is only revealed to us, never to the character herself. Cleopatra and Desdemona are unsurprised by their own self-revelations; and Lady Macbeth is mad. She has no part in the struggle to articulate her shadow and to reconcile it with her conscious Self. What is missing is the sense of an identity discovering itself, judging and shaping itself. The tragic heroes observe themselves—approving and disapproving of what they are, or noticing that they are no longer what they used to be. They feel some friction between what is and what was, or between what is and what ought to be. In Lady Macbeth the resurgence of the inner life destroys the Self that might have felt this friction. Her new identity is discontinuous with her old one. She is therefore the object of moral and psychological attention only; not, like the heroes, subject and object both.

The tragic hero is privileged not only with self-consciousness and the inner life, but with the capacity to change. His experience over the course of the play makes him seem a somewhat different character at the end from what he was at the beginning. Maynard Mack goes so far as to say that "the most important thing that happens in a Shakespearean tragedy is that the hero follows a cycle of change, which is, in part, psychic change."[10] Psychic change is a prerogative of the Self; whereas the Other seems stable, for good or for ill, the Self seems fluid and unfinished. In Shakespeare's plays only characters of the author's own sex may have the fluidity of the Self. Women do not change in Shakespearean tragedy; they do not respond to the events of the play, to the suffering, with new capabilities. Ophelia and Lady Macbeth go mad; the other women simply unfold from their original premises. They may surprise us, but only because we did not understand who they were to begin with, not because they seem to have become something new.

The point can be made by comparing two minor characters, Enobarbus and Gertrude. Enobarbus, of course, is not the hero of *Antony and Cleopatra;* the play is not about *his* changes. But unlike

Gertrude and like the tragic heroes, this male character does respond to his recognition by changing. Enobarbus and Gertrude are both guilty of betraying the tragic hero, but only Enobarbus changes in response to his guilt. Enobarbus's recognition is explicit: he calls Antony "Nobler than my revolt is infamous" (IV.ix.19) and kills himself for very shame. Gertrude's recognition is only implicit, but we can infer it from her responses to Hamlet toward the end of the closet scene. "O Hamlet," she says, "thou hast cleft my heart in twain. . . . What shall I do?" (III.iv.157, 181). At this point she is willing to take direction from Hamlet, to conspire with him; presumably, therefore, she has come to see the situation as he does. And from his point of view she has betrayed him. But Gertrude never changes in response to her sense of being at fault. In her final moments she appears to have forgotten the issue entirely. She feels no strain on her relationship with Hamlet, and her attentions to him in the last scene are unaffectedly cheerful:

> The Queen carouses to thy fortune, Hamlet.
> . . .
> Come, let me wipe thy face. (V.ii.291, 296)

But of course it is not Gertrude who is absent-minded about her betrayal of Hamlet; it is her author who chooses to forget it. Enobarbus's recognition changes him from a character defined by his irony and wit into one with profoundly serious feelings. Gertrude's recognition leaves her untouched and is itself soon forgotten.

It is not only the women of doubtful morality in Shakespeare who have fixed characters: the good women are as inviolable as the bad ones are incorrigible. Cordelia and Desdemona are no more likely to change for the worse than Goneril and Regan are to change for the better. The values and loyalties of these characters seem less an accomplishment than the principles of their dramatic identity. It does not seem that such women *exert* themselves—as the heroes do—to be true to their best selves. The tragic heroes seek out or flee from conscious images of themselves; Cordelia and Desdemona, like Lady Macbeth, are not moved by their own self-perceptions. Their identities are a part they cannot help playing, not something they achieve. Self-betrayal is never an option.

The Self is masculine, then, in Shakespearean tragedy, and women are Other. But as we have seen, this is a perspective from which most feminist critics choose not to see the plays. The feminist protest against the woman as Other began with Simone de Beauvoir, who opens *The Second Sex* with this ironic summary: "Humanity is male and man defines woman not herself but as relative to him. . . . She is the incidental, the inessential as opposed to the essential. He is the Subject, he is the Absolute—she is the Other."[11] Since it is masculine definitions that are adopted by our predominantly masculine culture, this is quite an unfortunate situation for women. Because our cultural institutions are dominated by men, the cultural perspective on the feminine is almost identical to the masculine perspective and women suffer from a dearth of cultural figures for the Self. But the problem cannot be solved by requiring men to abandon their masculine perspective on women. De Beauvoir herself considers Otherness, even sexual Otherness, "a fundamental category of human thought": "The subject can be posed only in being opposed—he sets himself up as the essential as opposed to the other, the inessential, the object."[12] What de Beauvoir calls for is not an androgynous vision on the part of men but a "reciprocal claim" to be made by women, "the other consciousness." This, says de Beauvoir, is what women have been unwilling to do; but of course since 1949, when she wrote *The Second Sex,* everything has changed. Since then the reciprocal claims of "the other consciousness" have been made with such frequency that they are actually beginning to be heard by the culture as a whole. The process is circular: the culture changes in response to the claims of individual women and women in turn respond to the changing culture. One way and another, we may finally be moving away from a society with a single focal point. The culture is no longer so firmly centered on the masculine Self.

But does this mean that women will cease to be the Other in fiction by men? I presume not. I presume that heterosexuality will always involve the projection of Otherness onto the opposite sex and that this projection will be reflected in the fictions we write. Certain authors like Henry James and George Eliot have tried to create opposite-sex characters with the attributes of the Self; but this is not the goal of many writers, nor are even Eliot and James always successful in achieving it. Male and female authors are both likely to imagine the Self in terms of their own gender and the Other in terms of the opposite sex. But as women participate more and more in the life of the culture, including its literary life, more and more fiction will presumably be centered on the female Self. More and more authors will thus be projecting their sense of Otherness onto men, not women, and the score will begin to even up. Male characters in fictions by women vary as greatly as female characters in fictions by men, and they will continue to do so. They may be dull and schematic or they may be alive with the energy of their authors' fantasies. Or they may be simply adequate to their function in the story, acceptable as sex objects, love objects, marriage objects for the authors' heroines. (Jane Austen's and Kate Chopin's men fit into this third category.) Women will not necessarily do better or worse than men have done at imagining the opposite sex. Whatever the quality of the imaginative product, however, as the female imagination becomes more and more a part of our culture, so will our consciousness of the masculine Other, called into being by the needs of the female Self. Then the dialectic that de Beauvoir calls for will take place within the world of fiction itself as each sex claims to be the Self and creates the other as an Other. The claims of each sex to be the subject will be heard more equally by the culture as more and more women make them.

Meanwhile, however, a kind of dialectic is also taking place in criticism. Feminists are pointing out that critical traditions are also gender-centered and are attempting to recenter these traditions on the feminine. This enterprise is at one level a crucial corollary to the dialectic within the world of fiction; but it is important to distinguish between gender-centered criticism and criticism that would center the work of opposite-sex authors in the gender of the critic herself. Gender-centered feminists are merely conscious that they perform their readings as women, and do so intentionally. Many feminists, however, go so far as to claim that the Self is feminine even in literature by men. Here it is not just the critic who is feminine but the representatives of the Self in the fiction. Such criticism refuses to accept the Otherness of the feminine even in the consciousness of individual men. This, I think, is a mistake. Only as a cultural idea is the idea of the woman as Other susceptible to change. At the level of the individual it is as inevitable an idea as the idea of the masculine Other is in the consciousness of women. Feminist criticism fights a losing battle when it tries to center the work of men on the feminine Self.

Two examples will illustrate my point. In "Egyptian Queens and Male Reviewers: Sexist Attitudes in *Antony and Cleopatra* Criticism," Linda Fitz makes powerful arguments against what are indeed sexist attitudes in *Antony and Cleopatra* criticism. But her own interpretation of the play is a kind of equal-but-opposite distortion. For Fitz argues that Cleopatra is a "tragic hero"[13] with all the privileges of the Self, comparable not to Juliet, Rosalind, or Portia but to Hamlet, Lear, and Antony. Cleopatra *is* the co-protagonist of the play, and Fitz is right to protest her diminishment at the hands of her critics; but even as co-protagonist she is better understood as an Other than as a version of Self. Like Fitz, I prefer to compare Cleopatra to Antony than to women characters from other plays; but I shall be emphasizing the differences between her accomplishment and Antony's, whereas Fitz emphasizes the similarities. Antony's accomplishments have to do with change and the inner life; Cleopatra is at her best if we understand her not as a character in the process of change but as one whose fixed identity we apprehend through her changing, dazzling performances. There is evidence for Fitz's argument that Cleopatra "learns and grows";[14] but Cleopatra as a learning, growing Self pales beside Hamlet, Lear, or Antony. Cleopatra as Other, however, as a stable element meeting the shifting challenges to her fixed identity, is brilliant and moving. I shall argue the point at greater length in Chapter Five; here I am only concerned to distinguish between Fitz's effort to recenter *Antony and Cleopatra* criticism and her effort to recenter the idea of the Self in the play.

Carol Thomas Neely's "Women and Men in *Othello:* 'What should such a fool/Do with so good a woman?'" is another effort to center Shakespeare's fiction on the feminine. As Neely reads *Othello,* Emilia is "dramatically and symbolically the play's fulcrum."[15] She is the potential mediator between romantic idealism and sexual cynicism; the play aspires to the synthesis that she represents. The project in *Othello,* says Neely, is the same as the project in the comedies; the correction by women of the foolish romanticism of the men. In this case, the project fails. Romanticism turns into its own murderous shadow, misogyny, and "the comic resolution of male with female, idealism with realism, wit with sex is never achieved."[16] Neely's article emphasizes the play's sympathy with the feminine, its criticism of the "isolated, rigid, hostile, foolish" masculine world. She calls attention, for instance, to the contrast between the "genuine intimacy of the women" and "the hypocritical friendship of the men." The male world is to blame for the tragedy: "The men see the women as whores and then refuse to tolerate their own projections." The women, on the other hand, are "all too tolerant" of the men.[17]

There are two issues here. One is whether or not Emilia is *right,* and the second is whether or not Emilia is the fulcrum of the play, the point of view from which everything assumes its proper shape. Emilia *is* right. Things are as she sees them. Othello is "ignorant" and the men in general are "coxcombs." Emilia shares with the comic heroines a clarity of emotion that guides her to the truth. But the play does not balance on the emotional clarity of its women, as the romantic comedies do. It is about confusion, not clarity; the interest is in the ignorant, erring, angry male, not in the knowing, right-feeling woman. The comic heroine from which Emilia is descended is so sure of her feelings that she sports along the edges of emotion, teasing and playing. In *Othello* emotion is deadly serious, worked up and worked upon, not, as in the comedies, playing freely. Emilia is to *Othello* only what Macduff is to *Macbeth:* a glimpse of sanity from the horrid fascination of our madness. Neely's reading implies that we are to center the play on sanity, on Emilia, on the feminine. If we do, Othello is exasperating, his story tedious, and his death good riddance to bad rubbish.

Why is feminist criticism so often hostile to the idea of the woman as Other? Possibly because this idea has been appropriated by those who would produce not just a gender-centered male writer but an actively misogynist one. Leslie Fiedler, for instance, makes extensive use of the idea in *The Stranger in Shakespeare.* Fiedler defines the Other (or stranger) as the creature of an unconscious psychological process:

Men . . . seem impelled to invent myths whenever they encounter strangers on the borders of their world, that is to say, whenever they are forced to confront creatures disturbingly like themselves in certain respects, who yet do not quite fit . . . their definition of what it means to be human. Such creatures are defined . . . as superhuman or subhuman, divine or diabolic. . . . In either case, however, there is a considerable margin of ambivalence, since the process which underlies the creation of stranger myths is, psychologically speaking, projection: more specifically, the projection onto the venerated or despised other of human possibilities not yet developed or rejected for the sake of something else by the defining group.[18]

The woman, of course, is the first and foremost of the strangers Fiedler deals with. Fiedler claims that in Shakespeare the feminine is merely a projection, a means of avoiding the encounter with something truly external to the Self. If this were true, the plays would indeed seem sexist. When the actual feminine Other disappears and is replaced by male projections of the Other, we inevitably get antifeminist fictions. But in Shakespeare there is an Other independent of the projections of the male Self. If Shakespeare participates in his characters' projections, he also distances himself from them and creates an impression of a feminine beyond these projections, external to the Self, impermeably Other.

In four plays, *Hamlet, Antony and Cleopatra, King Lear,* and *Othello,* the projection is contained by the heroes. In *Macbeth* and *Coriolanus* the projections pervade the whole plays—and yet even here, as we shall see, an independent Other is implied. In *Hamlet, Antony and Cleopatra, King Lear,* and *Othello* the phases of the tragic fable are congruent with phases in the heroes' relationships to women. Only in the heroes' worst moments—only when, as Maynard Mack puts it, the hero has "become his own antitheses"[19]— does the misogyny break out. In these four works the play itself makes the point that projection onto women is a function of incoherence within the male Self. It is only when his sense of his own identity is threatened that the hero projects onto women what he refuses to acknowledge in himself. Only when he finds himself cowardly, appetitive, shifty, and disloyal does the sexuality of women disgust him.

In the first phase of the tragic fable, which may take place before the action begins, the hero is confident of the rules governing his world and confident of his own preeminence according to these rules. In this phase the hero has no problems with women. Think, for instance, of prelapsarian Denmark, where Gertrude, as far as Hamlet knew, was a loving wife and Ophelia the innocent recipient of Hamlet's awful love poems:

> Doubt thou the stars are fire,
>   Doubt that the sun doth move;
> Doubt truth to be a liar,
>   But never doubt I love.   (II.ii.116–19)

It is typical of the hero in this phase to be so unconcerned with the woman's constancy as to protest his own, as Hamlet does here. But something happens to make the hero question himself and his orderly world, and when it does, he turns on his women in fury and disgust. In Lear's case, what happens is old age and the loss of power; in Hamlet's case it is the murder of his father; in Othello's case it is simply the undertaking of a sexual relationship, which destabilizes his whole world. Fortune is a strumpet, and when the downward cycle of the wheel sends men out from the manageable old world, they turn on the women in their pain and accuse them of being whores. It is in this phase that we find the famous sex nausea—Antony's "Triple-turned whore" (IV.xii.13); Hamlet's "Get thee to a nunnery" (III.i.137); and Othello's "Are you not a strumpet?" (IV.ii.81). The misogyny of the heroes, sometimes justified, sometimes not, is a signal of the chaos inside them at their worst moments. Misogyny and sex nausea are born of failure and self-doubt.

Lear's misogynist outburst is one of the clearest examples of the connection between misfortune and misogyny. The speech beginning "Down from the waist they are Centaurs" comes after Lear's misfortunes but before there is reason to suspect his daughters of sexual infidelity. It is an expression of what is within him, not a response to events. In "Satire on Women and Sex in Elizabethan Tragedy," E. C. Mason comments on that passage as follows:

What is remarkable about these ravings is their irrelevancy in the situation in which they are uttered. Lear has no such reasons as Hamlet, Othello, Posthumous, and Leontes have for being tormented by the thought of adultery and incontinence. He knows nothing about Goneril's and Regan's interest in Edmund, nor is his speech to be understood as referring to that particular case; it is a universal indictment. It is as though Shakespeare were bent on projecting at the eleventh hour into a tragedy of the tension between the generations the very different tragedy of the tension between the sexes, although he thereby further overcrowds his already over-crowded action and thematic pattern.[20]

But it is not that Shakespeare is "bent on projecting . . . a tragedy of the tensions between the sexes"; rather, in Shakespeare's tragedy there is a firm connection between self-hatred, reversal of fortune, and misogyny. The hero's view of women reaches bottom at the moment when he is out of control of himself and his world; women are whores to men when it is no longer possible for men to reconcile themselves to what they are.

It is less easy to generalize about the attitudes of the heroes toward the women in the final movements of the tragedies. Hamlet

and Antony, for instance, never find out whether Ophelia and
Cleopatra are finally good or bad, but they seem to accept these
women whatever they are. Simplicity is the mark of relations
between the sexes in the final phase of the tragedies. Lear tells
Cordelia, "You must bear with me. / Pray you now, forget and
forgive. I am old and foolish" (IV.vii.83–84). Hamlet says, "I loved
Ophelia" (V.i.269) and asks his mother simply, "How does the
Queen?" (V.ii.310). Antony, after all his rage and jealousy, dies advis-
ing Cleopatra to do whatever's best for her: "One word, sweet
queen. / Of Caesar seek your honor with your safety" (IV.xv.45–46).
The resolution of the woman problem is often undramatic; we cannot put our finger on the moment when the heroes become easy in
their mind about their women or on the way in which they achieved
this ease. Only in *Othello* is there a climactic moment of recognition,
during which, among other things, Othello lets go of his misogyny
and dies "upon a kiss" (V.ii.358). But however it comes about, the
tragic resolutions of these four plays include the resolution of the
woman problem. By the end of the play the hero can distinguish a
good woman from a bad one (*Othello, Lear*) or has lost interest in the
issue altogether (*Hamlet, Antony and Cleopatra*). Only during the
middle phase do the heroes obsess about the nature of women in general. Only then does the violent misogyny erupt.

In these tragedies, then, conventional attitudes toward women
are replaced temporarily by misogyny but finally by acceptance,
even love. This movement is paralleled by a movement redefining
the idea of manhood. The sexual hatred can be more clearly understood as projection if we notice that the phase in which it appears is
also a phase in which the hero experiences a disintegration of his
manhood. In the first part of the plays the heroes are notable figures
in the world of men. They are generals, kings, triple-pillars; they
are powerful in public life, and in a specifically masculine,
political-military public life. A central value in this world of men is
physical courage, with which the heroes are all well-endowed.
Othello makes Desdemona love him by telling her

> Of moving accidents by flood and field,
> Of hairbreadth scapes i' th' imminent deadly breach,
> Of being taken by the insolent foe
> And sold to slavery, of my redemption thence . . .
>
> (I.iii.134–37)

Antony's Roman manhood is defined by Caesar in the speech on Antony's retreat from Modena:

> Thou didst drink
> The stale of horses and the gilded puddle
> Which beasts would cough at. Thy palate then did deign
> The roughest berry on the rudest hedge.
> Yea, like the stag when snow the pasture sheets,
> The barks of trees thou browsed. On the Alps
> It is reported thou didst eat strange flesh,
> Which some did die to look on.   (I.iv.61–68)

Lear is too old for adventure, but he is the king, the patriarch. Hamlet's situation is more complicated; he has not yet come into this kind of manhood, although he longs to do so. Manliness based on aggression, power, and revenge is the only option Hamlet imagines for himself at the beginning of the play, however incapable he may be of exercising that option.

The surplus value in this manly world, and that which distinguishes a hero from a Laertes or a Ventidius, is some personal trait that complements his physical or political achievements. In Antony it is the graciousness and courtesy seen in his relationships with followers and colleagues: "Let us, Lepidus,/Not lack your company" (II.ii.170–71). In Othello it is a stylish, confident dignity: "Keep up your bright swords, for the dew will rust them" (I.ii.58). This quality of confidence or graciousness enables the heroes to fill the positions of public honor to which their physical accomplishments have promoted them. The standards of masculinity by which they are at first defined are thus by no means crude; but the heroes are hurt and astonished to find such standards inadequate to the tragic world they fall into.

In the second phase of the tragedies the heroes are plagued by questions that cannot be answered with what Robert Heilbrun calls the "man-honor-fight dogma."[21] Their images and self-images as public figures begin to crumble and they come face to face with their uncertainties as private men. In their personal relationships they do not know whom to trust or when to forgive and when to hold accountable. Their feelings are unsteady and their relationships (particularly with women) are vulnerable to sudden shifts in feeling. Lear's preference for Cordelia is muddied by his egotism and he forgets to love her best; Othello lacks the emotional

confidence to make his own judgment of Desdemona. But although in the second phase the heroes may fail in a traditionally
feminine sphere—the sphere of personal relationships—it would be
wrong to say that the action of the second phase de-emphasizes the
masculine values in favor of something more gentle. Although the
masculine values of the heroes are never enough, neither are they
ever dismissable. What the heroes lack is a principle to guide them
between "manly" self-assertion and "womanly" kindness. They are
committed to a code of manliness that is inadequate to the com-
plexity of their new situation. Their confused aggression ultimately
turns against the objects of their love.

In the final phase of the tragedies, manliness, self-assertion, and
honor are no longer in competition with love and forgiveness.
Antony dies loving and forgiving Cleopatra, but he also dies faithful to the Roman values Cleopatra has opposed: "a Roman, by a
Roman / Valiantly vanquished" (IV.xv.57–58). Othello kills himself
for his private sins against Desdemona, but in his final speech he
elevates his suicide to an act of public honor. Lear dies loving and
mourning for Cordelia, but his rage at her death and his refusal to
recognize Kent are still violent self-assertions. The most interesting
example of double manliness is Hamlet. At the end of the play
Hamlet has relinquished all the enmities he himself has stirred up
and directs his aggression only at Claudius. He calls Laertes his
"brother" (V.ii.246) and tells Horatio, "by the image of my cause I
see / The portraiture of his" (V.ii.77–78). He mourns Ophelia's
death and after the closet scene accuses Gertrude no more. But
when the time comes to kill Claudius he is ready for it. "Here," he
says in a passion of hatred, "thou incestuous, murd'rous, damnèd
Dane, / Drink off this potion" (V.ii.327–28). In the fifth act Hamlet
is, as he says, "dangerous" (V.i.262); he is also gentle, forgiving,
and sweet.

In all of these four plays, then, the heroes' confidence in conventional forms of manliness is shaken and they project their sexual
disorientation onto women. Whether or not their losses are caused
by women, their bitterness takes the form of misogyny and they
associate their changing fortunes with the disgusting changes of a
woman's appetites. In these plays the projections onto women are a
function of the heroes' situation and cannot be read as the playwright's own. What can we say, then, of the two major Shakespearean tragedies in which this is not the case? In *Macbeth* and

Coriolanus the heroes do not associate their losses with female sexuality; they never denounce women in general or insult the specific women in their stories, Lady Macbeth and Volumnia. In these two plays the misogyny seems to be within the text as a whole, not within the psyche of the heroes. It seems to be Shakespeare himself who projects aggression and cruelty onto the feminine. If Shakespeare had written only these two plays, Fiedler's analysis would seem correct. These plays do not draw back, as the others do, from their heroes' projections, and we are at one level justified in attaching those projections to Shakespeare himself.

But at another level we are not. Projection involves the subject's refusal to recognize what he is doing; the term is only relevant to the degree that the process is unconscious. *Macbeth* and *Coriolanus* pay the price of their projections quite systematically; and this reckoning of costs amounts to an awareness of projection. Within the play itself there is consciousness of projection as a form of pathology. Only in these two plays is the feminine *actually* as bad as the heroes of the other four plays imagine it to be: this is the projection. Only in these two plays does the dialectic between the Self and the Other fail to take place: this is the price of projection and the sign that the text is conscious of its own process. In *Macbeth* and *Coriolanus* there is no actual Other but only our projections of otherness. The outside world is nightmarishly repetitive of the inner world in these plays. Not only are the women projections of what is unacceptable in the male Self—vicious, single-minded aggression—but the external social world lacks the alternatives that elsewhere challenge the world of men. Coriolanus's Rome is not met by an Egypt, as Antony's Rome is in *Antony and Cleopatra,* but only by its own faint echo, Antium. Scotland, similarly, is entirely a world of men, a world of public affairs and military-political antagonisms. In these two plays both the feminine Other and the Other as outside world really *are* projections of the Self; but the plays pay the price of their projections in the sacrifice of both the dialectic between Self and Other and its outcome, change in the tragic hero. In the absence of the dialectic the Self collapses, like Coriolanus, or runs down, like Macbeth. Both heroes run out of steam before their ends and repeat themselves rather than go on. These plays sacrifice the final grandeur of the tragic Self to their own nightmare projections, including projections onto women, and the sacrifice alters the genre of the plays. *Coriolanus* is a kind of satire and *Macbeth* abandons the tragic focus on the individual toward the end. Where the feminine is a projection of the play itself, the tragic dialectic cannot take place. This, at least, is the argument I shall be making in Chapter Six. In all the tragedies where there is projection, there is also, at some level, recognition. Manliness in Shakespearean tragedy involves a detachment from the feminine, an independence from the Other. In *Macbeth* and *Coriolanus* that independence can never be achieved. There is no possibility of detachment because the Self is everywhere. The consequence is unmanliness in the heroes and an alteration in the structure of the tragedy. In the other four plays the heroes are finally detached from the feminine and the issue of their manhood is resolved. The resolution of the manhood issue, moreover, is simultaneous with the formal resolution of the drama as tragedy. Neither mode is preferable, of course, to the other; I am only arguing that the systematic differences between them amount to a recognition on Shakespeare's part of the projections within the alternative mode. At some level there is recognition—consciousness—that misogyny is a limitation on male identity and appears when masculinity is in disarray. It is because I feel the presence of this consciousness—strongly in some plays, dimly in others—that the tragedies do not seem to me, as they seem to Fiedler, symptomatic of their author's fear and hatred of the feminine. The antifeminist Shakespeare that Fiedler develops is unconscious of his own projections; in fact, however, Shakespeare's plays consistently relate misogyny—whether in the hero or in the play itself—to a radical failure of manliness.

So far I have been dealing exclusively with the tragedies, in which the author's relationship to the feminine is most problematic. This relationship can be further clarified if the tragedies are seen in the context of the other genres. In comedy, history, and romance, the nature of the feminine is also similar to the nature of the world outside the Self. In the comedies that world is manifestly reliable, orderly, a source of pleasure rather than a threat—and so is the nature of the feminine. In *As They Liked It* Alfred Harbage has made a statistical survey of Shakespeare's characters, dividing them by groups into good and bad. Of "characters of the high class," for instance, 69 percent are good and 31 percent bad. The highest percentage of good characters in any group is the percentage of good women in the comedies: 96 percent good, 4 percent bad.[22]

The possibility of betrayal in this world is very slight. The women will not betray the men, the comic world will not betray its chosen people, the playwright will not betray our expectations of a happy ending. The world of Shakespearean comedy is fundamentally safe and its women fundamentally good. We are free in this world to play, to court danger in sport. Sometimes it seems as though the games have gotten out of hand: Oberon's cruel love games in *A Midsummer Night's Dream,* Shylock's murderous bond in *The Merchant of Venice,* and Orsino's threat to Cesario's life in *Twelfth Night*—all these give us some bad moments. But an invisible hand unravels everything and we enjoy the thrill of danger without its dire consequences. Similarly, the woman problem is raised only to be dismissed. We are titillated with reminders that women might be unfaithful; the cuckoldry jokes of *Much Ado About Nothing* and Portia's ring trick in *The Merchant of Venice* remind us of what could happen. But it never does. The women are as transparently faithful as the plot is transparently comic. We are always on our way to the happy ending, to marriage, to the love of good women.

In the romances, the world is a much more serious place—not, as in the tragedies, because it may betray us, but because it may be lost altogether. The protagonist of Shakespearean romance loses his whole world; Pericles, Leontes, and Prospero live for a time in the absence of everything they care for. But although the world may be lost, it may also be found; and of course the most obvious property of the feminine in this genre is also its tendency to come and go. It is notable that in *The Winter's Tale* the two males who disappear from Sicilia, Mamillus and Antigonus, disappear for good; it is the women characters, Perdita and Hermione, who return. In Shakespearean romance the feminine is infinitely valuable, capable of being utterly lost but capable also of miraculous self-renewal. Again, the nature of the feminine is congruent with the nature of the world outside the Self.

The feminine in the history plays is more difficult to characterize briefly than it is in the comedies and romances; perhaps it is best described as unproblematic. The feminine Other may be unambiguously hated, as Joan is in *1 Henry VI;* cheerfully courted, as Katherine is in *Henry V;* or cleverly used to further a career, as Queen Elizabeth is in *Richard III.* But whatever role she plays, she never offers any metaphysical complications, never raises issues of identity for the masculine Self. Emotions toward women are unconfused; here the feminine Other does not call the masculine Self into question. Similarly, the world outside the Self in the histories is simple compared to the world of the tragedies. Because it is almost wholly a political world, it, too, offers few metaphysical problems. Desire and aggression are quite unmixed: the history heroes desire power and feel aggression toward those who keep them from it. The world divides up smartly into friends and enemies; everyone is playing the same game, however nastily. In tragedy, by contrast, the world becomes murkier, the masculine-historical enterprise loses its centrality, friends and enemies become hard to distinguish from each other, and the feminine becomes a problem.

In Shakespearean tragedy the world outside the Self seems to thicken. It becomes hard to make out. It is not necessarily evil, although it *may* be evil; in any case, it causes so much suffering that it will at certain moments at least *appear* evil. It is a world that is separate from us who inhabit it; it will not yield to our desires and fantasies no matter how desperately we need it to do so. This means that in tragedy, recognition—*anagnorisis,* the banishing of ignorance—is a major goal. We question the tragic universe to discover *its* laws, since they are what we must live by. The worlds of comedy and romance, by contrast, are shaped by our hearts' desires; and in history we are busily remaking the world to suit ourselves.

The feminine in the tragedies can be similarly defined in terms of evil, obduracy, and the issue of recognition. First of all, women in the tragedies constitute the *single* group in which Harbage finds more bad than good: 58 percent bad and only 42 percent good. (For Shakespeare, Harbage says sagely, "it meant woe to the world when women went wrong."[23]) Like the world outside the Self, the feminine causes suffering, appears evil, and may actually *be* evil. And like the world outside the Self, women in the tragedies are notably separate from us, governed by their own laws whether their natures are good or evil. The hero can only recognize them for what they are or fail to do so; he can only live with the feminine Other as she is or die from his own efforts to control her. The effort can only fail; neither the feminine Other nor the world outside the Self is within our power in Shakespeare's tragedy.

The tragic world thwarts and opposes the hero, refusing to rearrange itself around him. What the hero desires is centrality; what we see is his displacement from the center of his own story. Antony is displaced by Caesar, Lear by old age and bad children, Hamlet by his uncle's ambition and his mother's remarriage. The world grinds on, having its own purposes, indifferent to the suffering its progress is causing our hero. The women, too, pursue their own ends, even those who are bound by love to the hero. In *King Lear,* for instance, Cordelia loves her father as much as daughter ever loved; but she has her own ends even so and does not identify her interests with Lear's. This is what it means for her to love France as well as her father: that ultimately she is separate from both of them. In her own system, she is the sun; but Lear wants to be the only star in the sky. Lear's demands are obviously unreasonable, yet he is only expressing the unreasonable demands implicit in tragedy as a genre. The tragedy of our individualism lies in our efforts to make the whole world turn around us. In Shakespearean tragedy the woman is the microcosm of the tragic, eccentric outside world.

The point is worth developing in one more play. In *Antony and Cleopatra* the woman's purposes are by no means so clear and reasonable as they are in *King Lear.* Cleopatra's purposes are at times obscure and at times appear a bit suspicious. But what we are invited to ask of Cleopatra is not merely that her purposes leave room for Antony's but that they *merge* with Antony's. Linda Fitz points out how naively many critics have responded to the invitation:

Cleopatra is repeatedly criticized for thinking of anything but Antony [as she makes her choice in Act V]. . . . "Does she kill herself to be with Antony or to escape Caesar? It is the final question," Mills tells us. . . . Stempel, coming upon the lines "He words me, girls, he words me, that I should not/Be noble to myself" (V.ii.191–92) is . . . shocked that Cleopatra speaks two whole lines without reference to Antony: "No word of Antony here. Her deepest allegiance is to her own nature."[24]

Fitz points out that the critics apply a double standard. Antony is not expected to die entirely on Cleopatra's account, but Cleopatra is condemned for considering issues besides the death of Antony. The relationship between the critics and Cleopatra is similar to the one between Lear and Cordelia at the opening of *King Lear.* The woman's love is scorned because it is not her only emotion. Cleopatra *does* kill herself because she has lost Antony, just as Antony dies because he thinks he has lost Cleopatra; but just as Antony is also thinking of his humiliations at Caesar's hands, so too is Cleopatra. Only sexism, says Fitz, prevents the critics from noticing the similarity of their situations.

Mills and Stempel are, if not sexist, at least insufficiently alert to the problem.[25] But Fitz's criticism of their judgments leaves something out. The play *does* invite us to do what they do, to see things from Antony's point of view; and from Antony's point of view Cleopatra's motives are hard to swallow. Of the five motives for suicide that Fitz identifies, only two of them have to do with Antony. From Antony's point of view, they should *all* have to do with him, just as from Lear's point of view Cordelia should love only him. Fitz, of course, would say that there is no need for us to see things from Antony's point of view; but in tragedy we are invited to share the hero's fantasies of his own centrality. Simultaneously we recognize the fantasies for what they are and regret that they are not coming true.

But finally we are glad that the tragic world is obdurate. We do not really want it to yield to our desires; we want it to dish out its worst to our surrogate, the hero. We want to see what happens to him when his suffering has stripped away his habits and honors. The tragic world cracks the old mold in which the hero was cast; it sends him out on the heath to face himself and his death. It is there that he may become interesting. There, thanks to the resistance offered by the tragic world, we are in the presence of exciting possibilities. The hero may triumph over his losses; naked, he may be more splendid than he appeared when he was clothed. He may reclaim—with a difference—the center of his story. Or, like Coriolanus, he may collapse. The sense of risk and possibility is what excites us in tragedy; and this is just what animates relations with the feminine, too. The risk of betrayal is substantial, but so is its opposite, the possibility of endless love. For just as Lear and Antony reclaim their position in the story, so they reclaim, with a difference, the love of Cordelia and Cleopatra. (That is, Lear reclaims Cordelia's love. In Antony's case, the story and the woman seem to rearrange themselves around him after he is gone.) Finally we are glad that Cleopatra and Cordelia pursue their own purposes rather than yielding to the heroes' needs. Both the risk and the possibility depend on it. In Shakespearean tragedy, the satisfactions of the genre depend upon the alienation of both the tragic universe and the feminine Other from the tragic hero, the masculine Self.

The nature of the feminine, then, is similar to the nature of the world outside the Self, in tragedy as in comedy, romance, and history. What does this do to Fiedler's notion of "projection"? Projection involves a confusion between the internal drama and the external one; to project is to believe one sees in the external world what is really a repudiated element in one's own psyche. But in every genre the feminine is a version of the external world, not the internal one. The playwright associates the feminine with the nature of external reality itself; that nature seems to change as he looks at it through the prisms of the different genres. Thus, what seems like projection in the individual tragedies may be differently understood if the tragedies as a whole are compared with the comedies, histories, and romances. The feminine Other is not merely a projection of the masculine Self; she is *actually* Other—external, independent, and unpossessed.

At the next level of generality, of course, we might say that in fiction even the world beyond the hero's consciousness cannot be identified with a real, external world: tragedy, comedy, and romance are themselves forms of projection on the part of the author. The distinction between the two worlds (internal and external) is after all subsequent to the analogy between them. Freud himself gets trapped in a revolving door when he tries to distinguish between instincts, which are by definition internal, and stimulation that comes to us from the outside world. After a long, careful paragraph on the difference between the two he comments, "Of course there is nothing to prevent our assuming that the instincts themselves are, at least in part, the precipitates of different forms of *external* stimulation."[26] Our internal world is what it is because of what is outside it; our perception of the external world is determined by what is within. But if we retain the idea of projection, defined as a confusion between the two worlds, we also retain the possibility of distinguishing clearly between them. Genre by genre Shakespeare distinguishes clearly between the masculine Self and the world to which that Self brings his desires; genre by genre the nature of the feminine resembles the nature of this outside world. In general the feminine is no projection; it is a version of something outside the hero, outside the author, outside the Self. When we look at the women characters, then, we get contradictory answers to the question, "What is Shakespeare's image of women?" But if we ask, "What is the image of Otherness in this genre? What are the characteristics of the world outside the Self?," the women characters provide the best and most consistent answers.

It is possible to characterize not only genres but sub-genres by looking at the nature of the women within them. In tragedy, for instance, we may distinguish between *Macbeth* and *Coriolanus,* on the one hand, and the other four tragedies, on the other. We may go even further and make distinctions among the four plays I have been using to establish the tragic paradigm—*Hamlet, Antony and Cleopatra, King Lear,* and *Othello.* The first two, that is, may be distinguished from the other pair. In *King Lear* and *Othello,* the world outside the hero is starkly divided between good and evil, and so are the principal women characters, Goneril, Regan, Cordelia, and Desdemona. In *Hamlet* and *Antony and Cleopatra,* by contrast, the outside world is a mixture of good and bad; it is hard to tell manly strength from mindless ambition, and restraint may be confused with weakness. The women in these two plays are similarly a confusing mixture of good and evil, and finally may be neither. We never know the extent of Gertrude's guilt or whether Cleopatra, offered better terms, would have sold out to Caesar. But we know all along that Desdemona and Cordelia are perfectly good and Goneril and Regan, vile. In *Lear* and *Othello* kindness and constancy are to be found in their purest forms, as are their opposites, cruelty and malice.

In the black and white world of these two plays the heroes, appropriately, make absolute judgments of the women. Unfortunately, they are the wrong judgments. Lear banishes Cordelia, moves in on Goneril, rushes off to Regan; his decisions are immediate and final. Othello is similarly incapable of living with doubts: he must make a decision about Desdemona with violent speed, and having taken that decision, must act on it immediately.

Antony, on the other hand, rages at Cleopatra and forgives her, leaves her and returns to her. Hamlet is not a tolerant man, and he is indirectly the cause of Ophelia's death; but he, too, postpones judgments of women until he has passed the point where judgment is the issue. He speaks daggers but uses none, and when dealing with the feminine does not force himself to act on his suspicions. After the deaths of these two heroes we have Horatio telling Hamlet's story, Cleopatra making a myth of Antony, Dolabella (a Roman, and thus the enemy) feeling for Antony "a grief that smites my very heart at root" (V.ii.104–5), and Fortinbras (a partial Hamlet-figure) carrying on more or less with Hamlet's blessing. Such intimations of continuity are quite absent in *Lear* and *Othello.* In neither play has there been the partial accommodation of the outside world that we find in *Hamlet* and *Antony and Cleopatra,* mirrored in the partial accommodation of those plays' women.

In these four tragedies, then, the nature of the feminine is a major clue to the nature of the dramatic world. The feminine in one pair resists judgment, our own as well as the heroes'; in the other pair the feminine is transparently good or bad, and an error of judgment costs the hero everything. In *Antony and Cleopatra* and *Hamlet* there is more room for the heroes' errors; the worlds of Antony and Hamlet, like their women, can absorb more uncertainty than the worlds of Lear and Othello.

★

When we turn from tragedy to comedy both the Self and the Other must be redefined. The Self is elusive in the comedies; it is represented not by a major figure whose history organizes the whole drama but variously by a select social group, an unimpressive male hero, or an unearthly stage manager like Oberon or Puck. The Self is sometimes external to the drama altogether, hovering derisively or good-humoredly outside the action, identifiable with no less a figure than the playwright himself. But insofar as the Self is within the drama and human, it counts itself a member of the dominant social group; and this I take to be its defining feature. The comedies are not so much concerned with the inner life of the Self as with social surfaces, with disturbances and realignments within the society as a whole. When we look for a Self, then, we are looking for something larger than an individual ego. We are looking, let us say, for the centers of social power. Just as in tragedy we identify with the hero's power to imagine and affect his own identity, so in comedy we identify with the power of the dominant group to shape its own society. Of course, as readers and theatergoers we are indebted to whatever *disrupts* the society, challenges the sources of its power; for to the disruption we owe the process of the play. Just as in tragedy we owe our experience of the hero on the heath to the unforgiving outside world, so in comedy we owe the fun and games to whatever disrupts the existing social order. What disrupts the social order is Other to the social Self; the action of comedy can be described as a dialectic between the Other and the Self, between the forces for social disruption and the forces that reestablish the social order.

In comedy as in tragedy, the feminine is a version of the Other. The Otherness of the feminine is not, of course, the Otherness of the outsider, of the alien. Leslie Fiedler calls Portia's Belmont an "earthly paradise of absolute belonging";[27] the women are clearly not Other to society insofar as it ministers to our sense of community, to friendships and marriages, to whatever is voluntary and pleasurable in the bonds between its citizens. The feminine is Other to the social order only insofar as it restrains and compels us. The feminine is Other to society's rules and regulations, to its hierarchies of power, to the impersonality of its systems and sanctions. In comedy the feminine either rebels against the restraining social order or (more commonly) presides in alliance with forces that challenge its hegemony: romantic love, physical nature, the love of pleasure in all its forms. Rosalind presides over the love games in the Forest of Arden; Maria presides over the household conspiracies in *Twelfth Night* as Olivia presides over the whole crazy household; and Portia presides over Belmont, the realm of intimacy, music, and love. These characters are associated with what challenges the social order, and they invite us to suspend participation in the everyday social drama of class, power, money, and status. In Rosalind's forest, for instance, democratic primitivism challenges our usual insistence on hierarchy and degree; in Illyria romance and revelry put us all on the same social footing.

The feminine is not the only version of the Other in the comedies; it is not even necessarily the most important one. There are other dialectics in these plays besides the dialectic between the social Self as male and the Other as female. The Fool, for instance, presents a different kind of challenge to the social order from the one offered by the feminine Other; so, too, does the blocking figure. Blocking figures like Malvolio and Shylock do not so much disrupt the social order as struggle for the power to define it in their own terms; but the story of that struggle may engage us at least as much as the dialectic with the feminine. Just as the Self is more elusive in the comedies than it is in the tragedies, so is the Other. Shakespearean comedy is a decentralized form, and more than one dialectic may be operative at any given moment. But one version of the Other is certainly the feminine version, and what is challenged by the feminine is a social order defined and directed by the masculine Self. If we are interested in the feminine version of Otherness, then the Self is to be found where we find a vested interest in the social and political status quo, defined, in Shakespeare's time as in our own, as a hierarchical arrangement of society in which men outrank women. In the comedies, the feminine challenges the status quo either overtly or through its command of socially subversive forces like sexuality, romantic passion, household revels, and so forth.

The best example of the relationship between male dominance and the status quo comes in *A Midsummer Night's Dream,* which begins with a rebellion of the feminine against the power of masculine authority. Hermia refuses the man both Aegeus and Theseus order her to marry; her refusal sends us off into the forest, beyond the power of the father and the masculine state. Once in the forest, of course, we find the social situation metaphorically repeated in this world of imagination and nature. The fairy king, Oberon, rules the forest. His rule, too, is troubled by the rebellion of the feminine. Titania has refused to give him her page, the child of a human friend who died in childbirth. But by the end of the story Titania is conquered, the child relinquished, and order restored. Even here the comic upheavals, whether we see them as May games or bad dreams, are associated with an uprising of women. David P. Young has pointed out how firmly this play connects order with masculine dominance and the disruption of order with the rebellion of the feminine:

It is appropriate that Theseus, as representative of daylight and right reason, should have subdued his bride-to-be to the rule of his masculine will. That is the natural order of things. It is equally appropriate that Oberon, as king of darkness and fantasy, should have lost control of his wife, and that the corresponding natural disorder described by Titania should ensue.[28]

The natural order, the status quo, is for men to rule women. When they fail to do so, we have the exceptional situation, the festive, disruptive, disorderly moment of comedy.

A Midsummer Night's Dream is actually an anomaly among the festive comedies. It is unusual for the forces of the green world to be directed, as they are here, by a masculine figure. Because the green world here is a partial reproduction of the social world, the feminine is reduced to a kind of first cause of the action while a masculine power directs it. In the other festive comedies the feminine Other presides. She does not *command* the forces of the alternative world, as Oberon does, but since she acts in harmony with these forces her will and desire often prevail.

Where are we to bestow our sympathies? On the forces that make for the disruption of the status quo and therefore for the plot? Or on the force that asserts itself against the disruption and reestablishes a workable social order? Of course we cannot choose. We can only say that in comedy we owe our holiday to such forces as the tendency of the feminine to rebel, whereas to the successful reassertion of masculine power we owe our everyday order. Shakespearean comedy endorses both sides. Holiday is, of course, the subject and the analogue of each play; but the plays always end in a return to everyday life. The optimistic reading of Shakespearean comedy says that everyday life is clarified and enriched by our holiday from it; according to the pessimistic reading the temporary subversion of the social order has revealed how much that order excludes, how high a price we pay for it. But whether our return to everyday life is a comfortable one or not, the return itself is the inevitable conclusion to the journey out.

Does this make the comedies sexist? Is the association of women with the disruption of the social order an unconscious and insulting projection? It seems to begin as such; but as the form of Shakespearean comedy develops, the Otherness of the feminine develops into as powerful a force in the drama as the social authority of the masculine Self. For the feminine in Shakespearean comedy begins as a shrew but develops into a comic heroine. The shrew's rebellion directly challenges masculine authority, whereas the comic heroine merely presides over areas of experience to which masculine authority is irrelevant. But the shrew is essentially powerless against the social system, whereas the comic heroine is in alliance with forces that can never be finally overcome. The shrew is defeated by the superior strength, physical and social, of a man, or by women who support the status quo. She provokes a battle of the sexes, and the outcome of this battle, from Shakespeare's point of view, is inevitable. The comic heroine, on the other hand, does not fight the system but merely surfaces, again and again, when and where the social system is temporarily subverted. The comic heroine does not actively resist the social and political hegemony of the men, but as an irresistible version of the Other she successfully competes for our favor with the (masculine) representatives of the social Self.

The development of the feminine from the shrew to the comic heroine indicates a certain consciousness on the author's part of sexual politics; and it indicates a desire, at least, to create conditions of sexual equality within the drama even while reflecting the unequal conditions of men and women in the society at large.

Paradoxically enough, the movement toward equality between the feminine Other and the masculine Self includes a movement away from the feminist argument. For it is the shrew, not the comic heroine, who is a feminist. The feminism of the shrew seems to provoke her own author into a kind of dramatic retaliation against her. Consider, for instance, the debate between Adriana and Luciana in Act II of *The Comedy of Errors*. The shrew here is Adriana; Luciana speaks for the status quo. When Adriana complains that her husband is often late for dinner, Luciana remonstrates, "A man is master of his liberty" (II.i.7), and the following dialogue takes place:

Adriana	Why should their liberty than ours be more?
Luciana	Because their business still lies out o' door.
Adriana	Look when I serve him so he takes it ill.
Luciana	O, know he is the bridle of your will.
Adriana	There's none but asses will be bridled so.

(II.i.10–14)

Up to this point the exchange is perfectly balanced; the debate is contained within the extreme formalism of the stichomythia and at first seems merely to counterpoint the two women. It ends, moreover, in a draw: Adriana tells Luciana that her patience would soon wear thin if she herself were married, and Luciana replies equably, "Well, I will marry one day, but to try." But in the middle of the exchange, right after Adriana's witty and unanswerable observation, "There's none but asses will be bridled so," a solemn defense of male dominance is put in Luciana's mouth:

Why, headstrong liberty is lashed with woe.
There's nothing situate under heaven's eye
But hath his bound, in earth, in sea, in sky.
The beasts, the fishes, and the wingèd fowls
Are their males' subjects, and at their controls;
Man, more divine, the master of all these,
Lord of the wide world and wild wat'ry seas,
Indued with intellectual sense and souls,

Of more preeminence than fish and fowls,
Are masters to their females, and their lords;
Then let your will attend on their accords.   (II.i.15–25)

It is as though the author himself had suddenly become uneasy with
the debate, as though he heard what he had made Adriana say and
hastened to defend against it, abandoning witty exchange for a long
flat sermon. Luciana buries Adriana's liveliness with maxims that
had become platitudes by the time Chaucer invented the Wife of
Bath. With Luciana's speech all the air goes out of the balloon and
the heaviness of language descends simultaneously with the heaviness of the social hierarchy. Comedy challenges or suspends our
heaviness; but the feminist challenge, when it is as pointed and
effective as Adriana's is, apparently sends us running for cover
behind big guns: "Men are masters to their females, and their
lords," and so forth. At the conclusion of this play, moreover,
Adriana is held responsible for whatever has gone wrong between
her and her husband. The Abbess tells her authoritatively, "thy
jealous fits / Hath scared they husband from the use of wits"
(V.i.85–86)—and that is the end of that.

    In *The Taming of the Shrew* a feminist argument is not explicit,
but as we watch the battle between Kate and Petruchio, sexual
politics must be on our minds. Kate's resistance to Petruchio is at
least in part the resistance of the feminine to male dominance; as in
The Comedy of Errors, the feminist possibilities of his story provoke
the author's partiality for the status quo. Whenever Shakespeare's
comedies challenge the limits to sexual equality, they end by
strenuously reaffirming those limits. Shakespeare's later comedies,
however, seem to avoid both the feminist challenge and the
heavy-handed defense against it. In *Twelfth Night* and *As You Like It*
the feminine Other does not confront the political order; she simply
presides in its absence. In *The Taming of the Shrew* we are triumphant over the feminine; but when we leave the domain of the
comic heroine, we do so without triumph and without finality.
Illyria and the Forest of Arden are not, like Kate's resistance, shown
up as errors; they are states of mind that we visit and leave, revisit
and leave again. The later comedies do not share social and political
power with the Other; but they do emphasize areas of experience to
which other kinds of power—emotional, imaginative, personal—
are more relevant.

The Taming of the Shrew deserves extended consideration as the play in which the theme of the battle of the sexes is fully and finally elaborated. Here the rebellion of the feminine is sullen and point-less. It is not analogous, like Hermia's rebellion in *A Midsummer Night's Dream,* to the periodic rebellion of all citizens against the restraints of their society; it does not send us off into an alternative world in which we experience the terror and delight of life beyond the social order. Kate's challenge is entirely negative: she resists the arrangements of society but does not call to mind what is beyond society itself. If Kate were in love with another man, or even merely found Petruchio antipathic, she would call to mind the irrationalities of sexual attraction, something beyond the power of society to control. But Kate is no Juliet. Her antagonism to her father's choice is not based on her own sexual preference or on sexual antipathy to her father's choice. It does not resonate with anything larger than itself. Petruchio, on the other hand, represents not only his own desires but the arrangements of society itself. He does so by his cheerful insistence on society's archetypal institution, married cohabitation, which Kate resists. The dialectic between the two is unequal because Kate represents the Other very feebly while Petruchio is splendid and triumphant as a representative of the social Self.

Petruchio dominates Kate physically, socially, and economically; he is also the central consciousness of the play and the one character whose will prevails. Insofar as the play dramatizes the battle of the sexes, it ends in complete humiliation for the feminine; insofar as it is a power struggle, Kate loses. By the end of the play Kate herself speaks for wifely obedience. "Thy husband," she instructs her sister,

> is thy lord, thy life, thy keeper,
> Thy head, thy sovereign—one that cares for thee
>   . . .
> Such duty as the subject owes the prince,
> Even such a woman oweth to her husband,
> And when she is froward, peevish, sullen, sour,
> And not obedient to his honest will,
> What is she but a foul contending rebel
> And graceless traitor to her loving lord?
> I am ashamed that women are so simple
> To offer war where they should kneel for peace,

Or seek for rule, supremacy, and sway,
When they are bound to serve, love, and obey.

(V.ii.148–49, 157–66)

In *The Taming of the Shrew,* the Otherness of the feminine implies
only its inferiority to the powerful masculine Self. Kate is less
powerful, less wealthy, less cheerful, less in the playwright's
confidence—less everything than Petruchio. When the conflict
with the Other is stressed but unequal, as it is here, we are surely
justified in leveling the charge of sexism.

Many critics, however, have argued against doing so. One of the
most interesting articles to take up the issue is Coppelia Kahn's
"*The Taming of the Shrew:* Shakespeare's Mirror of Marriage."
Kahn's article illuminates both the play's intentions and its limitations when judged from a feminist point of view. Kahn's major
argument is that Petruchio "has gained Kate's outward compliance
in the form of a public display while her spirit remains mischievi-
ously free."[29] Surely the play *invites* us to accept just such a distinction between Kate's public and private selves and to agree that
Kate's taming has not crushed her spirit. If we do accept this
distinction, we may go so far as to read the final speech as though it
were ironic. Though the speech "pleads subordination," says
Kahn, "as a speech—a lengthy, ambitious verbal performance before an audience—it allows the speaker to dominate that audience."[30] But the distinction between Kate's public and private
selves seems to me a false one. The public forms of equality are
important (as Kahn, elsewhere in her article, agrees) because they
affect the life of the spirit itself. It is true, of course, that the limits
to Kate's equality as a wife are only public. As long as Kate publicly
defers to her husband, comes when he calls and says what he wants
her to say, their private relationship may be quite playful, equal,
and happy. Male dominance is merely a social form, irrelevant to
the private relationship—or so the play implies. But this is Shakespeare at his most self-flattering: he imagines the feminine offering
explicit social subservience without sacrificing its delightful equality as a sexual partner. Kahn sometimes seems to accept the bargain
Shakespeare offers in *The Taming of the Shrew:* if women will go
along with male dominance as a mere formality, we may all agree
that it is as silly a formality as you like. But the price is to go along
with it.

Elsewhere in her article Kahn refuses this easygoing bargain. Her objections to it are clearest in her discussion of the climactic scene of the play, Act IV, scene v. Here Petruchio and Kate argue over whether it is night or day, whether they see the sun or moon above them. When Petruchio threatens to punish Kate once again for her contrariness, Kate suddenly decides to let it be "moon or sun or what you please. / And if you please to call it a rush-candle, / Henceforth I vow it shall be so for me" (IV.v.13–15). There follows this dialogue, as Petruchio presses his advantage:

> *Petruchio* I say it is the moon.
> *Kate* I know it is the moon.
> *Petruchio* Nay, then you lie. It is the blessèd sun.
> *Kate* Then God be blessed, it is the blessèd sun.
> But sun it is not when you say it is not,
> And the moon changes even as your mind.
> What you will have it named, even that it is,
> And so it shall be so for Katherine.   (IV.v.16–22)

Kate has learned to maintain her independence through ironic exaggeration; if Petruchio says it is the moon, Kate *knows* it is the moon. When she cries "Then God be blessed, it is the blessed sun," her thankfulness is partly sincere. She feels blessed at having finally learned how to keep a pocket of freedom for herself within the limits of Petruchio's dominion over her. But as Kahn points out, Kate's solution is no solution at all. "Her only way of maintaining her inner freedom," says Kahn, "is by outwardly denying it, which thrusts her into a schizoid existence. . . . Furthermore, to hold that she maintains her freedom in words is to posit a distinction without a difference, for whether she remains spiritually independent of Petruchio or sincerely believes in his superiority, her outward behavior must be . . . that of the perfect Griselda, a model for all women."[31] Although the play presents Kate's capitulation as a gesture without consequence to her soul, it cannot seem so to a feminist reader. The battle of the sexes as a theme for comedy is inherently sexist. The battle is only funny to those who assume that the status quo is the natural order of things and likely to prevail. To the rest of us, Kate's compromise is distressing.

Perhaps Shakespeare himself was also dissatisfied with the resolution to *The Taming of the Shrew,* for after this play he abandons both the shrew and the feminist challenge for the comic heroine and the challenge of the green world. C. L. Barber's distinction between satirical and saturnalian comedy may be helpful here. Satirical comedy, he says, "tends to deal with relations between social classes and aberrations in movements between them. Saturnalian comedy is satiric only incidentally; its clarification comes with movement between poles of restraint and release in everybody's experience."[32] The shrew is a figure of satire and the comic heroine of saturnalia. The shrew is an aberration in the social order. At the end of the shrew comedy, "relations between social classes"—in this case the classes of men and women—are returned to the status quo. When the shrew challenges the social order, it reasserts itself in response; the comic heroine, by contrast, comes into her own when and where the social order may be taken for granted. The shrew is a representative of specific class interests rising against the power structure, whereas the comic heroine represents something beyond definition by class altogether, something that offers "release in everybody's experience." The comic heroine has a more general significance than the shrew, who is a local, political disturbance only.

Satirical comedy has a kind of righting moment: disorder is introduced into a society that rights itself like a balance toy that has been pulled over. The pleasure comes from seeing the center of gravity rejoin the center of resistance so that equilibrium is reestablished. But in saturnalian comedy the pleasure comes from a temporary release, as it were, from the laws of gravity altogether. The return to normalcy is implicit, but it does not provide the energy that drives the play. In *The Taming of the Shrew,* where the Other is a figure of satire, the return to normalcy is the goal throughout, and every action is directed toward it. In *As You Like It* and *Twelfth Night,* however, where the Other is saturnalian, our expectations of a return are muted or suspended during much of the action. We are occupied with the festivity or disorder, by the alternatives to the status quo, more than with the journey by which we return to it.

The movement on Shakespeare's part from the shrew to the comic heroine, from the satirical to the saturnalian Other, is a movement toward dialectical equality between the masculine and feminine elements of the drama. Although the comic heroine is less of a feminist than the shrew, as a representation of the Other she is a much more powerful figure. Feminists have objected, however, that the comic heroine is an essentially frivolous figure. Juliet Dusinberre, for instance, is unimpressed by the opposition she offers the established social order. In a discussion of the comedies she comments:

To be permanently providing light relief to serious men, to be in essence a symbol of that light relief in one's very being, allies women with professional Fools, as Shakespeare perceived when he depicted the peculiar sympathy between his Fools and his heroines: Celia and Touchstone, Viola and Feste, Cordelia and the Fool in *King Lear*. Both stand on the periphery of the serious world of men, assessing its wisdom from the perspective of not being of any account.[33]

Of course, an alliance with fools as wise as Feste and Touchstone is not entirely a disgraceful one. But it is true, as Dusinberre says, that the comic heroine "stands on the periphery of the serious world of men"; and if the world of men is the measure of our experience, the comic heroine need not be taken seriously. Saturnalia itself may be seen as a conservative form. As J. Dennis Huston puts it, "In a time of revelry the state buys long-term obedience at the cost of short-term license."[34] Similarly, the freedom that the comic Other is allowed to exercise for the duration of the play buys her long-term obedience at the play's conclusion as it returns to ordinary life. The most radical critique of the comic heroine as a figure of conservatism is Clara Claiborne Park's "As We Like It" in *The American Scholar*. Park calls the comic heroine a "shrew who will tame herself." "Her aggressiveness," says Park, "is only apparent, part of the delightful game that assures us that this prize is worth having."[35] Park finds the holiday brilliance of the comic heroines a distraction from the political realities of everyday life. The heroines are denied the opportunity to challenge the political hegemony of the men and so are a disappointment to feminists.

If there is to be an alternative to Park's point of view—if we are to see the subversiveness of the comedies as well as their conservatism—we must begin with a different understanding from hers of the relationship between holiday and the social order. Park and Dusinberre assume that everyday, social-political, serious life has more reality, more substance, than holiday. The comedies can only seem subversive if we understand the two possibilities— holiday and ordinary social life—as having equal metaphysical weight. Saturnalia is not merely a time of release, a temporary affair; it is also a permanent space within the social order. Holiday parallels our ordinary life, becoming available to us again and again. The festive spirit is always waiting for its moment; it is permanent as well as temporary. To the extent that holiday, play, festivity are endlessly recurring alternatives to the difficulty of ordinary life, the comic heroine is as significant a figure as the tragic hero himself. Insouciant, successful, self-delighted, the comic heroine reminds us of experience to which the intensities of the tragic hero are laughably inadequate. She subverts our tendency to focus on the conflicts of ordinary life and drains some of the seriousness from the "serious world of men." It is only when we forget how much festivity our social lives include that the comic heroine seems an insidious diversion from the painful experiences we call "real life."

The tragic hero looks at himself with a kind of horror. He can scarcely bear to contemplate the role he is forced to play. He feels he has betrayed himself and struggles for redemption. The comic heroine is on holiday from all this effort and judgment. When a Jessica or a Beatrice looks at herself she sees something perfectly common, perfectly acceptable. Instead of resolving to change, she laughs and invites our laughter. Rosalind, for instance, in *As You Like It,* is not disturbed to realize that as a married woman she will play a less flattering role than she plays as a lover. When Orlando promises to love her "forever and a day," Rosalind tells him,

> Say "a day," without the "ever." No, no, Orlando! Men are April when they woo, December when they wed. Maids are May when they are maids, but the sky changes when they are wives.
>
> (IV.i.142–45)

Whereas Rosalind blithely anticipates her transformation from a brilliant lover to an ordinary wife, the tragic hero is humiliated when he must play a poorer part than formerly. He feels reduced in his very being and resolves to make himself grand again somehow. Rosalind can gaily anticipate her reduction because she is less affected than the masculine heroic Self by *any* of her roles. The identity of the Other is assumed to be stable and invulnerable; whereas the Self may change, for good or ill, the Other will be itself. The comic heroine is therefore detached from the changing roles her Fortune requires her to play. She accepts them all gaily, without protest. She is naturally free and does not struggle, like the tragic heroes, to free her identity from the part she must play.

As self-judgment is the prerogative of the Self in tragedy, self-acceptance is the prerogative of the Other in comedy. The Self may change in response to his judgments but the Other shows us how to leave off trying to become what we are not. Being somewhat distant from the centers of female experience, Shakespeare does not deal with the flux of women's inner lives. But in a mode where life is not primarily inner he imagines women with the same distance on themselves that he has on them. The comic heroine shows us how to regard ourselves as Other, to be entertained by our own stories, the stories of our lives. She has no ambition to be other than as she sees herself. The heroines laugh to see themselves absorbed into the ordinary human comedy; the heroes rage and weep at the difficulty of actually being as extraordinary as they feel themselves to be.

The comic heroine is indeed allied to the fool, for the fool is the other figure who both understands and accepts his own role in the comedy. In *As You Like It,* when Jaques asks Touchstone, "Will you be married, motley?," Touchstone answers,

> As the ox hath his bow, sir, the horse his curb, and the falcon her
> bells, so man hath his desires; and as pigeons bill, so wedlock would
> be nibbling.   (III.iii.77–81)

Touchstone's role, as C. L. Barber puts it, is to be an example of "love reduced to its lowest common denominator, without any sentiment at all."[36] Because he calmly accepts his role, Touchstone is at leisure to entertain us extravagantly, hilariously, with his tour-de-force description of it. The comic heroine is not quite as detached as the fool. She does suffer her role as well as separate from it. In *Twelfth Night,* for instance, Viola is simultaneously involved and uninvolved with her role as the patient neglected lady. In the following exchange with Feste we can see both her detachment from and her commitment to her own experience:

> *Feste* Now Jove, in his next commodity of hair, send thee a beard.
> *Viola* By my troth, I'll tell thee, I am almost sick for one, though
>   I would not have it grow on my chin.
>   (III.i.45–48)

The tone of voice is downright, impatient, detached; but the strong emotion of the lover is nevertheless affirmed: "I am the lovesick maiden, damn it, not the beardless youth." Viola defines her role in the comedy, stamps her foot at the irritations of playing it, but nevertheless accepts herself in it without ado. It does not occur to her, as it occurs to the tragic heroes, to seek another role since she finds this one painful.

The Self is unique, the Other is typical. In tragedy we value the hero for being unique, but in comedy we value those who are content to be ordinary. The comedies deal with our problems as if they were ordinary difficulties rather than issues of life and death. The Otherness of the heroine makes her difficulties seem ordinary even to herself; she is gifted with the true comic perspective. In *Much Ado About Nothing,* for instance, Beatrice is described by Leonato as one who is "never sad but when she sleeps, and not ever sad then; for I have heard my daughter say she hath often dreamt of unhappiness and waked herself with laughing" (II.i.331–34). To those to whom life's difficulties present themselves as an everyday affair, unhappiness is a dream and laughter the property of wakefulness. Daylight laughter, which affirms even the difficulties of ordinary life, is regularly associated with the feminine Other in Shakespearean comedy. It is the tragic male Self who feels his difficulties to be unique, earth-shaking, and unbearable; the comic feminine Other refuses to find herself extraordinary.

The rejection of the extraordinary is made explicit in Beatrice's answer to Don Pedro a few lines earlier in *Much Ado About Nothing.* When Don Pedro proposes to her, Beatrice replies, "No, my lord, unless I might have another [husband] for working days; your grace is too costly to wear every day" (II.i.315–17). Beatrice rejects the pressures of the extraordinary, here imagined in terms of the rank she would assume as a nobleman's wife. She refuses, that is, the pressures of upward mobility. Social climbing is a common target of comic authors, who typically ridicule and abuse its practitioners. In comedy the effort to rise above oneself has none of the noble resonance it has in tragedy; it is a matter of changing classes rather than a grandly humanistic ambition to transcend one's limitations. The strain and effort of self-improvement is best represented in Shakespearean comedy by Malvolio, who simply wants to marry money. The feminine Other, lacking the ambition to be more than she is to begin with, is naturally free from the comic disgrace of status-seeking.

In the tragedies what happens is the effect of psychologically realistic causes; in the comedies what happens is clearly a plot complication and clearly to be resolved by the end of the play. In the tragedies we value the characters who take things seriously; we value the characters who seem to change in response to events. But in the comedies we value those whose changes are provisional, light-hearted and reversible—even as the changes brought about in the plot are reversible. The feminine Other has the freedom to play at change, to disguise herself and then to remove the disguise; the masculine Self has the substance really to change, to dissolve and reform in response to what he suffers. Before their final moments of grandeur, Lear loses his wits and Antony loses by turns his Roman dignity and his Egyptian generosity. We do not know, as Hamlet plays the Stoic, the Senecan, the Christian, and the Malcontent, who he really is; nor does he. Yet when Viola, Rosalind, and Portia dress up as young boys, we know all along that these are women and not men, and so do they. The comic heroines undergo a temporary and self-willed loss of identity; they stage finite and controlled performances at the end of which everything is as it was to begin with. Their provisional changes entertain us while their self-control guarantees a safe and comfortable return.

The feminine Other, then, is Shakespeare's natural ally in the mode of festive comedy. Precisely because she is Other, precisely because her inner life is obscure to her author, she seems gifted with precisely the qualities that make for comedy: a continuous, reliable identity, self-acceptance, a talent for ordinary pleasures. It has often been noticed that the comic hero seems dull next to the brilliant heroine; apart from Benedick (in *Much Ado*) and Berowne (in *Love's Labour's Lost*), who share many of her virtues, the heroes seem a little dazed and inept, as though they had wandered in from some other play. They are unfit for comedy because they take things too seriously; they are too much the male Self, imposing themselves aggressively on the situation. Think, for instance, of Orlando in Arden demanding food at sword's point, or Orsino threatening to kill Viola. These acts of aggression are the instinctive response of the male Self to Fortune's blows; the feminine Other, by contrast, does not take things so personally. In the comedies our experience is understood to be common, manageable, and an occasion for laughter; it is therefore the characters who do *not* take things so personally that appeal to us most. The detachment of the woman as Other, her distance from the centers of Self, is what makes her so useful an ally for the playwright in a mode that challenges our self-centeredness. To the extent that the comic mode presents a permanent possibility rather than a trivial escape, the comic heroine is a substantial alternative to the masculine Self. Only if we refuse the challenge of comedy is the comic heroine a figure by whom we avoid reality. In comedy we deal with experience that is no less real than our experience of conflict, difficulty, disaster, and death; the comic heroine is both a guide to this alternative experience and an image of it.

In the preceding pages I have argued that in Shakespeare the feminine as Other is something more than simply a projection of that which has been repudiated by the Self. I have argued that the Other in Shakespeare is for the most part a form of external reality, an embodiment of the world and not merely a vessel for what the psyche rejects. In tragedy the Other, the world, presents unmanageable difficulties; in comedy it challenges us to let go of our impression that our difficulties are extraordinary, unmanageable, tragic. At this point it is perhaps time to abandon my argument and, at the risk of seeming arbitrary, introduce the chapters to follow more simply. It is perhaps time to say that the idea of projection simply does not seem to me a fruitful one for feminist criticism. To my mind this idea puts an end to discussion rather than generating it. Once I have found an author guilty of projection I can think of nothing more to say than that he should not have done it, he should have been more conscious of the distinction between Other and Self. Thus I dismiss what I intended to discuss. If the discussion starts up again, it returns to the same conclusion. The arrow is shot from the bow again and again; again and again it lands a few yards from the feet. In other words, I have a rhetorical as well as a logical motive for abandoning the idea of projection: it offers me too short a ride. The idea of dialectic simply takes me further.

The idea of projection presents more difficulties than possibilities for the feminist critic, whose goal is to stick with the text rather than to turn away from it. The clinical analyst, of course, has completely different goals. The analyst does indeed turn away from the patient, again and again and again. There is no limit to the number of psychoanalytic sessions that can end quite productively with the discovery of projection on the patient's part. From the perspective of the analysand, the distinction between the Other and the Self is an endless mystery; the sensation of having penetrated that mystery is always exhilarating, therapeutic, hopeful. From the perspective of the feminist critic, however, the repeated discovery of projection on the part of a male author is by no means hopeful. The critic is in the position of the analyst whose patient refuses consciousness altogether. No matter how tactful or brutal, withdrawn or involved the analysis, the text remains exactly what it was to begin with.

From the perspective of the feminist critic, then, an author's projection onto the feminine is something that need only be discovered once or twice. After the first few times, the insight ossifies. Only if the author's projections are very similar to our own will the analysis seem worth returning to. In this case, of course, the idea of projection will be one we can never fully grasp. It will constantly slip our minds and we will be constantly excited to rediscover it. But the greater the distance between an author's projections and our own, the less likely we are to be led on by the idea of projection itself. Projections onto the feminine are therefore an unpromising topic for feminists, who presumably are the group of people least likely to project what the ego refuses onto the feminine. To feminists, projections onto the feminine must be a matter for political action, symptoms of our cultural pathology rather than an intriguing difficulty for literary criticism.

The Stranger in Shakespeare is, nevertheless, a brilliant book. It is Fiedler's genius to choose his subjects according to his own projections, and although his projections are different from my own, I can participate to some degree in the excitement of his analysis. *The Stranger in Shakespeare* is alive with the pleasure of its author's discoveries of otherness within the Self. But I have chosen my argument according to my desires rather than according to my projections. As a heterosexual feminist I want to imagine that there may be something *beyond* projection, that the conversation with the Other need *not* end with the discovery of the projected Self. I am interested in the possibility that the sexual Other, whether male or female, may indeed be the best representative of the world outside the Self—that the sexual Other may be real and not projected. To each his own, to each her own: I have found in Shakespeare what I want to imagine as a possibility in my life.

Antony and Cleopatra

Cleopatra, says Enobarbus, is to be understood in terms of her "variety" (II.ii.238). He means that she is a surprising person, that her moods are changeable and her personality many-sided. But Cleopatra is also various as an element in the drama. She is more than one kind of character, which may be why she provokes so much disagreement among critics. For my purposes there are three Cleopatras. At one level she is the embodiment of Egypt and a symbol of our antihistorical experience. At another level she represents the Other as against Antony's representation of the Self. As such, she appears indifferent to the destiny of the male Self; here, as in the other Shakespearean tragedies, the hero's encounter with this apparently indifferent Other is an important part of his tragic-heroic adventure. And finally Cleopatra is a character like Antony himself, facing failure and defeat, motivated by the desire to contain or rise above her losses. Let us begin with the first and most familiar Cleopatra, Cleopatra-as-Egypt.

This first Cleopatra is an alternative, for the reader and for Antony, to Caesar and Rome. She has had the lion's share of the critical attention, so it is unnecessary to deal with her at great length. This Cleopatra is the "serpent of old Nile" (I.v.25), a principle of pleasure, of fertility and decay, of artifice, of ambiguity. She opposes the cold, abstract certainties of Rome with the heat of her body; Caesar challenges Antony to be preeminent in the world of men whereas Cleopatra challenges him to his destiny as a lover. She represents the Egypt Antony describes to Lepidus when he returns to Rome:

> The higher Nilus swells,
> The more it promises; as it ebbs, the seedsman
> Upon the slime and ooze scatters his grain,
> And shortly comes to harvest.   (II.vii.21–24)

This Cleopatra is not so much a character in her own right as an experience of Antony's and a problem for his judgment. This is the one who might be good or bad, who attacks and eludes both the audience and the hero. Is she finally faithful to Antony or not? Is it worth giving up the honors of Rome to pursue something so shifty and unpossessable? We can never know. Take, for instance, the scene in which Cleopatra apparently plans to defect to Caesar. Thidias tells Cleopatra that Caesar "knows you embraced not Antony / As you did love, but as you feared him," and Cleopatra, as soon as she can collect her wits, responds, "He is a god, and knows / What is most right" (III.xiii.56–57, 60–61). This is enough for Enobarbus, who leaves to tell Antony that Cleopatra is "quitting" him. But Enobarbus only witnesses this speech in the first place because Cleopatra insists that he stay to hear it. Is it possible that Cleopatra *means* Enobarbus to report her to Antony? Could this be merely another ploy for Antony's attention and not really a betrayal? Furthermore, the scene ends with Enobarbus's desertion, not Cleopatra's: "I will seek," says Enobarbus, "Some way to leave him" (III.xiii.200–201). So we must ask ourselves, in retrospect, who was being faithful to Antony here, Enobarbus or Cleopatra? He actually does leave Antony (although he later returns in spirit) whereas she does not (or does she?). To hunt for this Cleopatra is to double back so many times that we forget what we were looking for. As Egypt, Cleopatra is radically ambiguous and can never be finally known.

The Cleopatra Antony perceives is this elusive one. He cannot wholly love her or wholly leave her; he can never bring himself to make final judgments of her, and yet he cannot put judgment aside. Only when he believes she is dead or when he is himself dying can he act from a love unmixed with fear and suspicion. Antony's fears are for his place in history as well as for the returns on his love. He has trusted his reputation to Cleopatra; if she is untrue to him, his fate will have been that of a strumpet's fool. He dies with his essential question about her unanswered, although at the moment of his death he is no longer interested in such questions.

If we read Cleopatra entirely as a principle, *our* question about her goes unanswered also. We do not know whether she is good or bad, important or trivial, Antony's greatest adventure or his "dotage" (I.i.1). John Danby is one of many critics who read Cleopatra as Egypt; his excellent essay on *Antony and Cleopatra* quite explicitly recognizes the consequences of doing so. That is, his essay deals with what *I* consider the consequences of doing so; Danby himself does not connect what I see as interpretive cause and effect. If Cleopatra is Egypt and the crucial dialectic is between Egypt and Rome, the play does not resolve, does not progress, does not reach any kind of tragic climax. Neither Egypt nor Rome represents values endorsed by the play as a whole:

> The Roman condemnation of the lovers is obviously inadequate. The sentimental reaction in their favor is equally mistaken. There is no so-called "love-romanticism" in the play. The flesh has its glory and its passion, its witchery. Love in *Antony and Cleopatra* is both these. The love of Antony and Cleopatra, however, is not asserted as a "final value." . . . To . . . claim that there is a "redemption" motif in Antony and Cleopatra's love is an . . . error. To the Shakespeare who wrote *King Lear* it would surely smack of blasphemy. The fourth and fifth acts of *Antony and Cleopatra* are not epiphanies. They are the ends moved to by that process whereby things rot themselves with motion—unhappy and bedizened and sordid, streaked with the mean, the ignoble, the contemptible. . . .
>
> *Antony and Cleopatra* is an account of things in terms of the World and the Flesh, Rome and Egypt, the two great contraries that maintain and destroy each other, considered apart from any third sphere which might stand over against them.[1]

King Lear, according to Danby, is eschatological, *Antony and Cleopatra* merely analytical. In the latter play opposite temperaments are merely weighed against each other, and each is found wanting the other's virtues. There is a "diminution of scope" from the earlier tragedies. What is missing from *Antony and Cleopatra,* according to Danby, is the theme of "Nature." By "Nature" he means "a reality that transcends the political and the personal," something that tests the soul of man. King Lear, says Danby, is tested and tempered by Nature, by the world beyond the Self; the characters in *Antony and Cleopatra* test only each other, commenting on each other's limitations. So "*Antony and Cleopatra* gives the impression of being a technical tour-de-force which Shakespeare enjoyed for its own sake."[2]

Danby's Nature seems very close to what I have been calling the Other: a reality external to the Self with which the hero is confronted in tragedy. We do battle with this Other because it seems to betray us, to make us less than we were; ultimately we transcend our antagonism to it, at which point it no longer seems implacably hostile to us. The dialectic between the Self and the Other, often reflected in the dialectical progression of the hero's relationship with women, does seem to resolve in tragedy. This dialectic— unlike the dialectic Danby finds between Egypt and Rome—does not simply exhaust itself. It creates something new: the tragic hero in his final phase, the Self transformed. If we read Cleopatra as the representative of the Other and not merely as Egypt, the diachronic movement of the play, which Danby sees as wholly "discreating," takes on a more positive aspect.

In a sense, of course, there is little difference between Cleopatra as Egypt and Cleopatra as the Other, for it is *as* Egypt that Cleopatra represents the Other. But in this reading Egypt and Rome are no longer equal but opposite options for the hero. In this reading Egypt is the new world, the world that calls into question all the old certainties, the heath on which Antony faces the indifference of the universe and his own falling off from what he means to be. Egypt replaces or rewrites Rome as experience replaces and rewrites innocence. When Antony returns to Rome, it is gone; the world in which physical courage and manly purpose prevail has been replaced by a world of drinking, matchmaking, speechifying, and deal-making. Roman honor, after Antony's time in Egypt, has become as elusive and dubious an ideal as Egyptian love. What it *had been* we may gather from Caesar's description of Antony before Egypt, on campaign:

> Antony,
> Leave thy lascivious wassails. When thou once
> Was beaten from Modena, where thou slew'st
> Hirtius and Pansa, consuls, at thy heel
> Did famine follow, whom thou fought'st against
> (Though daintily brought up) with patience more
> Than savages could suffer. Thou didst drink
> The stale of horses and the gilded puddle
> Which beasts would cough at. Thy palate then did deign
> The roughest berry on the rudest hedge.
> Yea, like the stag when snow the pasture sheets,
> The barks of trees thou browsed. On the Alps
> It is reported thou didst eat strange flesh,
> Which some did die to look on. And all this
> (It wounds thine honor that I speak it now)
> Was borne so like a soldier that thy cheek
> So much as lanked not.   (I.iv.55–71)

Prelapsarian Rome, like all the prelapsarian worlds of Shakespearean tragedy, was a world in which honor and manhood followed directly from the fulfillment of clear-cut criteria. In returning to Rome Antony means to return to a more clearly defined
manhood; he means to return to his old role as a fighting general.
"The beds i' th' East are soft," he tells Pompey,

> and thanks to you,
> That called me timelier than my purpose hither;
> For I have gained by't.   (II.vi.50–52)

But Rome can no longer be represented by the hardened body of
the general on campaign. In its own way it has gone as soft as the
beds in the East; it is pictured as a mean and drunken party on a
boat. After Egypt the corruption of Rome is revealed, to Antony
and to us. Antony's return to Egypt is inevitable; the old world is
gone and he has no choice but to live in the new.

If Egypt, then, is the new world—the world of the Other and
not merely an equal-but-opposite alternative to Rome—then
Cleopatra's identification with Egypt offers us the possibility of a
different interpretation from Danby's. In this case we may interpret
the phases of Antony's relationship to Cleopatra as phases in his
response to the new world. Seen from this point of view, the play
seems less committed than Danby thinks to "the sense of ripe-
rottenness and hopelessness, the vision of self-destruction [and] the
feeling of . . . fevered futility."[3] Danby charts the falling curve of
the dialectic between Egypt and Rome; this dialectic, as he points
out, loses energy as the play goes on. But the dialectic between Self
and Other gains energy until it reaches a kind of resolution. The
second dialectic begins with the refusal of the Other, develops into
misogynist rage, and resolves into kindness and connectedness.

It may seem paradoxical to refer to Antony's early relations with
Cleopatra as a species of denial. His first speech, after all, is one of
the most famous declarations of love in all of literature:

> Let Rome in Tiber melt, and the wide arch
> Of the ranged empire fall! Here is my space,
> Kingdoms are clay: our dungy earth alike
> Feeds beast as man. The nobleness of life
> Is to do thus; when such a mutual pair
> And such a twain can do't, in which I bind,
> On pain of punishment, the world to weet
> We stand up peerless.   (I.i.33–40)

But from this point until his reunion with Cleopatra in Act III, scene vii, Antony fights a losing battle to limit his relationship with her, to avoid the choice he so grandly claims, in the first scene, already to have made. He succumbs to the Roman view of his relationship, returns to Rome and marries Octavia. Antony does not deny his desire for Cleopatra; but he denies the revolutionary nature of his desire. He denies the radical changes in the Self that will be necessary to accommodate the Other; he denies the choice she imposes between Rome and Egypt, between an asexual and a sexual identity. Rome, of course, is opposed to sexuality not per se but only as it interferes with business. Caesar defines the Roman position as follows:

> Let's grant it is not
> Amiss to tumble on the bed of Ptolemy
> . . .
> . . . yet must Antony
> No way excuse his foils when we do bear
> So great weight in his lightness. If he filled
> His vacancy with his voluptuousness,
> Full surfeits and the dryness of his bones
> Call on him for't. But to confound such time
> That drums him from his sport and speaks as loud
> As his own state and ours, 'tis to be chid
> As we rate boys who, being mature in knowledge
> Pawn their experience to the present pleasure
> And so rebel to judgment.   (I.iv. 16–17, 23–33)

To Caesar and Rome, relationships with women are a leisure-time activity, something to fill up "vacancy." When serious business is broached—war or political realignments or the dividing up of land—a man who continues to "tumble on the bed" risks his place in the world of men. A sexual adventure is a luxury, an excursion one might make from a journey whose goals lie elsewhere. Antony's very decision to return to Cleopatra reflects the Roman attitude toward sexuality: "I will to Egypt," Antony says, "And though I make this marriage for my peace, / I' th' East my pleasure lies" (II.iii. 37–39). The imperial Self visits here and there, demanding "peace" in one place and "pleasure" in another. The Other is denied its dialectical relationship with the Self and valued only insofar as it brings pleasure. In this phase of the drama the Self refuses the Other and puts his faith in the firmness of his own boundaries.

Antony's first action of the play is his departure from Egypt. We are not really sorry to see him leave; we are pleased to see him recover his decisiveness and resist Cleopatra's wiles. But we should be troubled, I think, to notice that Antony's language as he leaves for Rome becomes transparently rhetorical. "By the fire/That quickens Nilus' slime," he tells Cleopatra,

> I go from hence
> Thy soldier-servant, making peace or war
> As thou affects. (I.iii.68–71)

This is simply untrue. Cleopatra has vigorously resisted Antony's departure; as a soldier he is precisely *not* her servant but makes peace or war as he himself affects. The speech is downright embarrassing; Cleopatra simply pretends not to have heard it: "Cut my lace, Charmian, come—" she says, "But let it be: I am quickly ill, and well,/So Antony loves" (I.iii.71–73). Antony's last words to Cleopatra are similarly specious:

> Our separation so abides and flies
> That thou residing here goes yet with me,
> And I hence fleeting here remain with thee.
> Away. (I.iii.102–5)

There is something silly, if not actually dishonest, about this scrap of an Elizabethan valediction poem. It makes a gesture in the direction of ideal love—but so cursory a gesture to so lofty an ideal is a kind of self-contradiction. And apart from its sing-song rhythm, easy rhyme, and conventional ideas, it is quite inappropriate at this moment. For the departure of the man into the man's world of business is an unpleasant inevitability in the lyric poems, whereas everything up to this point has emphasized the element of choice in Antony's departure. The grandeur of "Let Rome in Tiber melt" has been replaced by a feeble convention. In this movement Antony's relations with Cleopatra are only romantic; the flip side of his romanticism is his Roman instinct to limit relations with the Other.

If Antony's language in this first movement reflects the limitations of his relationship to the Other, so, too, do his actions. His marriage to Octavia is doubly significant in this respect. First of all, it is clearly a betrayal of Egypt and Cleopatra. Second, it is also an alliance with a woman who accepts her role as a leisure-time activity and offers no resistance to Antony's life in the world of men. To get things straight from the beginning, Antony intones to his new wife, "The world and my great office will sometimes / Divide me from your bosom" (II.iii.1–2). Octavia doesn't skip a beat:

> All the which time
> Before the gods my knee shall bow my prayers
> To them for you.　　　　　　　　　　　　　　　(II.iii.2–4)

Octavia will have no demands to make of her husband that conflict with his demands on himself. Leaving her for good, Antony will later tell her,

> If I lose mine honor,
> I lose myself: better I were not yours
> Than yours so branchless.　　　　　　　　　　(III.iv.22–24)

And poor Octavia will not hear the false note. Unlike Cleopatra she is not aware that the appeal to "honor," to his position in the world of men, may mask a breach of faith with her. She sends him off—to Cleopatra, as it turns out—without demur. In choosing Octavia over Cleopatra, Antony tries to choose a *limited* relationship with the Other. Unlike Cleopatra, Octavia offers no threat to the preexisting integrity of the Self.

In the next movement of the play Antony returns to Egypt for good. He does not exactly choose to do so, but his betrayal of Octavia makes another reconciliation with Caesar out of the question. Antony now has nowhere else to go. It is this knowledge that makes the next phase of his relations with Cleopatra so tumultuous and at the same time so much less theatrical than the opening movement of the play. There is no more striking of poses. The first time we see the lovers back together they are not, as we might have expected, dramatizing their reunion; they are holding a strategy session. Of course, it is because of Cleopatra that the strategy they settle on is a disastrous one; they will meet Caesar at sea. Enobarbus is horrified:

> Most worthy sir, you therein throw away
> The absolute soldiership you have by land,
> 　. . .
> 　　　　　　　　　　　　. . . quite forgo
> The way which promises assurance, and
> Give up yourself merely to chance and hazard
> From firm security.　　　　　　　　(III.vii.41–42, 45–48)

This is precisely what Antony has done by throwing in his lot with Cleopatra. In his relationship with her he is indeed at sea; he has forgone the assurance of success that Rome promises her sons for the "chance and hazard" of Egypt, Cleopatra, and a life centered on his own sexuality. He is indeed at sea, as all the tragic heroes are when they leave the "firm security" of the patriarchal system and confront the Other dialectically. And at sea Cleopatra is uncontrollable, unfathomable, and possibly unfaithful, even though Antony has committed his worldly fortunes to his relationship with her. Now the antagonism between his worldly affairs and his role as a lover can no longer be glossed over with courtly lies—"thy soldier-servant," etc. Now everything comes out into the open, and the results are those Shakespearean moments when the hero is taken over by sexual loathing:

> I found you as a morsel cold upon
> Dead Ceasar's trencher: nay, you were a fragment
> Of Gneius Pompey's, besides what hotter hours,
> Unregist'red in vulgar fame, you have
> Luxuriously picked out. For I am sure,
> Though you can guess what temperance should be,
> You know not what it is.   (III.xiii.116–22)

The opening of the sexual wound is here, as so often in Shakespeare, a symptom of the hero's confrontation with what Danby calls Nature and what I have been calling the Other. The new world—Egypt and Cleopatra—has become an inevitability for Antony and not merely a pleasure he may choose to enjoy or not. The difficulties of the new world—its ambiguity and its possible hostility to Antony—are now revealed, and Antony responds to the revelation with rage and disbelief. The intensity of his response is now unmistakably genuine; it is no literary convention that prompts his violent "Triple-turned whore!" or his fantasy of Octavia plowing up Cleopatra's face "with her prepared nails" (IV.xii.13, 39).

The final phase is one that the heroes never enter until it is too late. In this phase Antony simply abandons judgment of Cleopatra even though he has received no adequate explanation or apology from her. The last phase begins when Cleopatra, who may or may not have betrayed Antony in battle, thinks to avoid his anger by sending him word that she is dead:

> Mardian, go tell him I have slain myself:
> Say that the last I spoke was "Antony"
> And word it, prithee, piteously. Hence, Mardian,
> And bring me how he takes my death.   (IV.xiii.7–10)

The news abruptly turns the tide of Antony's emotions, which had been running heavily against Cleopatra. On hearing it Antony says, "I will o'ertake thee, Cleopatra, and /Weep for my pardon" (IV.xiv.44–45). Cleopatra's supposed suicide is proof to Antony that she has *not* "disposed with Caesar" (IV.xiv.123) and therefore that she has been loyal to himself. Cleopatra becomes "she which by her death our Caesar tells/'I am conqueror of myself'" (IV.xiv.61–62). When Antony learns that her suicide was a fake, however, his feelings toward her do not undergo another reversal. His anger and hatred do not return. "Bear me," he says immediately on hearing the news, "where Cleopatra bides" (IV.xiv.131); and his last words concern her safety after his death, not the unresolved question of her fidelity to him. In this phase of his story Antony is no longer concerned about Cleopatra as she controls his destiny. It is *her* destiny he thinks of at this point; his own he implicitly trusts to her.

Antony is Shakespeare's most sustained study in the temptation to limit or avoid sexuality where it conflicts with the hero's role in the world of men. The two halves of his life ultimately merge in spite of his efforts to keep them apart: by the second phase of the play Antony's political and personal destinies come together in Egypt. Antony alternately rages against the new world and sadly accepts it; in his dying moments his objections to it seem to have vanished altogether. Antony's final attitude toward Cleopatra is resonant with more than itself. If Cleopatra and Egypt stand for the world we fall into when we discover Nature, then Antony's final unprotesting love for Cleopatra affirms the value of our unsatisfactory natural lives. In his final moments Antony is at peace; he loves what he loves in spite of everything.

Where Danby sees a trend toward exhaustion, disintegration, and "rot[ting] with motion," then, I see a trend toward the recognition and acceptance of the Other. But I cannot claim that the trend I see is very pronounced or that it is powerful enough to counterbalance the disintegrative tendencies of the play. For our glimpse of Antony at peace is very brief. We cannot compare it to our vision of, for instance, Hamlet in *his* final phase. Antony has no graveyard scene, no long still moment when he performs for us his newfound ease. Furthermore, his death does not end the play. What happens to Antony is only part of the story; if we are looking for a sense of resolution we must look at what happens to Cleopatra as well. Does *her* story resolve? Does the fifth act halt the trend toward disintegration, offer an image of something permanent and valuable in human life? If not, then we must agree with Danby that it represents a kind of falling-off from *Hamlet* and *Lear;* Antony's dying words are simply not enough.

Of course, I disagree with Danby. *Antony and Cleopatra,* I think, resolves by offering us an image of a great love relationship. Just as Hamlet and Lear become greatly valuable to us in spite of everything, so too does the relationship between these lovers. This relationship, like whatever is grand about the heroes, endures the confrontation with Nature. It survives the test and resolves the play. But of course we cannot talk about the relationship apart from the lovers who enact it. The confrontation with Nature is endured by both Antony and Cleopatra; having seen something of Antony's relations with Nature we must now turn to Cleopatra's. Cleopatra confronts Nature not as Egypt nor as Antony's Other but as a character with her own destiny at stake.

Does this mean that Cleopatra, alone among Shakespeare's women, is a tragic hero, a version of the Self rather than the Other? Linda Fitz believes that she is. In her revisionist essay "Egyptian Queens and Male Reviewers," Fitz argues that we must understand Cleopatra from the inside since "Shakespeare . . . takes pains to let Cleopatra explain her contrary behavior and give the reasons for it (I.iii)." Cleopatra, according to Fitz, "struggles with her own inconstancy" and "learns and grows as Antony does not."[4] And yet where can we be sure we are getting an inside view of Cleopatra rather than a performance? Only, I think, in Act I, scene iii, the scene Fitz refers to above. This scene is very important to my interpretation as it provides us with an opening through which we can turn the play inside out; through this opening we may see things, as through the wrong end of the opera glasses, from Cleopatra's point of view. But the play does not maintain continuous contact with Cleopatra's point of view; it does not bring us close to Cleopatra for more than a few speeches; it does not give us any insight into the struggles of her inner life. The revelation moment merely tells us of her struggle to keep her lover:

> *Charmian*   Madam, methinks, if you did love him dearly,
>   You do not hold the method to enforce
>   The like from him.
> *Cleopatra*   What should I do, I do not?
> *Charmian*   In each thing give him way, cross him in nothing.
> *Cleopatra*   Thou teachest like a fool: the way to lose him.
>
> (I.iii.6–10)

What we see here is Cleopatra's strategy in dealing with what is outside herself, not any struggle "against her own inconstancy." This exchange does briefly but radically shift the perspective from Antony's to Cleopatra's; and this one shift gives us permission, as it were, to speculate on Cleopatra's motives and goals. It suggests a limited likeness between Cleopatra and the tragic version of Self. But we must acknowledge that our speculative reconstruction of Cleopatra's point of view is a wholly intellectual project. We are not close to Cleopatra, as we are to the tragic hero; we do not sympathize with her or share her hopes and fears. In fact, in the very scenes where the story might evoke most sympathy for her we are most carefully kept at a distance. Whenever Cleopatra suffers loss or defeat she is presented comically, unflatteringly, or ambiguously.

Consider, for instance, the scene in which Cleopatra learns that Antony has married Octavia. Clearly, *she* is *his* victim here and not the other way around. And yet we are dramatically prevented from taking her side, from sympathizing with her against him. She is presented as unreasonable, willful, capricious, and jealous—not as wronged, hurt, or sad. When the messenger arrives she flings herself at him melodramatically until he says in exasperation, "Will't please you hear me?"—to which she characteristically replies, "I have a mind to strike thee ere thou speak'st" (II.v.41–42). The scene proceeds:

> *Cleopatra*   Yet, if thou say Antony lives, is well,
>   Or friends with Caesar, or not captive to him,
>   I'll set thee in a shower of gold, and hail
>   Rich pearls upon thee.
> *Messenger*   Madam, he's well.
> *Cleopatra*   Well said.
> *Messenger*   And friends with Caesar.
> *Cleopatra*   Th'art an honest man.
> *Messenger*   Caesar and he are greater friends than ever.
> *Cleopatra*   Make thee a fortune from me.

> *Messenger*   But yet, Madam—
> *Cleopatra*   I do not like "But yet"; it does allay
>   The good precedence: fie upon "But yet";
>   "But yet" is as a jailer to bring forth
>   Some monstrous malefactor. Prithee, friend,
>   Pour out the pack of matter to mine ear,
>   The good and bad together: he's friends with Caesar,
>   In state of health, thou say'st, and thou say'st, free.
> *Messenger*   Free, madam, no: I made no such report;
>   He's bound unto Octavia.
> *Cleopatra*   For what good turn?
> *Messenger*   For the best turn i' th' bed.
> *Cleopatra*   I am pale, Charmian.
> *Messenger*   Madam, he's married to Octavia.
> *Cleopatra*   The most infectious pestilence upon thee!
>   *Strikes him down.*
>   (II.v.43–61)

We are elaborately prevented from sharing in Cleopatra's emotions at the very moment when it would be most natural for us to do so.

Another example is the very first skirmish of the play. In the first three scenes Cleopatra struggles to keep her lover from leaving her; by the fourth scene he is gone. And yet the dominant impression left by these scenes is of Cleopatra running circles around Antony, maneuvering him into professions of love only to jeer at them, taunting him with loving Fulvia and with not loving Fulvia, throwing up a fog of accusations and contradictions around Antony's efforts to make a judgment on his situation. Antony, says Danby, is "like the man innocent of jujitsu who thinks he is pushing when really he is being pulled." We may notice, if we like, that at the end of it all the innocent leaves the adept; but we are not free to sympathize very deeply with Cleopatra's loss. We are at least as pleased that Antony has broken away as we are sorry that Cleopatra has been left alone.

But although we do not feel Cleopatra's suffering, we may, if we wish, infer it. We cannot make Emilia the hero of *Othello,* as Carol Neely suggests,[5] nor even Cordelia the hero of *King Lear.* But we can, if we wish, shape a tragic fable around Cleopatra without violating or supplementing the data of the play. Through a glass darkly we can see that she, too, faces the challenge of an unsatisfactory Nature; she, too, resists her diminishment according to its laws. Although at one level she is herself a representative of the

Other, she also confronts the Other. The third Cleopatra is in fact the most important one for my interpretation. If we overlook her, the play does not resolve.

Nature (or the Other) in *Antony and Cleopatra*, whether Cleopatra represents it or confronts it, is quite different from Nature in *King Lear.* There Nature consists of starkest good and starkest evil; our difficulty is that the reality of the one may be concealed by the illusion of the other. Here we are faced with no such absolutes. Rather we are faced with an acceptable level of niggling everyday selfishness, with the perfectly understandable compromises we make, with ordinary failures of clarity and courage. Loss and defeat are undramatic here; no one stands on the heath and roars with astonishment and pain. In most of Shakespeare's tragedies, as A. C. Bradley notes,[6] we are confronted early on with "scenes of action or passion which agitate the audience with alarm, horror, painful expectation, or absorbing sympathies and antipathies." What is there of this in the first three acts of *Antony and Cleopatra*? "Almost nothing. People converse, discuss, accuse one another, excuse themselves, mock, describe, drink together, arrange a marriage, meet and part; but they do not kill, do not even tremble or weep." In *Antony and Cleopatra* the thing in nature that works against the characters is undramatic and diffuse; nevertheless it grinds away. In almost every scene some character is shown by his own or another's analysis to be smaller than he would like to think himself. Ventidius tells us that Antony is not free from jealousy of his own lieutenants (III.i); Antony tells us that the loyalties of the common people are shifty and perverse (I.iii); Pompey tells Menas that his own honor depends on technicalities (II.vii); Charmian reminds Cleopatra that she has loved before (I.iv); Antony notices his own inconstancy toward Fulvia:

> What our contempts doth often hurl from us,
> We wish it ours again. The present pleasure,
> By revolution low'ring, does become
> The opposite of itself: she's good, being gone;
> The hand could pluck her back that shoved her on.

> (I.ii.124–28)

All of these speeches imply that there are no absolutes, no unambiguous goods—or that even if there are, human nature can never adhere to them long enough to matter.

Such is the Nature that Shakespeare deals with in *Antony and*

Cleopatra, Danby to the contrary. And just as Lear's accomplishment is appropriate to the Nature of that play, so Antony's and Cleopatra's are appropriate to this. In *King Lear,* where warring cosmological forces seem in danger of overwhelming the significance of the human drama, Lear's search for value and joy takes on a kind of religious intensity. In *Antony and Cleopatra* it is much harder to know where to have the enemy, for here we are dealing not with the inhuman but with the all-too-human. If Lear's achievement is the depths to which he can root himself in such unfriendly soil, Antony-and-Cleopatra's perhaps, is in rising above the undergrowth of everyday failure into the sunshine of history, myth, story. Antony and Cleopatra do become famous, historical. Their ambition is to make themselves special, and as we shall see, they do.

Antony and Cleopatra, of course, do not struggle as a couple against Nature; they struggle individually, and they often appear to be struggling against each other. For if Cleopatra often represents Nature to Antony, often he represents it to her. But although at one level there is conflict between them, their separate and individual campaigns against Nature are at another level complementary. There is a third and final dialectic in the opposition between their different modes of meeting the challenge of Nature; it is the resolution to this dialectic that resolves the play.

Antony struggles with Nature by struggling with himself; Cleopatra has no quarrel with herself and struggles exclusively with the outside world. Whereas Antony resists his decline by struggling to become his own ideal, Cleopatra struggles only to keep her lover, to outfox Caesar, to win admiration from all. She is aware of no gap between what she is and what she ought to be, only of the gap between what she wants and what she has. Even when we put Cleopatra in the position of the striving Self, we must notice that she struggles as an Other, as a fixed identity. She is not self-divided, like the tragic heroes; she is at work on her destiny but not, like them, on herself.

Antony struggles to control his destiny by taking control of himself. "Ten thousand harms," he tells himself in Act I, scene ii, "my idleness doth hatch," and so he resolves to be less idle. He decides to become a good Roman again and urges the messenger

> Speak to me home, mince not the general tongue:
> Name Cleopatra as she is called in Rome;

> Rail thou in Fulvia's phrase, and taunt my faults
> With such full license as both truth and malice
> Have power to utter.   (I.ii.106–10)

Antony wants to hear his "ills" so he can mend them. He fights his sense of dissolving identity—of submission to the play's occasions—with the weapons of self-consciousness and will power. Although the decisions he takes about his character are often impossible to carry out, he is always sincere in his resolutions. It is the essence of the battle he wages against Nature that he should always believe he means what he says. He tells Octavia, "I have not kept my square, but that to come/Shall all be done by th' rule" (II.iii. 6–7), and he means it, even though thirty lines later he decides to return to Cleopatra. When he fails to live up to his resolutions he is bitter in his self-recriminations: "I have fled myself, and have instructed cowards/To run and show their shoulders" (III.xi.7–8). He is always ready to accept instruction; when Cleopatra, in the first words we see her address to him since he left for Rome, advises him that "Celerity is never more admired/Than by the negligent," he answers,

> A good rebuke,
> Which might have well becomed the best of men
> To taunt at slackness.   (III.vii.24–27)

Finally, when he thinks that Cleopatra has killed herself and sees Eros do so, he takes their deeds as a lesson:

> Thrice-nobler than myself,
> Thou teachest me, O valiant Eros, what
> I should, and thou couldst not. My queen and Eros
> Have by their brave instruction got upon me
> A nobleness in record.   (IV.xiv.95–99)

All these are efforts to be the man he thinks he should be; Antony is always at work on himself. Cleopatra, on the other hand, reproaches herself with nothing, rejects her past when it does not do her honor ("My salad days"—I.v.73), makes no resolutions for the future, and takes instruction from no one. She is fighting Nature with quite different weapons. If Antony tries to be a center that will hold, Cleopatra seems anxious to appear the least coherent thing on the landscape. Antony aims for constancy, of identity and of Fortune; Cleopatra reveals the constancy of her identity through her extravagant feigning and controls her Fortune by changing roles faster than it requires her to do. Instead of aiming for a solidity of personality that will control her universe, she risks everything on her capacity to fly faster than the Fortune that pursues her.

The crucial speech by which to distinguish between the two modes is Antony's great meditation on his own sense of shapelessness:

> Sometimes we see a cloud that's dragonish,
> A vapor sometime like a bear or lion,
> A tower citadel, a pendant rock,
> A forkèd mountain, or blue promontory
> With trees upon't that nod unto the world
> And mock our eyes with air.
>   . . .
> My good knave Eros, now thy captain is
> Even such a body: here I am Antony,
> Yet cannot hold this visible shape, my knave.
>
> (IV.xiv.2–7, 12–14)

Antony here is divided from himself, disappointed in himself and uncertain of his own identity. Cleopatra has no such speech; it is of the essence of Cleopatra, even of this third, possibly suffering Cleopatra, that she should have no such speech. Even as she passes through the phases of the tragic fable Cleopatra never comments on herself with disapproval, never shares with us the slightest dissatisfaction in herself. Her commentary is always (at least in part) a performance. Since we are aware of no seams in her personality, since there are no openings through which we can have at her innermost soul, she appears to us, as she does to Antony, mysterious and perfect-unto-herself. Antony's description of Egypt's emblematic animal, the crocodile, applies quite as well to Egypt's queen:

> It is shaped, sir, like itself, and it is as broad as it hath breadth; it is
> just so high as it is, and moves with its own organs.
>
> (II.vii.43–45)

Whereas Antony anatomizes himself for us, telling us his shape and breadth and height at each point in the play, Cleopatra never does. So though we seem to see as clearly as Antony the varying shapes he assumes, we can only say that Cleopatra, like the crocodile, is as broad as she has breadth.

The difference between Antony's and Cleopatra's styles of confronting Nature may be illustrated by a comparison between his
dealings with Caesar and hers. Both are underdogs when they first
face him; other than that the scenes that they stage have nothing in
common. Before the meeting between Caesar and Antony early in
Act II, Enobarbus suggests that Antony may lose his temper. "If
Caesar move him," says Enobarbus, "Let Antony look over
Caesar's head / And speak as loud as Mars" (II.ii.4–6). But of course
Antony does no such thing. His final speech of the argument is as
follows:

> As nearly as I may,
> I'll play the penitent to you: but mine honesty
> Shall not make poor my greatness, nor my power
> Work without it. Truth is, that Fulvia,
> To have me out of Egypt, made wars here,
> For which myself, the ignorant motive, do
> So far ask pardon as befits mine honor
> To stoop in such a case.   (II.ii.91–98)

Antony, as usual, is trying to bind together expediency, or responsibility, to the Idea of Antony. He uses his authentic self in the battle
for his destiny; his dignity and fair-mindedness rather than his
excuses are the answers that he makes to Caesar's accusations. It is a
very impressive and admirable speech; there is poise and confidence
in the way that Antony walks the line between chest-thumping and
self-deprecation. Yet, Nature being what it is in the play, the truth
that Antony achieves by confronting destiny this way is vulnerable
to an immediate and unanswerable attack:

> *Enobarbus* Or, if you borrow one another's love for the instant,
>   you may, when you hear no more words of Pompey, return
>   it again: you shall have time to wrangle in when you have
>   nothing else to do.
> *Antony* Thou art a soldier only; speak no more.
> *Enobarbus* That truth should be silent I had almost forgot.
> *Antony* You wrong this presence; therefore speak no more.
> *Enobarbus* Go to, then; your considerate stone.
>
>   (II.ii.103–11)

Because Antony opts for a version of sincerity, his compromises
with expediency leave him vulnerable to cynicism.

Cleopatra, on the other hand, never bothers to put the pieces of herself in truthful relation to one another and is therefore not vulnerable to an attack on the final assembly. She leaves the pieces of her identity false, because fragmentary, and flings them at the agents of her declining Fortunes. When she finds herself at a disadvantage before Caesar, she plays her part with an extravagance that would be unthinkable in Antony. Toward the end of the play, "I'll take my leave," says Caesar to Cleopatra after a few polite threats. Cleopatra dramatically and unnecessarily answers him,

> And may, through all the world: 'tis yours, and we,
> Your scutcheons and your signs of conquest, shall
> Hang in what place you please.   (V.ii.133–36)

The difference betwen Antony's balanced apology and Cleopatra's abandoned self-abnegation is not due to the deterioration of the political situation between the one and the other. It is due to the fact that Antony always plays himself as nearly as he can, whereas Cleopatra purposely keeps herself separate from her roles.

Antony takes the straight path to sincerity and finds it mined by his own slightly tainted motives. Cleopatra's brand of sincerity brings to mind a passage in Mailer's *Advertisements for Myself* in which Mailer comments on his own search for an authentic style: "To write about myself is to send my style through a circus of variations and postures, a fireworks of virtuosity designed to achieve . . . I do not even know what. Leave it that I become a quick-change artist, as if I believe I can trap the Prince of Truth in the act of switching a style."[7] But although Cleopatra is also a quick-change artist, Mailer's passage is actually a better description of Hamlet than of Cleopatra. Hamlet's variations and postures are designed to achieve . . . he does not know what. Cleopatra's are purposive rather than exploratory. They are not cultures to nourish the embryo of her final, fully developed being; they are deployed by a preexisting identity on missions in its own interests. Like the women in the comedies, and unlike Hamlet, Cleopatra is revealed and not changed by her actions. In a play that is crisscrossed by journeys all over the Mediterranean, Cleopatra alone stays at home. She is no quester; she makes no odyssey in search of herself.

The relevant comparison here is with Octavia, who journeys from Rome to Athens and back again in the effort to reconcile the two men by whom she is defined. It would seem, in Act V, that

Cleopatra is caught between these same two men, for it has been made clear through the imagery that an alliance with Caesar would be a sexual matter and amount to a betrayal of Antony. Caesar's metaphor, as he looks forward to his conquest of her, is of sexual capitulation:

> Women are not
> In their best fortunes strong, but want will perjure
> The ne'er-touched vestal.   (III.xii.29–31)

But Cleopatra, unlike Octavia, defines herself. Her changes of style are not experiments in a new identity as Caesar's ally but rather attempts to flush out the danger to her soul that she senses in Caesar. She is faced not with a choice between men but with a threat to her own identity. It is through her fidelity to herself that she is ultimately faithful to Antony, although it is no coincidence that this should be true. Antony recognizes her, Caesar would ruin her. Octavia, having no identity of her own, cannot be said to have been faithful to either man. *Her* fidelity simply doesn't matter, whereas Cleopatra's does.

And this, in fact, has been Cleopatra's goal all along—to make herself matter. Antony struggles with the problem of judgment, thinking that to make his mark on the world he must make correct distinctions between right and wrong, true and false, Rome and Egypt, honor and love. Cleopatra does not bother to make judgments. She meets her occasions with whatever she can find within herself, authentic or not, that will give her the edge. Just as she tries to make herself interesting rather than pleasing to Antony, so she tries always to be the one who elicits judgments rather than the one who makes them. She has no use for Charmian's advice, "In time we hate that which we often fear" (I.iii.12). It does not matter whether Antony's emotions toward her are good or bad; what matters is that he should not be able to leave off trying to figure her out.

At his death scene Antony gives Cleopatra a nugget of absolute, Roman advice: trust Proculeius. But like all his efforts to make absolute judgments, this one is a failure. Proculeius betrays and captures her. So Cleopatra once again switches styles. When Dolabella appears, he asks her to say that she has heard of him, but she refuses to make even such a trivial judgment of him as this. Instead, she forces him to judge her. At the end of her speech "I dreamt there was an Emperor Antony" (V.ii.76 et seq.), she asks him, "Think you there was or might be such a man / As this I dreamt of?" (V.ii.93–94), and Dolabella answers, "Gentle madam, no." But it does not matter that his judgment is negative; for what is at issue is not her truth, but the validity of her claim to be the center of attention, the topic of conversation, the object of judgment. And Dolabella, although he rejects her version of Antony, accepts her greatness:

> Your loss is as yourself, great; and you bear it
> As answering to the weight. Would I might never
> O'ertake pursued success, but I do feel,
> By the rebound of yours, a grief that smites
> My very heart at root.   (V.ii.101–5)

Seeing that her work is done, Cleopatra does not waste any further time: "I thank you, sir. / Know you what Caesar means to do with me?" (V.ii.105–6). And of course Dolabella tells her what she needs to know: that Caesar means to lead her in triumph through the streets of Rome. Now she knows how to behave.

Because Antony tries to define himself within Nature, his moments of authenticity, although they compel our sympathy and admiration, must be transient and qualified. Even the noble love in the scene where he thanks his followers is subject to a moment of irony: "What does he mean?" asks Cleopatra, and Enobarbus replies, "To make his followers weep" (IV.ii.23–24). Cleopatra, however, does not try to enact her "true self." She means to break through the limit on human stature—on the "true self" that is imposed by this play's Nature. To do so, she must abandon conventional standards of truth and decency, and she does so without regrets. So whereas we see in Antony a moving and admirable achievement given the restrictions of Nature and of his own human nature, Cleopatra presents us with a double vision of what lies outside the normal human limits. Her kind of truth is absolute and permanent, but it must coexist with patent lies. For instance, Mardian, sent to tell Antony that Cleopatra has killed herself, says, "My mistress loved thee, and her fortunes mingled / With thine entirely" (IV.xiv.24–25). This is simultaneously a disgraceful lie and the simple truth. In context it is monstrously untrue; in retrospect it describes the story. Or Enobarbus, anticipating hysterics when Antony announces his departure, says,

> Cleopatra, catching but the least noise of this, dies instantly; I have
> seen her die twenty times upon far poorer moment. I do think
> there is mettle in death, which commits some loving act upon her,
> she hath such a celerity in dying.   (I.ii.141–45)

This hits its mark at the time and yet it all comes true. For although
celerity is a Roman virtue and Caesar's weapon in the power
struggle with Antony and Pompey, Cleopatra is too quick for him.
He "hath sent—/ Too slow a messenger" (V.ii.321). "The stroke of
death" *is* at the end "as a lover's pinch" (V.ii.295), and Antony's
final departure *does* make Cleopatra's death inevitable. Again and
again we find ourselves having to say of Cleopatra's lies, "And that's
true, too."

These, then, are the two modes of confronting Nature in this
play: the one humanistic, synthesizing, responsible; the other self-
assertive, divisive, flamboyant, amoral. Antony is, or tries to be,
sincere; he struggles to know himself and to act in accordance with
his knowledge. Conversely, when his actions betray his sense of
Self he struggles to change. Cleopatra has no part in the effort to
accommodate action and inner life. She is not, like the tragic hero, a
divided self, struggling to pull herself together. Her struggle is only
to discover and ward off what threatens her, to do battle with the
outside world, not with the one within. Like all Shakespeare's
women, she is a finished product, a preexisting unified identity. We
become aware of Cleopatra's inner life only insofar as it serves her
conscious purposes; it is not, like Antony's, subversive, demanding, beyond his control.

Linda Fitz argues that Cleopatra's inner life *is* subversive of her
conscious purposes and that there is drama in her struggle to take
control of it. The triumphant outcome of her struggle, according to
Fitz, comes when Cleopatra says,

> My resolution's placed, and I have nothing
> Of woman in me; now from head to foot
> I am marble-constant: now the fleeting moon
> No planet is of mine.   (V.ii.238–41)

And just as this speech indicates the successful conclusion of her
struggle against her own inconstancy, so the following speech
represents the culmination of the spiritual growth we expect in a
tragic hero:

No more but e'en a woman, and commanded
By such poor passion as the maid that milks
And does the meanest chares.   (IV.xv.76–78)

It is worth noticing, however, that these two speeches contradict
one another. Marble-constancy is incompatible with milkmaid passion. To be commanded by passion is not to command oneself, as
Cleopatra claims to do. These two speeches are best understood, I
think, as performances which *use* the inner life rather than as direct
expressions of it. What is moving is neither Cleopatra's marble-
constancy nor her new simplicity, but the sheer energy, talent, and
effort she puts into her performances.

Cleopatra herself comments on the energy it takes to perform as
she does. The comment comes after the one moment in which she
abandons or fails at performance; when Antony is leaving her in
Act I she is at a loss for words:

Courteous lord, one word.
Sir, you and I must part, but that's not it:
Sir, you and I have loved, but there's not it:
That you know well. Something it is I would—
O, my oblivion is a very Antony,
And I am all forgotten.   (I.iii.86–91)

The broken sentences create the effect of an emotion beyond even
Cleopatra's prodigious capacities to perform; in contrast to Antony's glibly rhetorical farewell speeches, Cleopatra's farewell is
a demonstration of speechlessness. Antony, with Othello-like
obtuseness, responds to this one display of naked emotion with
disapproval:

                    But that your royalty
Holds idleness your subject, I should take you
For idleness itself.   (I.iii.91–93)

Cleopatra responds,

                    'Tis sweating labor
To bear such idleness so near the heart
As Cleopatra this.   (I.iii.93–95)

Cleopatra, unlike Antony, does not deny that she performs her
love, plays roles, puts on shows. She only claims that it is hard
work, "sweating labor," to put on these particular shows, and that it

is hard because the performance concerns something "so near the heart." She only says so this once; but we would do well, I think, to remember this speech when we come to Act V, where the project near her heart is the preservation of her own integrity. If we are too aware of the sweating labor, of course, we lose the effect of the performance—just as we lose the effect when we become aware of the actual sweat on a ballerina. But if we are unaware of the effort and risk of her performance altogether, then it must seem to us, as it seems to Antony, idle. Like our appreciation of live ballet, our appreciation of Cleopatra's act depends on our understanding of how hard it is to do it.

In *The Dickens Theatre,* Robert Garis identifies two schools of performance, one of which he associates with Duse and the other with Bernhardt. Duse, he says, offers the continuous illusion of realism, whereas Bernhardt is overtly theatrical. Garis quotes Shaw on Bernhardt to illustrate his point:

One is not sorry to have been coaxed to relax one's notions of the dignity of art when she gets to serious business and shows how ably she does her work. The coaxing suits well with the childishly egotistical character of her acting, which is not the art of making you think more highly or feel more deeply, but the art of making you admire her, pity her, champion her, weep with her, laugh at her jokes, follow her fortunes breathlessly, and applaud her wildly when the curtain falls. It is the art of finding out all your weaknesses and practising on them—cajoling you, harrowing you, exciting you—on the whole, fooling you. And it is always Sarah Bernhardt in her own capacity who does this to you. The dress, the title of the play, the order of the words may vary; but the woman is always the same. She does not enter into the leading character: she substitutes herself for it.[8]

If Cleopatra's role is the enactment of her inner life, Shaw's description of Bernhardt may illuminate her method. Whereas Antony tries to enact his feelings as accurately as he can, Cleopatra, à la Bernhardt, seems to substitute herself for her feelings. "Here I am Cleopatra"—is the message of the "marble-constant" speech— "feeling the thrill of my own resolution." And in the milkmaid speech: "Here I am Cleopatra feeling the bittersweet pleasure of illusionlessness." I do not mean that Cleopatra is pretending to feel something she does not; I only mean that her feelings do not threaten her consciousness of being herself, Cleopatra, as broad as she has breadth, at all times and places. Under similar circumstances of loss, the tragic Self, by contrast, invariably suffers a loss of identity more painful than the material loss itself.

Cleopatra's style of confronting Nature is, of course, a function of her gender. Only the feminine Other faces the challenge of Nature, of the world outside the Self, with an identity as fixed and unyielding as Nature itself. Insofar as she does confront this challenge, Cleopatra is a rarity among Shakespeare's women characters and has some affinity with the masculine tragic Self. But insofar as she faces it with performances à la Bernhardt, insofar as her performances remain perfectly self-centered and in her own control, she remains Other even in the face of the Other, in the face of Nature and the challenge of tragedy. Although she is certainly the co-protagonist of the play, she is not the representative of the Self; she is not, as Linda Fitz suggests, a tragic hero.

It is time to return to the question raised by Danby's essay, the question of tragic climax or resolution. Neither Antony nor Cleopatra as individuals provides us with a resolution, with an image of human value so impressive as to triumph over and transform our sense of Nature. But what is between them, their relationship, does endure, does restore them to history. The forward motion of the play destroys them both as individuals; nevertheless, it "proves" the relationship between them. This relationship is complex; they are both married and not married. They are not married in that each would sacrifice the other, if they could, for the sake of their own separate destinies; they are married in that they cannot. Antony follows Cleopatra out of the sea battle against his will because "My heart was to thy rudder tied by th' strings" (III.xi.57), and Cleopatra remains faithful to Antony because, although she could wish it were otherwise, it is the only way of being "noble to myself" (V.ii.191). But out of the antagonism between their immediate purposes comes the accomplishment of their ultimate purpose, the achievement of distinction or historicity. They defeat themselves in the short run; Cleopatra destroys Antony in her attempt to possess him, and Antony cannot deny her even when he knows she is doing so. Yet they succeed in becoming famous, not individually, but as a pair. In trying to serve themselves, they have served the third thing, their story, and thus have served each other as well as themselves.

If Antony had not resisted Cleopatra's spell, he would have lost his citizenship in the world of men, and Cleopatra would not have had an Emperor Antony to dream of when she needed one. But if Antony had succeeded in breaking away, if, Othello-like, he had taken decisive action against the treacherous witch, there would have been no Cleopatra to make a myth of Antony and to pay him the returns on his love that she finally does. In other words, Antony controls his fortune by allowing its agent, Cleopatra, to destroy him, for it is only after his death that she is in a position to choose Antony without qualification. Had he not realized this, Antony's fate would have been that of a strumpet's fool; but because he cannot help giving her her due, she lives to make her choice and to give him a noble fate. Her death for his sake is ambiguous, for it is primarily a self-protective measure; his death for her sake is equally ambiguous, for he fights it every step of the way. Yet in this play, it is the negative way to love that leads to significance, to a place in the story. The Octavias and Lepiduses get lost precisely because they lack images of themselves that would command their first loyalty, whereas Antony and Cleopatra are each ennobled by the other's love only because each pursues a private destiny. Danby remarks that in *Antony and Cleopatra* "Opposites are juxtaposed, mingled, married; then from the very union which seems to promise strength, dissolution flows." Yet if we see Cleopatra as opposite to Antony, we see that here is one pair of contrarieties that do *not* mingle, and the fame that each earns from his connection with the other depends on the space between them.

The third Cleopatra, then, is the one we must turn to in order to account for our sense of resolution at the end of the play. This Cleopatra faces Nature independently of Antony and differently from him; ultimately, it is her own self-centeredness that leads her back to him. He, by contrast, repeatedly returns to Cleopatra by *de*centering, by abandoning his pride, his sense of his due, the images he has of himself. This double movement of each, in their opposite ways, toward the other provides us with the resolution we have come to expect in Shakespearean tragedy. As in *King Lear,* the third thing is love.

Hamlet

Of all Shakespeare's tragedies, *Hamlet* is the one in which the sex nausea is most pervasive. The other heroes all have to be brought by the action of the play to that low moment when their pain is translated into misogyny; Hamlet compares his mother to a beast in his very first scene:

> O God, a beast that wants a discourse of reason
> Would have mourned longer . . .
>   . . .
>   O, most wicked speed, to post
> With such dexterity to incestuous sheets!
>   (I.ii.150–51, 156–57)

And from the first his encounters with Ophelia are spattered with hostility and disgust:

> I have heard of your paintings, well enough. God hath given you one face, and you make yourselves another. You jig and amble, and you lisp; you nickname God's creatures and make your wantonness your ignorance.   (III.i.143–47)

In the closet scene with Gertrude, Hamlet's loathing comes to its climax:

>   Nay, but to live
> In the rank sweat of an enseamed bed
> Stewed in corruption, honeying and making love
> Over the nasty sty. . . .   (III.iv.92–95)

Furthermore, there is no reconciliation with women at the end of the play, as there is in the other tragedies. Lear and Othello at least recognize Cordelia and Desdemona, even though too late; Antony forgives Cleopatra. In *Hamlet* there are no such reconciliations. Hamlet does throw himself into Ophelia's grave, but clearly this is more an act of aggression against Laertes than of reconciliation with the dead Ophelia. And his recovery of relationship with Gertrude is so understated that we cannot be sure it is present at all.

Hamlet is therefore the example most critics use to discuss sex nausea in Shakespeare. Robert Ornstein, for instance, puts *Hamlet* in the context of Jacobean tragedy and argues that its revulsion against sexuality was part of the pathology of the age.[1] But if Shakespeare does give rein to misogynist emotion in *Hamlet,* he also dissociates the play as a whole from that emotion. The sex nausea is here, as in the other tragedies, a corollary to the hero's psychological and spiritual suffering. It is isomorphic not with the play as a whole but only with the second phase of the tragic fable. It is present from the beginning because *Hamlet* actually begins in the middle of the second phase. The first phase has ended with the death of Hamlet's father, two months prior to time present. That death has ended the old world, comfortably centered on the masculine Self and based on an identity of interests between father and son. In the new world the presence of the Other destroys the hero's sense of centrality. Misogyny is a version of the anger the hero directs toward the Other for destroying his old, self-centered world. Hamlet, like the other heroes, rages against women when he loses his place in the sun.

Of course, it was not Hamlet who was central to the old world; it was his father. But in the old world, as we have seen in the history plays, the father and son share power with one another. In the new world the continuum is broken: Claudius does not share power and position with Hamlet, as the late king had done. Hamlet's loss is perhaps more grave than even Lear's or Antony's; he loses what he has never actually had.

But only the second phase of the tragic fable is defined by the hero's rage at his losses. In the third and final phase the hero is beyond his anger. And it is notable that after a certain moment in Hamlet the sex nausea simply vanishes. After Act IV, scene iv, Hamlet's last scene before going to England, we hear no more about the frailty of women. The sexuality of the play, violent and disgusted up to this point, suddenly becomes clear and elegiac. In the very next scene Ophelia sings her sweet mad songs, and from here on she becomes an icon of positive femininity. The play seems not to know that up to now sexuality has been perverse and loathsome; from here on it seems so natural that it hardly needs much notice. The sexuality of the final movement is natural first of all, in that Ophelia's femininity is defined by its association with natural things—with the flowers that she gives away, hangs on the willow tree, and has thrown on her grave. Ophelia becomes a kind of inverse Perdita, a pathetic May Queen. Bridget Lyons calls her a Flora figure and remarks on the similarities "between Perdita's language in giving away flowers that she considers appropriate for her visitors and Ophelia's gestures and remarks on the flowers she dispenses."[2] Ophelia says,

> There's rosemary, that's for remembrance. . . . And there is pan-
> sies, that's for thoughts. . . . There's fennel for you, and colum-
> bines. There's rue for you, and here's some for me. . . . I would
> give you some violets, but they withered all when my father died.
> (IV.v.175–77, 180–81, 183–85)

Compare this to Perdita's

> Here's flow'rs for you:
> Hot lavender, mints, savory, marjoram,
> The marigold that goes to bed wi' th' sun,
> And with him rises, weeping; these are flow'rs
> Of middle summer, and I think they are given
> To men of middle age. You're very welcome.
> (*The Winter's Tale,* IV.iv.103–8)

Perdita understands that she is playing the role of a fertility goddess: "Methinks I play as I have seen them do / In Whitsun pastorals"
(IV.iv.133–34). Ophelia, having lost her wits, cannot be expected
to have the same understanding of her role; but as the play's representative of young womanhood, Ophelia has the May Queen's authority over the flowers, a female version of Adam's authority to
name the beasts. Ophelia, of course, represents possibilities that
have been lost in the *Hamlet* world, whereas Perdita stands for triumphant fertility, rebirth, renewal. Perdita's marigolds sleep and rise
rhythmically with the sun; Ophelia's violets wither once and for all.
The deaths in *Hamlet* are final, including the death of sexual possibility; but that possibility, we now feel, was for something innocent
and valuable, not for something rotten to the core. Ophelia in the last
part of the play evokes responses very far from the ones we had in
sympathy with Hamlet's "I say we will have no moe marriage"
(III.i.147–48).

The sexuality of the last movement, then, seems natural because
it is associated with natural processes. Furthermore, those who

refer to sexual matters have no sense that anything *un*natural has happened. When Gertrude speaks over Ophelia's grave, for instance, she gives no hint of anything but the most ordinary sexuality between Hamlet and Ophelia:

> Sweets to the sweet! Farewell. [*Scatters flowers*]
> I hoped thou shouldst have been my Hamlet's wife.
> I thought thy bride bed to have decked, sweet maid,
> And not have strewed thy grave.   (V.i.243–46)

Gertrude's simplicity here is absolute. She sees herself participating in a fertility rite honoring the sexuality of the next generation. That the next generation has thought *her* sexuality bestial; that she has been an accomplice to the disruption of "her" Hamlet's love affair; that there has been something dark and ambiguous between her and her son—none of this is present to her consciousness here, nor should be—to ours. Here everything is in perfect order, although very sad. Gertrude imagines herself yielding her place to a daughter-in-law, stepping aside in her season to do so. What has been lost through Ophelia's death is something natural, lawful, desirable.

This speech of Gertrude's has given a lot of trouble. G. F. Bradby puts it most succinctly when he asks, "Is that the language of a murderess?"[3] Clearly it is not; nor is Gertrude's speech describing Ophelia's death:

> There is a willow grows askant the brook,
> That shows his hoar leaves in the glassy stream:
> Therewith fantastic garlands did she make
> Of crowflowers, nettles, daisies, and long purples,
> That liberal shepherds give a grosser name,
> But our cold maids do dead men's fingers call them.
> There on the pendent boughs her crownet weeds
> Clamb'ring to hang, an envious sliver broke,
> When down her weedy trophies and herself
> Fell in the weeping brook. Her clothes spread wide,
> And mermaidlike awhile they bore her up,
> Which time she chanted snatches of old lauds,
> As one incapable of her own distress,
> Or like a creature native and indued
> Unto that element. But long it could not be
> Till that her garments, heavy with their drink,
> Pulled the poor wretch from her melodious lay
> To muddy death.   (IV.vii.166–83)

It has surprised many commentators that Gertrude is the one to make this speech. It seems too gentle for her. Bradby remarks,

[Shakespeare] does not generally allow his characters to wander so far from dramatic probability if he has visualized them clearly. The Queen is not so visualized. . . . One feels tempted to suppose that, when he wrote the ghost scene, Shakespeare meant her to have connived at least at her husband's death; that he afterwards changed his mind and thought of her as guilty only of adultery—perhaps not even of that; and that he failed to reconcile the two ideas in the final acting version of the play.[4]

The problem that Bradby is dealing with here is a critical problem only, not a failure of coherence on Shakespeare's part. Gertrude's innocence or guilt is not really an issue in the play. She, like Cleopatra, is a character of ambiguous morality whom we can never fully know; but whereas *Antony and Cleopatra* continually invites our judgment of Cleopatra, *Hamlet* continually deflects our impulse to judge Gertrude. First of all, we have no firsthand evidence. Although Hamlet sees his mother as a disgustingly sensual creature, the relationship that we see between Gertrude and Claudius is domestic and ceremonial, never sexual at all. There is less evidence of sexuality here than there is between some of the kings and queens in the history plays. The Gertrude that we see—as opposed to the one that Hamlet imagines—is her son's mother and a worried, affectionate partner to her husband, who happens to be going through a period of political danger. Of course, this proves nothing. Though we see nothing in Gertrude to corroborate Hamlet's image of her, we still see nothing inconsistent with it. My point is not that Hamlet is wrong, or that we should feel an ironic distance from his visions of Gertrude's lust. But since we see the evil version of Gertrude entirely through his eyes, we lack the investment in it that we would have if we came to it on our own. We accept Hamlet's version more or less passively, and scarcely notice when we are required to abandon it.

Not only is the evidence for judgment lacking; we are hardly even moved to seek for it. Again the comparison with Cleopatra is relevant. There is finally insufficient evidence for judging Cleopatra, too, but in her case we are constantly teased into the effort to judge. Cleopatra is discussed throughout the play by other characters; no one exchanges words over Gertrude. Hamlet talks to himself about her, and we adopt his feelings as long as he displays them; but we are not involved as we are by the debate over Cleopatra. Enobarbus

gives Agrippa one version of Cleopatra; Caesar gives Lepidus another; Demetrius and Philo agree on her nature; Antony and Mardian
disagree; everyone has an opinion. In *Hamlet* there is no such fallout
from Gertrude's presence. Nor does she discuss herself or reveal herself in private, behind-the-scenes moments. We simply do not worry
over her much, and therefore our feelings about her do not take root.

In all the tragedies, including *Hamlet,* the idea of Woman is a kind
of spiritual barometer. As long as the hero's world lacks grace,
Woman is a monster of lust and deception. Toward the end of the
plays, however, she seems good and true, worthy of love. How
does Shakespeare change the image of Woman without dramatic
inconsistency? Sometimes, as in *Othello,* the hero simply learns that
his image of Woman has been wrong. There is no dramatic inconsistency here because the audience has known all along that Desdemona is "heavenly true" (V.ii.135). Sometimes, as in *Antony and
Cleopatra,* the audience is newly impressed with the integrity of the
female character. Sometimes, as in *King Lear,* the primary representative of Woman shifts as the play goes on. Whereas Goneril and
Regan dominate in the middle section of *Lear,* Cordelia is the more
important woman in the final movement. Something like this
happens in *Hamlet,* too. Until Hamlet's departure for England, the
more important woman is Gertrude, but afterwards it is Ophelia.
Gertrude's one womanly function after Act IV, scene iv, is to
respond to Ophelia; her responses confer honor both ways.

But Ophelia, of course, has been no Cordelia. She is a woman
whose own honor has been at least momentarily doubted, and
Gertrude, unlike Regan and Goneril, is present to the very last
scene. What is unusual in *Hamlet* is that we end up feeling mild
toward Gertrude and enthusiastic about Ophelia without either
woman having cleared her name of the sins we held against her in
the first acts. The question is not Bradby's "Which is the Real
Queen, Gertrude-the-good or Gertrude-the-bad?," but rather
"Why is there not more *sense* of inconsistency between the women
of the first and last movements of the play—given that they look so
bad at first and so good later?"

One reason, I think, is that the very issue of Woman fades into
the background toward the end of the play. This greatly lessens the
sense of disjunction that we feel. Hamlet has forgotten about
Woman *as* an issue, and so do we, unless we make it a point not to.

Women here are only a grace note, a fragrance. The point can be clarified by a comparison to the ending of *Antony and Cleopatra*. Here the resolution depends entirely on sustained tension about Cleopatra's nature. Is she good or bad, for or against Antony? Gertrude and Ophelia, however, cease to be objects for judgment, ours or Hamlet's. They function only to evoke a mood, and excite no admiration or censure at all.

But a more important reason, I think, is that Gertrude and Ophelia are psychologically and morally neutral characters who take on the coloration of the play's moods. Often they are simply there to advance the plot, swell the crowd, or hold up an end of conversation. This neutrality has often been mistaken for a character trait. Leo Kirschbaum, for instance, complains that Ophelia "has no depth in her at all" and is "pitifully incompetent in the *Hamlet* spiritual milieu."[5] A. C. Bradley calls Gertrude "very dull and very shallow";[6] Granville-Barker says she is "passive."[7] Refuting Caroline Heilbrun's defense of Gertrude, Baldwin Maxwell comments, "Perhaps . . . her obedient rising at the King's 'Madam, come,' suggests her domination by him. Such a suggestion is supported by her leaving the stage in three later scenes upon similar words from the King ('Come, Gertrude' IV.i., 'Let's follow, Gertrude' IV.vii, 'Sweet Gertrude, leave us' III.i) and by her only once speaking as she makes her exit."[8] But why should this suggest that Gertrude is psychologically "dominated" by Claudius? Is it not rather a sign of Gertrude's "attendant lord" status in the play? Of the dramatic necessity to sweep her off the stage without calling much attention to her? It is not that Gertrude and Ophelia have no personality, make no distinguishing gestures; rather, we have so little direction in interpreting their gestures that they are no sooner made than they are dissipated. Is Ophelia spunky or dull? Does her skill in parrying with Hamlet ally her with the comic heroines or is she just a conventional, obedient daughter? When Laertes warns her to "be wary" of her chastity, she replies,

> I shall the effect of this good lesson keep
> As watchman to my heart, but, good my brother,
> Do not, as some ungracious pastors do,
> Show me the steep and thorny way to heaven,
> Whiles, like a puffed and reckless libertine,
> Himself the primrose path of dalliance treads
> And recks not his own rede.   (I.iii.45–51)

Bradby says this is the one time Ophelia "shows a touch of spirit,"[9] but to Kirschbaum this "buoyant raillery"[10] suggests Ophelia's affinity to the "shallow" Laertes. How can we decide? If we adopt Bradby's interpretation we can point to the Ophelia who speaks back fearlessly when Hamlet torments her:

> *Hamlet* I did love you once.
> *Ophelia* Indeed, my lord, you made me believe so.
> *Hamlet* You should not have believed me, for virtue
>   cannot so inoculate our old stock but we
>   shall relish of it. I loved you not.
> *Ophelia* I was the more deceived.   (III.i.115–20)

This is more than spirited; Ophelia parries Hamlet's blows with courage, skill, and self-respect. If we adopt Kirschbaum's view, however, we can emphasize her role as her father's tool, the court spy. But in fact we come closest to the play by avoiding these issues altogether. Ophelia's personality, like Gertrude's morality, has no resonance. It does not matter that various clues are contradictory because each clue falls into silence.

Morally and psychologically, then, Gertrude and Ophelia cast no shadow either before or behind themselves. Their characters are without dramatic issue. Take, for instance, the closet scene, the climax to the Hamlet-Gertrude theme. Here Hamlet accuses his mother of everything he holds against her and she capitulates to him. He swears to "set you up a glass / Where you may see the inmost part of you" (III.iv.20–21), and we might expect that we, too, will finally see "the inmost part" of Gertrude. But in spite of her acquiescence to Hamlet's accusations, she remains as bland as ever, as much a vessel for Hamlet's feelings and as little a character with her own moral shape. First of all, she loses the initiative ten lines into the conversation and spends the rest of the scene reacting to Hamlet. Her reactions do not fall into any sort of pattern; they reveal neither courage nor cowardice, self-knowledge nor denial. She confesses once, briefly, and to the vaguest of crimes:

> O Hamlet, speak no more.
> Thou turn'st mine eyes into my very soul,
> And there I see such black and grainèd spots
> As will not leave their tinct.   (III.iv.89–92)

We know as little as ever about Gertrude after this. As Bradby says, "The Queen is directly accused of murdering her husband. She neither admits the charge nor denies it, and it is not mentioned again."[11] From here on Gertrude has almost nothing to say about herself. Typically her speeches do nothing but break up Hamlet's passionate monologues:

> O Hamlet, thou has cleft my heart in twain.
>
> . . .
>
> What shall I do?
>
> . . .
>
> Be thou assured, if words be made of breath,
> And breath of life, I have no life to breathe
> What thou has said to me. (III.iv.157, 181, 198–200)

The mountainous labors of Hamlet's rage elicit nothing but this little mouse of self-accusation. The scene immediately following the closet scene, where we would be most receptive to some sign of Gertrude's real response to it, is maddeningly noncommittal. Gertrude does what Hamlet has asked her to do: she conceals from the King that Hamlet is only "mad in craft" (III.iv.189). But her role here is essentially the neutral role of the messenger; she really does nothing but tell the King that Hamlet has killed Polonius. She offers no protest to Claudius's intention to ship him away; all she adds is the utterly irrelevant " 'A weeps for what is done" (IV.i.27). With this little embroidery on the truth, Gertrude becomes again the anxious intermediary between her erring son and his disapproving stepfather; and nothing in the rest of the play indicates that she is merely playing the role. In Act V, scene i, she strikes the same note of motherly excuse after Hamlet fights Laertes in Ophelia's grave:

> This is mere madness;
> And thus a while the fit will work on him.
> Anon, as patient as the female dove
> When that her golden couplets are disclosed,
> His silence will sit drooping. (V.i.284–88)

Gertrude's dramatic function here, as in her speeches about Ophelia, is to sound the note of poignant femininity; clearly this speech is not meant as a cunning bit of role-playing.

If the closet scene has no issue, Ophelia's betrayal of Hamlet has no prologue. We are never encouraged to wonder whether or not Ophelia will cooperate with her father or defy him on Hamlet's behalf; therefore the answer to the question "How will Ophelia choose?" goes unnoticed. Ophelia is not developed as a woman with a choice to make; her position is not even given the glancing

attention Shakespeare pays to Octavia's in *Antony and Cleopatra*.
Octavia has at least a speech or two to enunciate her dilemma:

> A more unhappy lady,
> If this division chance, ne'er stood between,
> Praying for both parts.
> The good gods will mock me presently
> When I shall pray "O, bless my lord and husband!"—
> Undo that prayer by crying out as loud,
> "O, bless my brother!" Husband win, win brother,
> Prays, and destroys the prayer; no midway
> 'Twixt these extremes at all.   (III.iv.12–19)

Shakespeare is very fond of putting women between two men, a
lover (or husband) and a father (or brother); the choice this situation
demands is a kind of female parallel to the tragic choices forced
upon the men. But to compare Ophelia to other women in the
same position is to realize how unemphatic Ophelia's choice is next
to theirs.* We are never encouraged to speculate whether Ophelia
could do other than she does; therefore we scarcely have any
opinions at all about what she does do.

Furthermore, until the decoy scene we never see Ophelia with
Hamlet, so our sense of the relationship she betrays is minimal. The
strongest evidence of it is the reported appearance of Hamlet in
Ophelia's closet, and there is no way of knowing what this means.
We know that he went to her in the grip of emotion, but backed
away; we do not know why. The relationship is almost a convention right up to the decoy scene itself, where it begins to take on
some substance. Until then it is a matter of Hamlet's conventional
love letter, Laertes's conventional concern for Ophelia's virginity,
and such conventional, spiritless exchanges as this between Ophelia
and the Queen:

> *Gertrude*   And for your part, Ophelia, I do wish
>   That your good beauties be the happy cause
>   Of Hamlet's wildness. So shall I hope your virtues
>   Will bring him to his wonted way again,
>   To both your honors.
> *Ophelia*   Madam, I wish it may.
>   (III.i.38–42)

---

*Isabella (in *Measure for Measure*) is the woman character whose choice is most
emphatically presented to us. In her case the choice is between her brother's life and
her own sense of sexual and religious integrity. Shakespeare orchestrates her situation to make us as curious about and judgmental of Isabella as possible.

In Act III, scene i, Ophelia does encounter Hamlet, and technically she betrays him. She has agreed to lead him on while Claudius and Polonius listen. But Hamlet refuses to be led. This scene, like the closet scene, is Hamlet's; Ophelia here, like Gertrude there, is quickly reduced to one-liners while Hamlet berates and confuses her at will:

> What means your lordship?
> . . .
> I was the more deceived.
> . . .
> O help him, you sweet heavens.
> . . .
> Heavenly powers restore him.   (III.i.106, 120, 134, 142)

Ophelia's sins, like Gertrude's in the closet scene, are simply not in focus here. Hamlet's feelings about her are all that count.

In the last part of the play two things change: first, the associations surrounding the idea of Woman become unambiguously pleasant; and second, Ophelia takes on some resonance as a character. She becomes an icon of positive sexuality rather than a moral character; what she does and suffers as such echoes the major themes and events of the play. What she does, of course, is go mad and die; her madness and death are significantly like and unlike Hamlet's. She is part of the quarrel between Laertes and Hamlet; Laertes blames Hamlet for her madness, and each man is enraged by the other's claim to be her chief mourner. So she is with us to the end of the play, when Hamlet and Laertes kill one another. But the theme of her death is most prominent from Act IV, scene vii, to Act V, scene i; it begins with Gertrude's watery, flowery report and climaxes when Hamlet and Laertes fight in her grave. Throughout the graveyard scene she is an underground source of suspense; we are partly waiting for Hamlet to discover that the grave he is philosophizing over so calmly has been prepared for her. Right before he does, the exchange between Laertes and the priest continues the flower imagery and establishes Ophelia as an unequivocal good:

> *Laertes* Must there no more be done?
> *Doctor*   No more be done.
>   We should profane the service of the dead
>   To sing a requiem and such rest to her
>   As to peace-parted souls.

Laertes   Lay her i' th' earth,
And from her fair and unpolluted flesh
May violets spring! I tell thee, churlish priest,
A minist'ring angel shall my sister be
When thou liest howling!   (V.i.235–42)

This speech is as out-of-character for Laertes as Gertrude's flower speeches are for her; his passion is characteristically blunter and less impressive. But this is our farewell to Ophelia, and it must strike a full, rich chord of love and beauty. Gertrude scatters flowers on her grave; the play takes leave of its only young woman and all the possibilities she stands for. In this scene Ophelia is mourned, defended by her brother, debated by the gravedigger, fought over, and, in dramatic terms, awaited. As tragic May Queen, Ophelia clearly counts for more than either she or Gertrude does as a moral individual.

Here, then, is the reason why the audience is not shocked by the change in the idea of Woman in *Hamlet*. Until the orchestration of the Ophelia theme at the end of the play, neither woman takes hold in our imagination. We experience our disgust vicariously, through Hamlet, and we are ready to abandon it when the time comes. In fact, Gertrude and Ophelia may almost be understood as figures in Hamlet's dreams, so little resistance do they offer to the affect he attaches to them. At least this is true until Act IV, scene iv, when he loses interest in them. And when Hamlet ceases to guide our feelings toward these characters, we may perhaps continue to understand them as figures in the internal drama, as anima figures. Gertrude and Ophelia are not, of course, simply projections of Hamlet's, emanations of his poor and then improved mental health. Hamlet has not dreamed his whole tragedy; he is a hero, not a neurotic. But this is a play in which the outside world is almost exactly congruent with the landscape of the hero's soul. The ghost, for instance, is a real ghost, visible to the audience as well as to the hero; but it is not by coincidence that it appears only during Hamlet's confusion. Hamlet's inner life seems to shape the play itself, not just our reactions to characters in it. The best way to understand the change in the image of Woman, I think, is to see it as a function of a change in Hamlet—even though Hamlet is no longer the filter for our response.

The sexual atmosphere of *Hamlet* improves because the hero ceases to be appalled by his own condition, by the human condition, and by sex as a central feature of the human condition. Why does the hero's mood improve? No one knows. Robert Ornstein says, "The question of action in an evil society, one might say, is resolved by an expedient dear to Victorian novelists: a change of air, a sea voyage from which the hero returns calm if not resolute, buoyed by a vaguely optimistic fatalism that is half-Christian, half-Stoic."[12] Ornstein's point is that Shakespeare is not a didactic author whose plays illustrate a thesis; but the point might equally be made that transformations such as Hamlet's are so mysterious and yet so common that they are best represented as simply as possible. The less cause-and-effect logic we attach to the coming and going of grace the better. However, there *is* a psychosexual logic to Hamlet's transformation that I should like to explore. It must be understood, however, that this logic can never replace the more significant spiritual *il*logic of the change in Hamlet.

In Shakespeare's tragedies, men who have proved themselves according to a rather limited code of manliness suddenly find that code inadequate to their difficulties. Their physical courage and soldierly or statesmanlike honor is no longer enough, and they struggle with more inward definitions of courage, honor, integrity. In *Hamlet,* however, the hero must simultaneously live up to the dogma of "man-honor-fight"[13] and also transcend it. Hamlet must simultaneously prove himself according to both history and tragedy. He must become single-minded and successfully self-assertive on the one hand, and move beyond the world of masculine aggression on the other. Until he does so, he lives in a state of anger, self-doubt, and sexual rage.

Hamlet has not yet proved himself according to the original code of manliness, so he cannot reject it; indeed, he glamorizes it and does his best to envy those who exemplify it. He finds Fortinbras a "delicate and tender prince" and attributes to him "divine ambition" (IV.iv.48–49). Of himself he keeps asking, "Am I a coward?" and concluding, "it cannot be / But I am pigeon-livered and lack gall / To make oppression bitter" (II.ii.577, 582–84). Of course, Hamlet is not a coward. A coward would lie low; Hamlet has made *himself* the issue, whirling about the court abusing everyone. He has insulted Ophelia, harangued Gertrude, mocked and killed Polonius, revealed to Rosencrantz and Guildenstern that he knows who they are, publicly accused Claudius of murder—in other words, he has been openly hostile to everyone in the play but

Horatio. Far from being cowardly, his behavior has been recklessly provocative. But Hamlet accuses himself of cowardice because he lacks single-mindedness about his revenge mission. The code of manliness is to Hamlet like a parental imperative that offers false but unavoidable standards of judgment.

The revenge code is no use to Hamlet because his problem is much larger than Claudius. Hamlet's sense of meaning and order has been destroyed by the success of his uncle's villainy. Nothing is "very strange" to him any more,

> for my uncle is King of Denmark, and those that would make mouths at him while my father lived give twenty, forty, fifty, a hundred ducats apiece for his picture in little. 'Sblood, there is something in this more than natural, if philosophy could find it out.
>
> (II.ii.370–75)

Hamlet suffers from the metaphysical flimsiness of a world in which there is nothing to "set things right" but oneself; merely setting things right would not assuage his suffering.

Hamlet, then, seeks a way simultaneously to fulfill the code and to transcend it. He wants to know that he is a man, able to kill his enemies and make his presence count; but he also wants to know that there is something beyond displays of manliness, some "divinity" beyond the "divine ambition" of a Fortinbras—and therefore also beyond the diabolical ambition of a Claudius. Hamlet's soul seeks a way of being simultaneously active on his own behalf and passive before Providence. He finds what he seeks on the trip to England. Here the manly code ceases to be a parental imperative, a duty laid on one generation by the other, and supports Hamlet in his own battle. After Hamlet returns from England, he no longer feels the slightest doubt of his "manliness"—just as he no longer expresses the slightest doubt of Woman's integrity. On the trip to England Hamlet discovers that Rosencrantz and Guildenstern intend to have him murdered, and he arranges for their murder instead of his. With this gesture of single-minded aggression against his enemies, Hamlet finally proves himself as a history hero, a man of action. The event is narrated by Hamlet himself with Horatio as his audience:

> *Hamlet*   Up from my cabin,
>   My sea gown scarfed about me, in the dark
>   Groped I to find out them, had my desire,

Fingered their packet, and in fine withdrew
To mine own room again, making so bold,
My fears forgetting manners, to unseal
Their grand commission; where I found, Horatio—
Ah, royal knavery!—an exact command,
Larded with many several sorts of reasons,
Importing Denmark's health, and England's too,
With, ho, such bugs and goblins in my life,
That on the supervise, no leisure bated,
No, not to stay the grinding of the ax,
My head should be struck off.
　　　. . .
Being thus benetted round with villains,
Or I could make a prologue to my brains,
They had begun the play. I sat me down,
Devised a new commission, wrote it fair.
　　　. . .
　　　　　　　　　　　Wilt thou know
Th' effect of what I wrote?
Horatio　　　　　　　　Ay, good my lord.
Hamlet　An earnest conjuration from the king,
　　　. . .
That on the view and knowing of these contents,
　　　. . .
He should those bearers put to sudden death,
Not shriving time allowed.
Horatio　　　　　　　　How was this sealed?
Hamlet　Why, even in that was heaven ordinant.
I had my father's signet in my purse,
Which was the model of that Danish seal,
Folded the writ up in the form of th' other,
Subscribed it, gave't th' impression, placed it safely,
The changeling never known. . . .
Horatio　So Rosencrantz and Guildenstern go to't.
Hamlet　Why, man, they did make love to this employment.
They are not near my conscience.　　　　(V.ii.12–58)

A notable feature of these lines is the swelling confidence of the
verse rhythms, especially in the fourteen-line sentence beginning
"Up from my cabin. . . ." These are the rhythms of a natural
forward momentum, exactly what Hamlet has longed for and what
has been missing from his soliloquies. There the rhythms are either
meditative, repetitive, meandering, or (as in "O what a rogue and

peasant slave am I") self-excited. Here the story—a male adventure story at last!—sweeps Hamlet along just as the "divinity" swept him along at the time. "Or I could make a prologue to my brains," he says, "They had begun the play." This metaphor recalls the end of "O what a rogue and peasant slave am I," where Hamlet abjures his own rhetoric and plans to take action. But the action he takes is only mental; he plans to write a play:

> About, my brains!
> Hum—
> I have heard that guilty creatures sitting at a play
> Have by the very cunning of the scene
> Been struck so to the soul that presently
> They have proclaimed their malefactions.   (II.ii.594–99)

After the trip to England Hamlet no longer lays plots, writes plays. He reacts to events as they occur; and one of his reactions happens to be the longed-for execution of Claudius.

Lionel Abel calls *Hamlet* the first example in Western literature of "metatheater."[14] In "metatheater" the characters see themselves *as* characters and choose or fail to choose the roles they will play. *Hamlet* is not quite *Six Characters in Search of an Author,* but there is no question of Hamlet's preoccupation with the act he is putting on in life, with his "True Story" as well as with the roles he wears as disguises. He is constantly looking at himself from the outside, assessing his own performance. His evaluation is usually negative: he calls himself "a whore . . . a very drab,/A scullion!" (II.ii.592–94), or he berates himself for having less passion in his own life than an actor reciting lines in a play. The idea of *Hamlet* as metatheater is a useful tool for understanding the Rosencrantz and Guildenstern adventure as a turning point in the play. Hamlet may be seen as a character in search of a genre and the killing of Rosencrantz and Guildenstern as a crucial action in the making of *Hamlet* as a tragedy. As a metatheatrical consciousness, Hamlet "knows" that a tragic hero begins from the point of successful aggression against his equals in the world of men, begins only *after* he has established himself according to history. As a metatheatrical consciousness, Hamlet is aware that he must move simultaneously backwards toward the achievements of history and forwards toward the tragic transcendence of history and the world of men. The killing of Rosencrantz and Guildenstern settles the question of origins if not of ends. Hamlet's feverish activity has shaken loose a pair of enemies he can kill with unconflicted zest, as a history hero kills, as Prince Hal kills Hotspur and Clifford kills York. This action does not, of course, resolve what is unresolved between Hamlet and Claudius. Claudius is a father figure, a version of the Other; the proper object for the aggression of the history hero must be a version of the Self. Rosencrantz and Guildenstern are Hamlet's own age and gender, fellow students at his own university; whereas Claudius has betrayed Hamlet's father, Rosencrantz and Guildenstern have betrayed Hamlet himself. Since Hamlet does not, like the history hero, wholeheartedly accept the inheritance of injuries bequeathed to him from the past, he must make and kill his own enemies. The tragic hero ultimately finds his aggression inadequate to his situation; but he must have *some* experience of wholehearted and successful aggression before confronting what is beyond its reach.

Why should this be so? We do not usually think of aggression as a goal in tragedy but rather as the starting point of the tragic action, or the cause of the catastrophe. *Oedipus Rex* begins when Oedipus kills three men who jostle him on the road; *King Lear* begins when Lear banishes and disinherits Cordelia; the catastrophe in *Othello* comes about because Othello murders Desdemona. Usually the hero's aggression is at odds with his morality or inner life or his love of another character; the overt values of the play run against it. Covertly, however, tragedy absolutely requires the hero's aggression. It is worth pausing to ask why this should be so.

First, the hero's aggression helps to make him stand for the Self, the individual. The hero's aggression is the other side of his self-love; it makes us understand the rate at which he values himself. Of course, if the hero's aggression goes on too long or too successfully—*Macbeth* and *Tamburlaine* are examples—it ceases to exhilarate us. The hero's ego must be very large but firmly defined at its boundaries by morality or social sanctions. The hero's aggression, then, provides tragedy with one of its sources of moral tension. In tragedy we are close enough to the boundaries of ego to feel some anxiety lest they be overstepped.

Second, aggression helps to establish the hero's metaphysical stature. From the metaphysical perspective we see the hero alone on the stage battling with time, change, history, death. He refuses the limitations of his mortality, refuses to relinquish control to what is clearly more powerful than he is. The best example, of course, is

King Lear, who battles with the storm itself, defying and insulting it:

> Rumble thy bellyful. Spit, fire. Spout, rain!
>   . . .
> But yet I call you servile ministers,
> That will with two pernicious daughters join
> Your high-engendered battles 'gainst a head
> So old and white as this.   (III.ii.14, 21–24)

Even if he realizes what he is up against, as Lear does on the heath, the hero continues to act as if his will and desire might be central. In his enormous antagonism to his fate, the hero comes to seem as large as Fate itself. In tragedy the battle between the human and the superhuman must seem an almost even match.

In Shakespearean tragedy there comes a moment when the hero understands the uselessness of his aggression, his powerlessness to revenge himself against his destiny. Coriolanus has no such moment, and he gradually loses our interest; but the other heroes, even Macbeth, stop before the end of their stories to notice their own smallness in the universe. Lear on the heath, Hamlet in the graveyard, Antony before his last battle—all realize, in their own ways, the puniness of their own wills. But the heroes always return from these moments to the fight. After the spiritual recognitions come Lear killing Cordelia's jailer, Hamlet killing Laertes and Claudius, and Antony's murderous anger at Cleopatra.

The hero's successful aggression is, in fact, what makes him a hero. Without it he would merely be a victim and not the agent of his story. It is the hero's business to make sure that he is *not* more sinned against than sinning, to bring the house down with him when he goes. Because of its emphasis on aggression, tragedy, no less than history, may be said to be a male genre. Women writers do not seem to imagine themselves in terms of heroic aggression. *Men* may imagine women who assert will and desire unequivocally; but Phaedra, Antigone, and Medea are male creations. No woman's heroine has the strengths and weaknesses of these characters' selfishness. Of course I do not mean that women are less selfish and aggressive than men; but lacking the positive cultural images for female aggression, women do not imagine themselves heroically. The image that lies behind the code of manliness is of single combat between equals, of aggression cleansed by courage and backed by the body itself. Physical combat between two women, however, has been a matter for comedy, not for epic or tragedy, from Aristophanes to contemporary film. How many cultures have found it heroic? The image of the Amazonian is unique. Female aggression is traditionally domestic or sexual—directed, that is, against men and children, against physical superiors and inferiors. Success is always, therefore, impure, suspect. It depends either on sheer physical superiority (if the battle is with a child) or on the antagonist's inhibitions and taboos (if the battle is with a man). Our images for feminine aggression are incomplete; we can imagine only a woman's aggression against the Other, only sexual and cross-generational aggression, never aggression against versions of the Self. Until the final movement of the play, Hamlet may be said to occupy the position of the cultural feminine.

Until Hamlet dispatches Rosencrantz and Guildenstern to their deaths, his aggression is mostly sexual, directed against women who have withdrawn from him. In Abel's terms, it is Hamlet's "job" to get himself out of this unmanly situation, to turn his aggression against characters who stand in a political relationship to him, not a sexual and domestic one.* As soon as he does so his metaphysical problems resolve. The graveyard scene shows him dealing with questions of life and death in a completely new manner; his responses come naturally to him now and no longer need to be worked up or denied. He suddenly seems at home in the world, involved, confident that he is playing his own role whatever he does. His situation is no longer something thrust upon him; he has

---

*This, of course, is a transition that women, having so little tradition of public life, rarely imagine themselves making. And if the classical heroines are transparently male creations, many male characters in women's writing betray just as clearly the sex of their author. One such is George Eliot's Daniel Deronda, a more or less sexless male onto whom Eliot projected many of her own attitudes. Here is her analysis of Daniel's failure to find a vocation, a place for himself in the social context: "His early-wakened sensibility and reflectiveness had developed into a many-sided sympathy, which threatened to hinder any persistent course of action: as soon as he took up any antagonism, though only in thought, he seemed to himself like the Sabine warriors in the memorable story—with nothing to meet his spear but flesh of his flesh, and objects that he loved. His imagination had so wrought itself to the habit of seeing things as they probably appeared to others, that a strong partisanship, unless it were against an immediate oppression, had become an insincerity for him." (George Eliot, *Daniel Deronda* [Baltimore, Md.: Penguin, 1967], p. 412.)

With some modification, this could be a description of Hamlet himself. The difference between Deronda and Hamlet is that Hamlet has a powerful sense of free-floating aggression that he uses to heat up the story until it comes to a boil in an "immediate oppression." Deronda does not, and remains trapped in a sexual no-man's-land. Lacking any political antagonism, Daniel is utterly unconvincing as a Zionist, as a lover, as a man.

partly created it himself, by killing his enemies. In the nick of time he stops being his uncle's victim and becomes the agent of his own destiny.

It is always dangerous to talk about how "conscious" an author is of what he is saying in his fictions, and in the case of Shakespeare it is particularly risky. The "consciousness" implied by Shakespeare's work is superhuman, angelic, divine. To avoid worshiping the man as a god we concentrate on the work and only occasionally wonder how it came to be written in the first place. But it would be useful to be able to discuss the degree to which a given pattern is, as it were, near the surface of a play. Perhaps we might say that the play itself may be more or less conscious of certain elements within it. The sexual patterns in *Hamlet,* then, are something of which the play itself is hardly aware at all. The connection between Hamlet's misogyny and his own confused manliness is not one the play explicitly makes. The play itself does not emphasize what I have emphasized, the contrast between Hamlet's sexuality before and after his trip to England. The sexuality of the last movement is disembodied—fragile, wraithlike, and far removed from Hamlet himself. His positive sexuality is never in focus; we can only notice that his negative sexuality has disappeared and notice the coincidence between its disappearance and Hamlet's offstage adventure. It is only if we know what to look for that we find the familiar pattern; only if we come to *Hamlet* after *Antony and Cleopatra* or *King Lear* that it stands out. But there is one moment when these issues float upward in the consciousness of the play, toward, if not to, its surface. When Hamlet tells Horatio how he robbed Rosencrantz and Guildenstern, the language implies a heavy investment of libido in the action:

> . . . in the dark
> Groped I to find out them, had my desire,
> Fingered their packet. . . .   (V.ii.13–15)

Hamlet's most manly act of aggression is vaguely, but unmistakably, imagined as a rape; after this his sexuality is purged of its aggression. For this one moment—the pivot point in Hamlet's sexual history—the play almost makes the connection.

FOUR

Macbeth and *Coriolanus*

In *Macbeth* and *Coriolanus*, the two most important representatives of the feminine are even more committed than the heroes to a code of manliness that emphasizes power, honor, war, and revenge. They both prefer a bloody ambitious sort of honor over traditionally feminine values in general and womanly love in particular. When Coriolanus goes to war Volumnia announces,

> If my son were my husband, I should freelier rejoice in that absence wherein he won honor than in the embracements of his bed where he would show most love. (I.iii.2–5)

And in the violence of her ambition Lady Macbeth renounces womanly love for the spirit of murder:

> Come, you spirits
> That tend on mortal thoughts, unsex me here
>
>   . . .
>
> Come to my woman's breasts,
> And take my milk for gall (I.v.40–41, 47–48)

Both women value the world of men above everything else; at various points in these plays each urges the hero beyond the limits of decency in his struggle for power in that world. Both Volumnia and Lady Macbeth are the opposite of the Jungian feminine. Instead of connecting us to natural fertility, family love, or a sense of the body, they represent fanaticism according to the dogma of "man-honor-fight."[1]

In Shakespearean tragedy, as we have seen, the feminine is not necessarily congruent with the Jungian feminine; the dialectic is not necessarily between the world of men and the world of Woman. But in tragedies like *Hamlet, Othello,* and *Antony and Cleopatra* the feminine is always Other to the male Self, if not thematically then circumstantially. Women characters in these plays have their own purposes, whether or not these are notably or necessarily "feminine" purposes. In *Macbeth* and *Coriolanus,* Lady Macbeth and Volumnia are the heroes' collaborators or stage managers rather than independent centers of self-interest. There is no dialectic between the masculine Self and the feminine Other in these plays because the primary representatives of the feminine are not Other to the hero. They are identified with the masculine-historical project in general and the heroes' own careers in particular. They do not present him with the challenge of the Other but merely repeat the demands these heroes make upon themselves. In *Coriolanus,* to be sure, the identity of interest between the hero and the principal woman does not last all the way through. By the end of the play the plot has separated Volumnia and Coriolanus; indeed, they are finally mortal antagonists. But, as we shall see, by this time it is too late for the dialectic between Self and Other to begin. There simply is not time for the hero to take account of his separation from the feminine, abuse women for whores, and move beyond his anger and loss. The tragic process, always paralleled in Shakespeare by the process of separation from the feminine, cannot begin as late as the third scene of the fifth act. Coriolanus does not have time before the end of the play to register the news his mother brings him of the Other.

Coriolanus and Macbeth do not quarrel with their plays' representatives of the feminine as the other heroes do. Antony, Lear, Hamlet, and Othello quarrel with the feminine "for being separate," as Stanley Cavell puts it in the case of Othello's quarrel with Desdemona, for being "outside [themselves], beyond command."[2] Macbeth and Coriolanus are unaware of any painful separation from the feminine. Macbeth calls his wife his "dearest partner of greatness" (I.v.11), and Coriolanus salutes his mother as "the honored mold / Wherein this trunk was framed" (V.iii.22–23). Here it is the women who quarrel with the hero—and that only when they find him slow to serve his own interests. When Coriolanus refuses to placate the tribunes, for instance, his mother scolds him for political stupidity:

> I have a heart as little apt as yours
> But yet a brain that leads my use of anger
> To better vantage   (III.ii.29–31)

And when Macbeth hesitates, of course, his wife goads him on to kill the king: "When you durst do it, then you were a man" (I.vii.49). The feminine does not represent the Other in these plays. It opposes neither the hero's sense of Self nor the world of men he moves in; indeed, Volumnia and Lady Macbeth seem rather to block the heroes' exits from the world of men than to enact or require alternatives to that world.

The one woman in *Macbeth* who does represent the feminine as Other is Lady Macduff. Like Cleopatra, and unlike Volumnia and Lady Macbeth, Lady Macduff is hostile to the hero's public role when it calls him away from her. Consider, for instance, her response to Ross when he reports that Macduff has gone to England:

Lady Macduff	What had he done, to make him fly the land?
Ross	You must have patience, madam.
Lady Macduff	He had none:
	His flight was madness.

(IV.ii.1–3)

The dramatic purpose of Lady Macduff's one scene (IV.ii) is clearly to increase our sympathy for the Macduffs and our loathing of Macbeth, under whose orders Lady Macduff is murdered. Another playwright might therefore have pictured a more tender Lady Macduff, teaching her son to honor his father as she controlled her tears of loneliness and anxiety. But Shakespeare's Lady Macduff enters on the attack.

Macduff has left his family in order to do what is best for his country; Lady Macduff thinks only of his obligations to herself:

> Wisdom! To leave his wife, to leave his babes,
> His mansion and his titles, in a place
> From whence himself does fly? He loves us not;
> He wants the natural touch: for the poor wren,
> The most diminutive of birds, will fight,
> Her young ones in her nest, against the owl.
> All is the fear and nothing is the love;
> As little is the wisdom, where the flight
> So runs against all reason.   (IV.ii.6–14)

Although the arguments in favor of Macduff's rescue of Scotland—even at the expense of his family—are implicit in the play as a whole, Shakespeare does not bring them up against Lady Macduff. Ross can only make soothing noises: "your husband . . .

is noble, wise, judicious, and best knows/The fits o' th' season"
(IV.ii.15–17). Macduff may be noble, but he is no wiser or more
judicious than the next man, and he has precisely *mis*judged the
season; he never meant to sacrifice his family for his country. Lady
Macduff is left unanswered in her quarrel with her husband. The
claims of the feminine Other are perfectly valid in this play; they are
simply ignored by the entire cast.

Although Lady Macbeth is her husband's "dearest partner of
greatness" and Lady Macduff a demanding and critical wife, the
reaction of the two husbands on hearing of their wives' death is the
reverse of what we might expect. Macduff is dazed by the bad
news: "My wife killed too?," he asks in horror. "All my pretty
ones? Did you say all?" (IV.iii.213, 216–17). Macbeth, by contrast,
has no tears to spare for his "dearest partner." "She should have
died hereafter" (V.v.17), he says blankly. Lady Macduff opposes
her husband's enterprise whereas Lady Macbeth collaborates with
her husband; it is the feminine as Other who is loved.

In *Coriolanus* the closest we come to the feminine as Other is
Virgilia. If Volumnia speaks for Rome—for military glory, honor,
and the readiness to kill—Virgilia speaks for the opposition to
Rome, as Cleopatra does in *Antony and Cleopatra*. But the comparison with Cleopatra is very unflattering to Virgilia; compared to the
glamorous and fully articulated world of Cleopatra, Virgilia's protest seems faint indeed. Cleopatra is the queen of her own country;
Virgilia lives at her mother-in-law's. Virgilia must submit to Volumnia's demands, her speeches, her values. The following exchange, in which Volumnia triumphs at the level of language and
action both, is typical:

> *Gentlewoman* Madam, the Lady Valeria is come to visit you.
> *Virgilia* Beseech you give me leave to retire myself.
> *Volumnia* Indeed, you shall not.
>   Methinks I hear hither your husband's drum;
>   See him pluck Aufidius down by th' hair—
>   As children from a bear, the Volsces shunning him.
>   Methinks I see him stamp thus, and call thus:
>   "Come on, you cowards, you were got in fear,
>   Though you were born in Rome." His bloody brow
>   With his mailed hand then wiping, forth he goes,
>   Like to a harvest-man that's tasked to mow
>   Or all or lose his hire.
> *Virgilia* His bloody brow? O Jupiter, no blood!

> *Volumnia*   Away, you fool! It more becomes a man
>   Than gilt his trophy. The breasts of Hecuba,
>   When she did suckle Hector, looked not lovelier
>   Than Hector's forehead when it spit forth blood
>   At Grecian sword, contemning. Tell Valeria
>   We are fit to bid her welcome.
>   *Exit Gentlewoman.*
> *Virgilia*   Heavens bless my lord from fell Aufidius!
> *Volumnia*   He'll beat Aufidius' head below his knee,
>   And tread upon his neck.   (I.iii.26–47)

Linguistically Volumnia rides triumphantly over Virgilia's mild opposition to her military fantasies; dramatically she forces Virgilia to receive the unwanted caller. Where Virgilia prays and beseeches, Volumnia commands. Volumnia is profusely and passionately certain; Virgilia has room only to register a line at a time of protest.

Virgilia's insignificance is evident even in the scene where she is reunited with her husband. Here Coriolanus greets her with a speech often quoted as evidence of her importance to him:

>   O, a kiss
> Long as my exile, sweet as my revenge!
> Now, by the jealous queen of heaven, that kiss
> I carried from thee, dear, and my true lip
> Hath virgined it e'er since.   (V.iii.44–48)

This is in fact a very unusual speech for a Shakespearean hero to make a woman in the fifth act of a tragedy. It exhibits the easy confidence about a sexual relationship that the earlier heroes lose when their Fortunes plummet—that is, by the middle of the third act at the latest. Hamlet's silly poem to Ophelia ("Doubt that the stars are fire"), Antony's love rhetoric in the opening scene—these are, like Coriolanus's greeting to Virgilia, conventional protestations of the heroes' own qualifications in love. But when sexual relations become serious in Shakespearean tragedy, the heroes focus angrily on the question of the *woman's* constancy—not complacently on the issue of their own. Although Virgilia is Other to Coriolanus at a symbolic level, standing for life values as opposed to masculine-historical honor, she does not trouble him with her difference. When the other heroes become aware of the woman's difference, their anger and suspicion focus their attention on the feminine; but Coriolanus never notices Virgilia. Antony and Hamlet quickly shift to the question of Cleopatra's, Ophelia's, and

Gertrude's constancy, but Coriolanus, in the final moments of the play, still imagines that his own "true lip" is the issue.

Of course, the false note in this speech is only one indication of Virgilia's unimportance. The role that she plays is small throughout; she is only ornamental to her husband's life, not essential to him as Cleopatra is to Antony. Virgilia's opposition to Coriolanus's militarism is patient and passive. Like Octavia, and unlike Cleopatra, she only awaits and welcomes her husband; she plays a ceremonial rather than a sexual role. Virgilia, like Lady Macbeth, fails to enact the intransigent separateness of the Other.

The absence or insignificance of the feminine as Other is a crucial characteristic of both *Macbeth* and *Coriolanus*. In neither play does the masculine Self engage in a dialectic with the feminine Other. In *Macbeth* the dialectic is between Macbeth and an opposing party of men; in *Coriolanus* the dialectic is between the hero and Aufidius, his opposite number in the world of men. The dialectic in both plays, confined as it is to the world of men, is inconclusive—as it is in the history plays, where one conqueror replaces another without creating a sense of transcendent loss. The deaths of Macbeth and Coriolanus, like the deaths of the history heroes, are lacking in general significance. They do not, like the deaths of Hamlet and Lear, reaffirm us in our humanism, our sense of the value of our lives to us. Macbeth and Coriolanus simply exhaust the possibilities of their mode; they repeat themselves until, like Marlowe's Tamburlaine, they are dramatically played out. Then they die. Whereas Hamlet's story culminates at the time of his death, Macbeth's and Coriolanus's stories simply end. In retrospect we might say that Coriolanus has repeatedly fought battles and abused the commoners and Macbeth has killed and killed and killed. These heroes, unopposed by the Other, solipsistically repeat themselves; in both cases the price of solipsism is tedium. In the middle of the road Macbeth says,

> I am in blood
> Stepped in so far that, should I wade no more
> Returning were as tedious as go o'er.   (III.iv.136–38)

To Macbeth it is tedious rather than dangerous and exciting to murder, scheme, and terrorize. Coriolanus, a much less sensitive and intelligent character, does not suffer from the tedium himself, but he does make himself tedious to us. O. J. Campbell points out that he is in the grip of a "reflex mechanism": "The mob produces a rhythmical recurrence of Coriolanus's grotesque rage; and this stimulated repetition of a vice or folly turns Coriolanus into a jack-in-the-box. Every time his self-esteem is depressed, it springs back with the same choler-distorted face."[3] As different as the two plays are, they share this sense of recurrence rather than forward motion. Coriolanus keeps fighting the same battles with the same weapons; Macbeth keeps murdering his enemies open-eyed. For Hamlet and Lear the terms of the problem keep changing; not for Coriolanus and Macbeth. Jarold Ramsey uses the same key terms in discussing Macbeth that Campbell uses about Coriolanus: he says that the hero enters "a doom of reflex and repetition" and that "a principle of repetition and re-enactment governs the entire drama."[4] The compulsion to repeat is a function of the absence of the Other. In these two tragedies the hero does not appear to change.

Many readers, of course, would disagree. Indeed, in the case of *Coriolanus,* the opposite argument has been made. Jan Kott, for instance, believes that the dialectic between history and personal relationships does take place in this play and that Coriolanus is tempered into a renunciation of the world of men. His interpretation is worth considering at some length; it is concerned with both the issue of genre and with the question of Coriolanus as a tragic hero.

Kott divides the play into two movements, Acts I–III and Acts IV and V. The first movement, he says, is a kind of history play with "a republican moral." The conflict is between the mob-hating aristocrat and the people of Rome. As the first movement ends,

History has proved the plebeians right; the enemy of the people [Coriolanus] has become the enemy of Rome. In the first three acts of *Coriolanus* a bare drama of class attitudes has been played out. One could call it also a drama of historical inevitability. There is no discrepancy between social situation and action, or psychology. Coriolanus could be nameless, just as the First, Second, and Third Citizens are nameless. He is just an ambitious general who hates the people and went over to the enemy camp when he was unable to achieve dictatorial power.[5]

Kott's analysis, of course, leaves out the people's tribunes, a pair of slimy politicians who are as ambitious and self-centered as Coriolanus himself. But his sympathy for the Citizens themselves is well founded. Whenever we see them in close-up, they seem both

quick and fair. For instance, when Coriolanus asks them belliger-
ently what their "price o' the' consulship" is, the First Citizen
replies, "The price is to ask it kindly" (II.iii.75–76). If it is these
individuals who represent Kott's "people," then his analysis is
correct. They are right and good, Coriolanus is wrong and bad.
And whether or not we agree to omit the tribunes and to see the
class conflict in these stark terms, we must agree with Kott that in
the first three acts the characters are primarily interesting as representatives of conflicting classes. It is, as Kott says, "a drama of
historical inevitability." But after the third act, according to Kott,
this drama recedes and another one replaces it. As Kott reads the
play, the second movement deals with a moral victory on
Coriolanus's part that gives him stature as an individual and lifts
him out of the drama of historical inevitability. He "outgrows both
Romans and Volscians, plebeians and patricians," and we come to
value him as a man, however much we had opposed him as the
representative of a class. According to Kott, we realize at the end
that "there is no common system of values for the polis and for the
individual."[6] Coriolanus has become so impressively a man that he
cannot be judged by political criteria any longer.

Let us examine the play from Kott's point of view. At the end of
the third act Coriolanus is banished from Rome; in Act IV, scene i,
he is about to go into exile. This is the familiar tragic pattern: the
hero is leaving the old world, where the rules are favorable to his
success, for a new and more difficult world. He will be on his own
version of Lear's heath, outside the city walls; that which has
defined his identity will be left behind. The values of Rome will
have to be replaced by something else because Rome has expelled
him. These, at least, are the expectations we bring to this moment
from the other tragedies. As we shall see, they are not fulfilled. But
there is at this moment something new about Coriolanus that
reinforces these expectations. Up until now he has been entirely
self-centered, unaware of much that is outside himself. In the scene
where he must beg the citizens' votes, for instance, he is oblivious
to their good will. As they later agree, "He mocked us when he
begged our voices . . . / He flouted us downright" (II.iii.161–62).
But as Coriolanus says goodbye to his "friends of noble touch"
(IV.i.49), he seems more in touch with them than he ever has
before. In fact, he has something of Antony's manner in defeat

toward *his* followers. Coriolanus speaks to his friends in turn, praising them, reassuring them, promising to live up to their expectations of him:

> While I remain above the ground you shall
> Hear from me still, and never of me aught
> But what is like me formerly.   (IV.i.51–53)

For the first time Coriolanus *sounds* like a tragic hero.

Our expectation of tragic stature for Coriolanus is heightened in Act IV, scene iv, by his one and only soliloquy, his one moment of reflectiveness:

> O world thy slippery turns! Friends now fast sworn,
> Whose double bosoms seems to wear one heart,
> Whose hours, whose bed, whose meal and exercise
> Are still together, who twin, as t'were, in love
> Unseparable, shall within this hour,
> On a dissension of a doit, break out
> To bitterest enmity. So fellest foes,
> Whose passions and whose plots have broke their sleep
> To take the one the other, by some chance,
> Some trick not worth an egg, shall grow dear friends
> And interjoin their issues. So with me:
> My birthplace hate I, and my love's upon
> This enemy town.   (IV.iv.12–24)

This is not a terribly profound speech, but it is as effective as any of Hamlet's soliloquies in simply allying us with its speaker as a man who wonders at himself. Here for the first time the hero becomes self-reflexive. In Act IV, scene v, Coriolanus sounds even more like Hamlet; there he uses that riddling, mocking, and self-mocking language that is characteristic of Hamlet in distress:

> *Third Servingman* Where dwell'st thou?
> *Coriolanus* Under the canopy.
> *Third Servingman* Under the canopy!
> *Coriolanus* Ay.
> *Third Servingman* Where's that?
> *Coriolanus* I' th' city of kites and crows.
> *Third Servingman* I' th' city of kites and crows! What an ass it is!
>   Then thou dwell'st with daws too?
> *Coriolanus* No, I serve not thy master.

Third Servingman   How, Sir! Do you meddle with my master?
Coriolanus   Ay; 'tis an honester service than to meddle with thy
    mistress.   (IV.v.40–52)

The new graciousness (to his friends), the soliloquy, the cool
distanced wordplay are familiar from the earliest tragedies; these
things tend to mark out men who are at work on themselves. But
even more important than these hints of a new Coriolanus is the
plot structure of the last two acts. For the plot no longer proceeds
through conflict between two classes or two cities, as it did in the
political part of the play; these conflicts are now, as in the tragedies,
givens, a middle ground to the fate of the hero. Class warfare is
actually treated comically (or at least ironically) in the second
movement. For instance, in Act IV, scene vi, the tribunes taunt
Menenius with "Your Coriolanus is not much missed" or "Caius
Marcius was . . . insolent, / O'ercome with pride," and Menenius
gives them subdued answers: "All's well"; "I think not so." But the
next moment the positions are reversed; it develops that Coriolanus
intends to retaliate against Rome, and it is Menenius who becomes
vituperative while the tribunes stand about uncomfortably. "You
have made good work," shouts Menenius,

> You and your apron-men; you that stood so much
> Upon the voice of occupation and
> The breath of garlic eaters!   (IV.vi.96–99)

Confrontation between representatives of the opposing classes is
presented no longer for its own sake but for the sake of illustrating
the theme of Coriolanus's soliloquy: "O world thy slippery turns!"
This scene focuses our attention not on the actual claims of the two
classes against each other, but rather on the irony of history that
alternately credits and discredits opposing positions and that will
soon ruin Coriolanus. This same irony—that 'our virtues / Lie in th'
interpretation of the time" (IV.vii.49–50)—is emphasized repeatedly in this portion of the play, and the conflict between Menenius
and the tribunes is just another vehicle for doing so. It is no longer
the conflict between the liberal aristocrat and the self-interested
populists, as it was in the earlier part of the play. The political
dimension has been lost.

As the political tensions slacken, the play's resources go toward
constructing a tragic situation around Coriolanus. By Act V, scene

iii, everything is in place. Expelled from Rome, Coriolanus has joined forces with Rome's enemies and is on the point of sacking his native city in revenge. Various embassies have failed to change his mind; at the last minute his mother appears to petition him for mercy. Volumnia, who has always stood for honor and revenge, now pleads the cause of family love; Coriolanus's wife and daughter stand near her as she speaks:

> Think with thyself
> How more unfortunate than all living women
> Are we come hither; since that thy sight, which should
> Make our eyes flow with joy, hearts dance with comforts,
> Constrains them weep and shake with fear and sorrow,
> Making the mother, wife, and child, to see
> The son, the husband, and the father, tearing
> His country's bowels out.
>   . . .
>   Alack, or we must lose
> The country, our dear nurse, or else thy person,
> Our comfort in the country. We must find
> An evident calamity, though we had
> Our wish, which side should win; for either thou
> Must as a foreign recreant be led
> With manacles through our streets, or else
> Triumphantly tread on thy country's ruin,
> And bear the palm for having bravely shed
> Thy wife and children's blood. For myself, son,
> I purpose not to wait on fortune till
> These wars determine. If I cannot persuade thee
> Rather to show a noble grace to both parts
> Than seek the end of one, thou shalt no sooner
> March to assault thy country than to tread
> (Trust to't, thou shalt not) on thy mother's womb
> That brought thee to this world. (V.iii.96–103, 109–25)

Under the threat of his mother's suicide, Coriolanus calls off his revenge, knowing that he risks his own death by doing so. According to Kott, Coriolanus puts aside the political motive for the personal relationship. He "outgrows both Romans and Volscians" and becomes an individual. He is no longer "just an ambitious general, a theoretically nameless representative of his class"; he has become a man. His death—for Aufidius does indeed have him murdered for his change of heart—is therefore significant of more than itself. Coriolanus has transcended the masculine-political code and become a tragic hero.

So Kott reads the end of the play. Yet the final drama of the play is unconvincing. The conflict between Coriolanus and his mother seems fatally compromised by the identity of interests that has existed between these two characters up to this point. It is too late for us to read Volumnia as a representative of the Other; we have known her too long as the source of the male Self, as the Mother in Coriolanus's mind, as the hero's coach or trainer. His renunciation for her sake cannot seem a triumph over his own class attitudes but can only seem a return to origins. In fact, we have already seen her persuade him to a kind of self-violation; his sense of identification with her has always counted with him for even more than the identity she has successfully urged upon him. Once before he has put aside his rigid pride at her request: in Act III, Volumnia persuaded him to apologize, as a matter of policy, to the plebeians he had insulted. To do so utterly violates his sense of honor, but Volumnia says,

> I prithee now, sweet son, as thou hast said
> My praises made thee first a soldier, so,
> To have my praise for this, perform a part
> Thou has not done before.   (III.ii.107–10)

Coriolanus answers, "Well, I must do't." But it sticks in his craw so badly that ten lines later he cries,

> I will not do't;
> Lest I surcease to honor mine own truth,
> And by my body's action teach my mind
> A most inherent baseness.   (III.ii.120–24)

Volumnia triumphs, here as in the reconciliation scene, by threatening to withdraw and leave Coriolanus with the consequences of independent choice. "At thy choice then," she says, "Come all to ruin! . . . Do as thou list." But Coriolanus cannot act on a desire that conflicts with hers. He answers her,

> Pray, be content.
> Mother, I am going to the marketplace.
> Chide me no more.   (III.ii.130–32)

The resolution to the conflict in Act V must be read in the light of the resolution to the conflict in Act III. Coriolanus does not appear to change, to confront and move beyond the opposition offered by the Other. There is no dialectic, only capitulation to what is after all a more important version of Self.

One of the regularly recurring signs of change in the hero, of course, is violent denunciation of the mutability of women. Coriolanus has perhaps more justification than most of Shakespeare's heroes for accusing a woman of mutability: Volumnia changes the rules on him right in the middle of his end game. A Hamlet or a Lear—even a Titus Andronicus—would at this point revile the sexual treachery of women in general. But the quarrel between Coriolanus and Volumnia, unlike the quarrel between Hamlet and Gertrude, has no sexual dimension. It is a quarrel with the hero's other Self and not with the sexual Other. Volumnia's choice of her own interests over his, mortal though it proves to Coriolanus, does not strike him with the force of a sexual betrayal. The principal feminine is not Other in this play. Her opposition to the hero brings about his death without awakening his consciousness to the world outside the Self.

The absence of the woman as Other in Shakespearean tragedy apparently indicates the absence of the Other altogether. No conflict in *Coriolanus* reminds us of the dialectic between the hero and the world outside the Self. Even at the level of locale we have only projections of the Self: Antium is merely Rome writ small. (The obvious contrast, of course, is with *Antony and Cleopatra*, where Rome is opposed by Egypt, its Other.) And in Antium we find the hero's primary antagonist, Aufidius, an exact reflection of the masculine Self. Aufidius only opposes Coriolanus circumstantially, not as an alternative idea. He is not a separate and competitive center around which the world may turn but only a competitor for the brass ring of political and military power. He merely repeats the hero. As many critics have noticed, there is a narcissistic and homoerotic dimension to the relationship between these two warriors. When Coriolanus comes to Antium, Aufidius welcomes him in highly sexualized language:

> Here I clip
> The anvil of my sword, and do contest
> As hotly and as nobly with thy love
> As ever in ambitious strength I did
> Contend against thy valor. Know thou first,
> I loved the maid I married; never man

Sighed truer breath. But that I see thee here,
Thou noble thing, more dances my rapt heart
Than when I first my wedded mistress saw
Bestride my threshold. Why, thou Mars, I tell thee,
We have a power on foot, and I had purpose
Once more to hew thy target from thy brawn,
Or lose mine arm for't. Thou hast beat me out
Twelve several times, and I have nightly since
Dreamt of encounters 'twixt thyself and me.
We have been down together in my sleep,
Unbuckling helms, fisting each other's throat,
And waked half dead with nothing.   (IV.v.113–30)

Aufidius is Coriolanus's Cleopatra, his mortal enemy and—at the
level of the imagery—his lover. Aufidius, says a servingman,
"makes a mistress" of Coriolanus (IV.v.204). But whereas Cleopatra represents the Other, Aufidius is a version of the Self.

There is no single character, then, who represents the Other in
this play. It is worth noticing, however, that the Roman mob
stands in for the feminine Other as the target of the hero's excessive
rage. "The fires i' th' lowest hell fold in the people!" he cries in
Act III:

Let them pronounce the steep Tarpeian death,
Vagabond exile, flaying, pent to linger
But with a grain a day, I would not buy
Their mercy at the price of one fair word,
Nor check my courage for what they can give,
To have't with saying "Good morrow."

(III.iii.68, 88–93)

This is the kind of irrational fury that the other heroes seem to
reserve for their women. And if it does not cross Coriolanus's mind
that Volumnia or Virgilia might be unfaithful to him, he is obsessed
with the mutability of the mob:

He that depends
Upon your favors swims with fins of lead
And hews down oaks with rushes. Hang ye! Trust ye?
With every minute you do change a mind,
And call him noble that was now your hate,
Him vile that was your garland.
      . . .

You are no surer, no,

Than is the coal of fire upon the ice,
Or hailstone in the sun.   (I.i.181–86, 174–76)

This might be Antony at his worst to Cleopatra. Moreover,
Coriolanus's disgust is physical as well as moral. Just as Gertrude is
"rank" as well as "mutable" to Hamlet, the mob is the "mutable,
rank-scented meiny" (III.i.66) to Coriolanus. Coriolanus directs
his strongest feelings, then, toward an abstraction rather than a
human being. The abstraction he hates is, of course, a projection of
the Self; he quite specifically refuses to deal with the people as
individuals but ideologically lumps them all in a heap. Whereas the
rage of Antony, Lear, and Hamlet is resolved by love and sorrow,
Coriolanus's anger can never resolve. There is nothing outside
himself to love or to mourn; the mob does not exist except in his
mind. And clearly his decision to spare Rome does not indicate any
grand reconciliation with her people, his Other. The theme of the
mob simply disappears at the end of the play. It is not a factor in
Coriolanus's choice.

In *Macbeth,* as in *Coriolanus,* the absence of a significant feminine
Other is a sign of the hero's failure to engage in a dialectic with the
outside world. The hero of this play is entirely taken up by the
internal dialogue; from beginning to end his attention is fully
claimed only by his own inner life. Lady Macbeth neither claims
nor receives his attention—nor, indeed, does she "deserve" it. She
does not represent an alternative either to his mode of being or to
his sense of Self. As the play goes on he loses interest in her
altogether. The absence of dialectic between the Other and the Self
is in turn related to the inconclusiveness of the hero's death. Macbeth's death does not, like Hamlet's and Lear's, release the Self
from our reservations about it; it does not reaffirm the *reader* as Self
the way the other deaths do. Macbeth is the one hero of Shakespearean tragedy whose own self-love is weakened by the action of
the play. By the end of the play his own passion for life has worn
away:

> I 'gin to be aweary of the sun,
> And wish th' estate o' th' world were now undone.
> Ring the alarum bell! Blow wind, come wrack!
> At least we'll die with harness on our back.   (V.v.49–52)

In the absence of any dialectic with the Other, Macbeth has simply
run down. Even his apocalyptic fantasy is listless: "Blow wind,

come wrack!/At least we'll die with harness on our back." The comparison with Lear is obvious. The feminine Other provokes that old man to love and rage beyond his physical capacity to endure. Macbeth, by contrast, can hardly summon the energy to resent the thought of his own death.

As the play goes on, however, a different kind of dialectic develops from that between the Other and the Self. Instead of a dialectic between the hero and the world outside, we see a dialectic between two different worlds—Macbeth's and that of Macduff's alliance. If Macbeth never meets with an Other as absorbing and terrifying as the life he finds within himself, Macduff and company, by contrast, meet and conquer Macbeth. The one is all sensibility and inner life, the others are defined in terms of their courageous action. We are allied with Macbeth on account of his feelings and in spite of his vicious action; we are allied with Macduff patriotically, as activists in a cause. There is a dialectic within the play as a whole, if not between the hero and the world of his play. Here the absence of the feminine as Other does not indicate an absence of dialectic altogether; although the hero is undialectical, the play is not. Whereas *Coriolanus* simply ends with the death of its protagonist, *Macbeth* conclusively resolves at its end.

The resolution of Macbeth has some affinities to the resolutions of comedy. At the end of the play the social order is restored and life goes on as before. John Hollander has even suggested that Macduff's army enacts a variant of the theme of "bringing in the May."[7] The advancing soldiers camouflaged in greenery bring new life to replace what has gone rotten. Of course in the comedies the Maying rituals are a kind of creative disorder from which we emerge refreshed; here the army of green rises up *against* the confusion and disorder. The greenery here is in aid of good government, not saturnalian license. The alliance that opposes Macbeth, then, is obviously not a comic society. It is entirely male and entirely devoted to the social ideal. It is in fact a world of history-play heroes. The comic society is less ideological, less heroic, more various. The tendency to narrowness of this alternative world is epitomized in Siward's reaction to his son's death:

> *Siward*   Had he his hurts before?
> *Ross*   Ay, on the front.
> *Siward*   Why then, God's soldier be he!
>   Had I as many sons as I have hairs,

> I would not wish them to a fairer death:
> And so his knell is knolled.   (V.viii.46–50)

This is chilling. Although Macduff's alliance is a benign version of the masculine-historical ideal, the ideal nevertheless demands the sacrifice of full emotional responsiveness. The alliance against Macbeth, like the world of the history plays, is characterized by its emphasis on the relationship between fathers and sons. Siward and his son remind us of Talbot and young John; Fleance's escape is Banquo's triumph; Malcolm and Donalbain learn of their father's death through images of the vital connectedness of father to son: "The spring, the head, the fountain of your blood/Is stopped; the very source of it is stopped" (II.iii.98–99). Macbeth is dramatically neither a father nor a son; the dialectic in this play is between Macbeth's individualism and the social cohesion of the world of the fathers and sons. The feminine is for once irrelevant to the dialectic of the tragedy; but it is important to notice that this is a tragedy in which, for once, the resolution of the play is not to be located in the death of the hero. Where Shakespeare creates the illusion of tragic growth, of the resonant death, of life valued according to our individualism, the hero's value at the moment of his death is a function of his interaction with the Other; and the feminine is the foremost representative in Shakespeare of the challenge by the Other of the Self.

FIVE

The Comic Heroine and the Avoidance of Choice

In Shakespeare's comedies, and only in the comedies, we see the feminine Other face to face. In the tragedies we respond to the women characters very largely on the basis of our interest in the hero; our vision of the feminine is mediated by our desires on behalf of the men. Our strongest feelings for Cordelia, for instance, come when we see *her* feelings for Lear; Cleopatra, for another instance, is never quite free from our hopes of her on Antony's behalf. In the histories we see the feminine primarily in relation to the masculine struggle for power. In the romances the loss and recovery of the feminine is experienced through our sympathy with the male Self who has lost and found his feminine Other. Miranda and Marina are most moving as figures that may be lost to Prospero and Pericles; Hermione is most important as a figure who may be lost and found by Leontes. But our response to the comic heroine is direct and unmediated by her father, lover, or husband. We do not judge Rosalind by her loyalty to Duke Senior; Viola does not move us by being restored to Sebastian; Portia's fidelity to Bassanio is not what impresses us about her. The interest we feel in these heroines is in an Other quite apart from her relationship to the desires of the Self—which is to say, apart from the fact of masculine unfulfill-ment. In comedy we are always sure of getting what we want, so masculine unfulfillment does not shape our response to the Other. In every other genre, it does.

The closest we come in the comedies to judging a woman by her loyalty to a man is in Act III, scene i, of *The Merchant of Venice,* where Shylock hears that Jessica has traded his ring for a monkey. He cries,

> Out upon her! Thou torturest me, Tubal. It was my turquoise; I
> had it of Leah when I was a bachelor. I would not have given it
> for a wilderness of monkeys. (III.i.116–19)

Shylock, of course, is the closest thing to a tragic Self in all of the comedies; just as we have in him a glimpse of the tragic hero's rage and grandeur, so we also have a hint of the hero's tendency to deflect our feelings toward the feminine. If we dwell on this passage we may feel some of Shylock's anger at his daughter. But only if we dwell on it. In context it is so thoroughly surrounded with reminders of Shylock's hatefulness that we scarcely have time, when Shylock makes this appeal, to respond. Earlier in the scene Shylock revolts us by wishing Jessica dead with "the jewels in her ear . . . the ducats in her coffin!" On learning that Antonio will go bankrupt, he gloats, "I am very glad of it. I'll plague him; I'll torture him. I am glad of it." Then come the touching lines about his ring; but immediately afterwards his attention returns most unpleasantly to Antonio: "I will have the heart of him if he forfeit, for were he out of Venice I can make what merchandise I will." Shylock is so completely our antagonist that it is all we can do to *notice* his personal feelings in this scene. They scarcely have the power to turn us against Jessica.

In this scene we have a glimpse of masculine unfulfillment; but for the most part the comedies absorb masculine desire into what Charles Frey defines simply as "a sense of humor": "a sense of proportion and propitiation celebrating the huge ongoingness of life."[1] In the tragedies, where unfulfillment is rampant and life may end abruptly, the feminine Other is the object of intense suspicion; in the comedies, where life goes on and on, eventually giving us much of what we want, the feminine is treated to almost perfect trust. It is true that the comedies exhibit a continuous low-grade anxiety about cuckoldry, located mostly in the margins of the drama, in jokes and songs. But since the anxiety almost never focuses on a particular woman, it seems free-floating and unrelated to its ostensible object. Fear of cuckoldry seems to stand for a general discontent; it is the fly in the ointment, the uneasiness that keeps us from full enjoyment of the gifts of the earth. This is certainly its function in the final song of *Love's Labour's Lost*, "The Owl and the Cuckoo." Here the threat of cuckoldry spoils the perfect spring:

> When daisies pied and violets blue
> > And lady-smocks all silver white
> And cuckoo-buds of yellow hue
> > Do paint the meadows with delight,
> The cuckoo then, on every tree,

> Mocks married men; for thus sings he, "Cuckoo!
> Cuckoo, cuckoo!" O word of fear,
> Unpleasing to a married ear!   (V.ii.892–99)

Clearly the cuckoo's song does not speak ill of the women in this play, Rosalind and her ladies; it speaks of sexual anxiety per se and of the self-preoccupation that spoils nature for us. In *Much Ado About Nothing,* the only play in which a woman's virtue is in question, the cuckoldry jokes seem more substantial than elsewhere, more indicative of a possible Woman Problem. But Benedick comes to see his own fear of cuckoldry as one of the little disturbances of man; he plans to live with it rather than allow it to dominate his life. "Prince," he cries at the end of the play, "thou art sad. Get thee a wife, get thee a wife! There is no staff more reverend than one tipped with horn" (V.iv.122–24). Benedick refuses sadness and accepts his own anxiety as nothing more serious than a limitation on his pleasures.

If Lear's speech beginning "Down from the waist they are Centaurs" is the classic example of sexual anxiety in the tragedies, Bottom's comment on the song he sings to cheer himself up is the classic response to sexual anxiety in the comedies:

> The finch, the sparrow, and the lark,
>   The plain-song cuckoo gray,
> Whose note full many a man doth mark,
>   And dares not answer nay—
>
> for, indeed, who would set his wit to so foolish a bird? Who would give a bird the lie, though he cry "cuckoo" never so?
>   (*A Midsummer Night's Dream*, III.i.129–35)

Bottom does not even realize what the song of the cuckoo means, and he feels a certain superiority to those who would converse with winged creatures. To worry about sexual betrayal in the comedies is to box with shadows, to talk to birds. The anxiety is there in the culture, identifiable in songs such as Bottom sings; but it need not affect our relations with the particular Other, the woman in question, who is without exception chaste, faithful, good.

Shakespeare's attitude toward women in the comedies is irreconcilable with the misogynist rage Fiedler discovers in the tragedies. In the comedies, Fiedler says, Shakespeare's hatred of women is concealed by the conventions of the genre.[2] But if we compare Shakespeare's comedies to their sources or to the comedies his contemporaries were writing, it becomes clear that Shakespeare's attitude here is not conventional at all but quite particularly good-humored. Every change from the source is a change away from ambiguity and toward a feminine chastity that can be taken for granted.

Good humor toward the feminine in the comedies is part of a more general good humor toward the general conditions of life. When Parolles complains to Lafew, "I am a man whom Fortune hath cruelly scratched," Lafew asks him, "Wherein have you played the knave with Fortune that she would scratch you, who of herself is a good lady . . . ?" (All's Well That Ends Well, V.ii.26–31). In the comedies Lady Fortune smiles down like the noonday sun, casting no shadows onto the feminine Other who so often represents her in Shakespeare's drama. When Orlando is invited to "sit down with me and . . . rail against our mistress the world," he firmly refuses: "I will chide no breather in the world but myself, against whom I know most faults" (As You Like It, III.ii.277–81). There is no call to rail against one's mistress the world, and there is no call to rail against one's mistress. In comedy both will be true.

The psychosexual confidence of the comedies, however, is no more to be identified with Shakespeare himself than the psychosexual doubt of the tragedies. His confidence, like his doubt, is a matter of genre. In the tragedies anxiety develops because the feminine Other, like the masculine Self, is forced to make choices, and these choices may go against the hero. In the comedies, however, choice is almost unnecessary. The comic world is frankly controlled and unified by its creator; it is a world of "both/and" rather than of "either/or," as in tragedy. Our confidence in the feminine Other is partly the effect of the world she lives in, a world in which we need not fear her choices because no choices confront her. Consider, for instance, Shakespeare's favorite love triangle, the constellation of father, daughter, and prospective son-in-law. In the tragedies the women are forced to make a choice between the father and the lover; in the comedies the choice is almost always avoided. The distinction is worth developing at some length.

In Othello and King Lear, Desdemona and Cordelia must explain to their fathers, however gently and reasonably, that they can no longer expect the best of their daughters' love. Desdemona tells Brabantio,

> You are the lord of duty,
> I am hitherto your daughter. But here's my husband,
> And so much duty as my mother showed
> To you, preferring you before her father,
> So much I challenge that I may profess
> Due to the Moor my lord.   (I.iii.182–87)

And Cordelia tells Lear,

> Good my lord,
> You have begot me, bred me, loved me. I
> Return those duties back as are right fit,
> Obey you, love you, and most honor you.
> Why have my sisters husbands, if they say
> They love you all? Haply, when I shall wed,
> That lord whose hand must take my plight shall carry
> Half my love with him, half my care and duty.
> Sure I shall never marry like my sisters,
> To love my father all.   (I.i.95–104)

Cordelia's choice is the epitome of all those motions by which the universe lets us know that we are not central to its concerns. What happens in *King Lear,* including Cordelia's own death, all follows from Lear's perception that he does not matter to Cordelia as she matters to herself—and, of course, from his recognition that he matters not at all to her sisters.

In *Othello* as in *King Lear* the situation requires the feminine Other to choose, and Desdemona's choice is orchestrated by Iago into a prototype of sexual betrayal. He tells Othello, "she did deceive her father, marrying you" (III.iii.206), implying that Desdemona is ipso facto a practiced adulteress. And Brabantio himself sounds the same note:

> Look to her, Moor, if thou hast eyes to see:
> She has deceived her father, and may thee.   (I.iii.287–88)

Leslie Fiedler, discussing the resemblance of Act I to the boy-gets-girl plot of New Comedy, comments as follows on this theme:

For marriage to occur, a girl must abandon her father, and that abandonment necessarily implies revealing capacities for deceiving men which terrify her husband forever, making assurance in marriage impossible. Behind the conventional happy ending of New Comedy, therefore, lies a potential disillusion which the genre itself cannot contain, yielding to farce when the consequence is cuckoldry, tolerated or ignored, and to tragedy when it is adultery, discovered and bloodily revenged.[3]

In *Othello,* of course, the disillusion is itself an illusion and adultery is bloodily revenged without ever having been discovered. There is something ludicrous about Fiedler's paradox, that marriage is in itself proof of the wife's "capacities for deceiving men"; but in *Othello* jealousy *is* ludicrous as well as tragic. As Stanley Cavell has noticed,[4] Desdemona is victimized merely for being a choice-making creature, merely for having the sexuality on which to base her choices, merely for choosing Othello himself. It is her choice of Othello that teaches him that she is capable of choice and therefore capable of choosing someone else.

The choices that Desdemona and Cordelia make are so natural in Shakespeare as to amount to a female rite of passage; and yet even so they bring on tragedy. The choices of other women in the tragedies are much more problematic. Gertrude, Ophelia, Cleopatra, and Cressida make choices whose outcome is much less predictable and may be much less acceptable to us. In *Troilus and Cressida,* Cressida's choice *is* Troilus's tragedy. In tragedy the best and the worst of women will make their choices, and the feminine itself is therefore cause for alarm.

But in the comedies, the women tend to avoid making choices. If a father opposes a daughter's marriage at the beginning of the play, he is sure to come around by the end. Two examples are Aegeus in *A Midsummer Night's Dream* and the Duke of Milan in *Two Gentlemen of Verona.* (It is not true, of course, in *Romeo and Juliet,* where Capulet's coming around would be sufficient to turn this tragedy into comedy.) Often in comedy there *is* no father to be hurt by the daughter's marriage: in *Twelfth Night,* for instance, there is a brother instead of a father; far from betraying Sebastian, as the daughters betray the fathers, Viola provides him with a wife. But the perfect contrast to *Othello* and *King Lear* is *As You Like It,* where the sexual tensions in the father-daughter theme are nothing but an occasion for jokes and flourishes. When Celia mentions "the duke your father," Rosalind asks, "But what talk we of fathers when there is such a man as Orlando?" (III.iv.36–37). Rosalind's cheerful self-irony would be impossible if she were actually forced to choose between the two. These words would be impossible from women who live in a tragic universe; Desdemona and Cordelia must be deeply serious about the essentially ordinary business of leaving home. For them, everything is charged. But Rosalind need feel no conflict between being a daughter and being a lover. In Act V she explicitly flaunts her freedom from the double bind that ruins Desdemona:

> (*To Duke*)   To you I give myself, for I am yours.
> (*To Orlando*)   To you I give myself, for I am yours.

And the men respond obediently,

> *Duke Senior*   If there be truth in sight, you are my daughter.
> *Orlando*   If there be truth in sight, you are my Rosalind.
> (V.iv.116–19)

In the comic universe the comic heroine need *not* choose between men; she is therefore without terrors for the masculine Self. There are two exceptions to this rule: in *Much Ado About Nothing* there is a moment when sexual tensions arise between Hero and Leonato; and in *The Merchant of Venice,* of course, Jessica betrays Shylock. Both exceptions are worth pausing over.

In *Much Ado About Nothing,* Don John, informing Claudio of Hero's betrayal, calls her "Leonato's Hero, your Hero, every man's Hero" (III.ii.101–2). Here the prior possession of the girl by her father is a kind of rhetorical advantage to her slanderer: because Don John can name two men who have "had" Hero, the phrase "every man's Hero" seems to confirm, not just to introduce, the idea of her duplicity. And Leonato, hearing her slandered, certainly falls into a frenzy of injured possessiveness. Clearly he takes her alleged betrayal of Claudio as a betrayal of himself as well. The following speech, with its obsessive repetition of the word "mine," is more appropriate to a cuckolded husband than to a father.

> Why ever wast thou lovely in my eyes?
> Why had I not with charitable hand
> Took up a beggar's issue at my gates,
> Who smirchèd thus and mired with infamy,
> I might have said, "No part of it is mine;
> This shame derives itself from unknown loins"?
> But mine, and mine I loved, and mine I praised,
> And mine that I was proud on, mine so much
> That I myself was to myself not mine,
> Valuing of her.   (IV.i.129–38)

Leonato here recalls Brabantio, and Shakespeare is hinting at the theme of the betrayed father. But whereas Brabantio feels betrayed by Desdemona's marriage, Leonato feels betrayed by Hero's failure to marry. Her sexuality is not in itself the problem; only its supposed unlawfulness is cause for alarm. In any case he soon announces, "My soul doth tell me Hero is belied" (V.i.42), and from then on he takes her part. His pride of possession works in favor of his daughter's marriage; Brabantio's claim on Desdemona requires her to choose between himself and her husband.

The one woman in the comedies whose marriage actually does involve a betrayal of her father is Jessica. Two things, however, distinguish her choice from that of the women in the tragedies: first, it is so lightheartedly made that we hardly perceive it as a choice; and second, Shylock is such a villain that we rarely take his feelings into account. The following exchange is illustrative of both Jessica's insouciance and the general assumption in *The Merchant of Venice* that Shylock is a dreadful person:

> *Launcelot* . . . look you, the sins of the father are to be laid upon the children. . . . you may partly hope that your father got you not—that you are not the Jew's daughter.
> *Jessica* That were a kind of bastard hope indeed! So the sins of my mother should be visited upon me.
> *Launcelot* Truly then, I fear you are damned both by father and mother. Thus when I shun Scylla your father, I fall into Charybdis your mother. Well, you are gone both ways.
>   (III.v.1–18)

In this fantasy the betrayal of Shylock is pushed back a generation from Jessica to her mother; Jessica is thoroughly justified in her desertion of her father; and the whole issue is cheerfully dismissed in Jessica's last remark: "I shall be saved by my husband. He hath made me a Christian" (III.v.19–20). In this exchange heavy themes are orchestrated very lightly; salvation and damnation are subjects for witty repartee. Similarly, the theme of the betrayed father is so lightheartedly developed as to defuse anxieties even as it provokes them.

Furthermore, Shylock and Jessica are not the only father and daughter in the play. They are only the father and daughter appropriate to Venice, to realism, to the world of hard choices. The late Duke of Belmont and Portia present the Belmont version of the father-daughter theme. Portia's father has left a will that would seem to require her to choose between love and family loyalty. But whereas Jessica actually makes such a choice, Portia is spared the trouble of doing so. Her will *happens* to coincide with the terms of her father's will. In Belmont Fiedler's paradox does not apply, and Belmont has the last word in this play. Jessica's betrayal of Shylock is balanced by the happy outcome of Portia's obedience to her father's will.

How are we to understand the feminine avoidance of choice in Shakespeare's comedies? On the one hand it may seem to depotentiate the women; the comic heroine may seem a masculine wish-fulfillment, an Other who may be loved at no risk to the Self. But on the other hand, the avoidance of choice is a positive gift and a comic prerogative. In the world of comedy the barriers are lowered between our alternatives, and it is the characters who take advantage of the situation that appeal to us most. In *A Midsummer Night's Dream,* for instance, the barrier is temporarily lowered between the world of reality and the world of the imagination. Bottom appeals to us because he moves with such aplomb between the real and the fantastic, stepping over the barriers as if they were not there. This is what we long to do in comedy: *not* to choose between competing worlds but to move between them with Bottom's stupendous calm. In tragedy, of course, the situation is different. In tragedy our alternatives are mutually exclusive, and characters who refuse to choose between them write themselves out of the story. Octavia and Ophelia, for instance, are much reduced by their failures to choose between men—Antony and Caesar in Octavia's case, and Hamlet and Polonius in Ophelia's. In tragedy we reserve our admiration for those who face their choices squarely, like Cordelia and Desdemona. But in comedy we are attracted to characters who minister to our sense of freedom from choice, and it is no coincidence that these characters are often women. It is the feminine Other who is most at home in the alternative world; the male Self, as we shall see, is less than brilliant in this setting. Bottom is an exception, a male character whose presence dissolves all oppositions; but Bottom is hardly a male Self. His unconsciousness (not to say stupidity) makes him Other to the reader just as his lack of social status makes him Other to the Athenian lovers. When the feminine Other represents the avoidance of choice she does so more consciously than Bottom—although not necessarily more appealingly.

In *The Merchant of Venice,* for instance, Portia spares us the choice between love and law, Belmont and Venice, stepping Bottomlike over the barriers between the two worlds. Just as Bottom goes from being a real tinker to being an imaginary ass-headed creature, Portia goes from being a Belmont heiress to being a Venetian judge. But Bottom is at home in the world of the fantastic because he refuses to dwell on its differences from ordinary life. Portia, on the other hand, is at home in Venice because she knows exactly what the differences are between this public world and the world she has come from. She is perfectly conscious of the choices that face us in this play; she is merely confident that they need not be made.

In this play, general philosophical choices arise from specific choices made by the male hero, Bassanio. Bassanio is faced with a conflict between his concern for his friend and his own desire to marry Portia. He chooses Portia, allows Antonio to become bound to Shylock, and is about to suffer the consequences when Portia sweeps into Venice and saves him from them. At the same time she saves *us* from the philosophical choice between love and law. Because of her, we do not have to choose between our desire for social order and our desire to see our representative excused from society's bargains. On the one hand,

> The duke cannot deny the course of law;
> For the commodity that strangers have
> With us in Venice, if it be denied,
> Will much impeach the justice of the state,
> Since that the trade and profit of the city
> Consisteth of all nations.   (III.iii.26–31)

In other words, it will be bad for business, bad for all our business, if Antonio is let off from his bond. But on the other hand, Antonio is a good man, a dear friend, and does not deserve to die at Shylock's hands. The conflict is absolute; when Portia arrives from Belmont it simply melts away. The course of law is upheld *and* Antonio is saved; because of the comic heroine we can have things both ways.

In Shakespearean comedy the successful avoidance of choice is a feminine prerogative, and the men are burdened with a graceless tendency to choose. During Antonio's trial, for instance, Bassanio blunders into this strange speech:

> Antonio, I am married to a wife
> Which is as dear to me as life itself;
> But life itself, my wife, and all the world

Are not with me esteemed above thy life.
I would lose all, ay sacrifice them all,
Here to this devil, to deliver you.   (IV.i.281–86)

In a passion to show his friendship for Antonio, Bassanio offers up
his love for Portia, gratuitously creating a conflict between the two.
No one has demanded the sacrifice of Portia, nor is it clear how it
could possibly be of any help. Portia, in disguise as Bellario, is
understandably annoyed to hear her husband say these lines. She
tells him coolly, "Your wife would give you little thanks for that / If
she were by to hear you make the offer." In mock revenge, Portia
later pretends to have sacrificed Bassanio to a figure from his own
public life: "Pardon me, Bassanio, / For by this ring the doctor lay
with me" (V.i.258–59). Of course, Portia herself is the "doctor."
As Bellario she demands the ring from Bassanio; as Portia she
produces the ring to prove her own infidelity. The point is Bassanio's failure to be two things at once as Portia has been. Since he
has betrayed her by choosing between love and friendship, she
pretends to have betrayed him by choosing between men. The
contrast is striking between the two characters at this moment.
Bassanio seems heavy, puzzled, slightly unfit for the world of
comedy; he has chosen Portia over Antonio, Antonio over Portia,
and now he wants Portia again. Each time he has clumsily identified himself with a single desire. Portia, on the other hand, is
talented and desirous as both a woman and a man, Bassanio's wife
and, as it were, his lawyer. It is the feminine Other who can avoid
choice in comedy, who can perform alternative identities, who can
move gracefully between worlds that the hero finds mutually exclusive. The male Self seems tainted in the world of comedy by the
lingering necessity to choose. He expects to be one thing only, like
a tragic hero; in comedy we are blessedly free to be this and then
that, or both at once.

In the courtroom scene, Bassanio fabricates a conflict where none
exists; but the comic hero's choice is not always unnecessary. The
typical choice faced by the hero in comedy is the one between love
and friendship, between a woman and a man. But with the exception of *A Midsummer Night's Dream*, no play deals with a conflict for
women between friendship and love. The final word on female
friendship comes in *The Merry Wives of Windsor* when Mr. Ford
derides the intimacy between Mrs. Page and his wife. Mr. Ford tells
Mrs. Page, "I think if your husbands were dead, you two would

marry," and Mrs. Page snaps back, "Be sure of that—two other husbands" (III.ii.13–15). Marriage is marriage; friendship is friendship. The feminine Other is confident she may simultaneously enjoy relationships that may be mutually exclusive for the male Self.

The exclusion of the masculine from the privileges of comedy is clearest in *Much Ado About Nothing*. Here Shakespeare develops his best and blithest comic hero; and yet Benedick's freedom from choice is heavily qualified. There are two sides to Benedick. On the one hand he is an individual male; on the other hand he is the male half of a couple. The couple is analogous to a comic heroine: Beatrice-and-Benedick both mock love and experience it, are self-aware but capable of spontaneity. Of course, they must be tricked into their spontaneous emotions; their friends must bring about the change in them from confirmed-bachelor-and-spinster to happily-engaged-couple. But Benedick-and-Beatrice, unlike the tragic Self, accept the change without a sense of lost identity. Benedick finally refuses the choice between the old self and the new, distancing himself like a comic heroine from all his roles even as he plays them:

> In brief, since I do purpose to marry, I will think nothing to any purpose that the world can say against it; and therefore never flout at me for what I have said against it; for man is a giddy thing, and this is my conclusion. For thy part, Claudio, I did think to have beaten thee; but in that thou art like to be my kinsman, live un-bruised, and love my cousin.   (V.iv.104–11)

The high-spirited self-consciousness of this passage allies Beatrice-and-Benedick with Rosalind and the other quick-change artists. But the circumstances of the play force Benedick into a choice from which detachment and high spirits cannot rescue him. The men in the play are confronted by a discrepancy between the illusion of Hero's infidelity and the reality of her love; like Antony and Othello they must choose between a woman and the world of men by whom she is condemned. Claudio chooses the old world of male solidarity; his friendship with Don Pedro teaches him to trust Don John instead of Hero. But Benedick, like Antony, chooses on the basis of his relationship to a woman, even though it costs him his place in the world of men to do so. He decides to defend Hero on the basis of his love for Beatrice. We are more sympathetic to Benedick's choice than to Claudio's because, of course, Don Pedro is wrong about Hero and Beatrice is right. But in the crucial scene where Benedick is persuaded, Beatrice is certainly less attractive than Don Pedro, who after all has been acting in good faith. In Act IV, scene i, Beatrice's good faith is sunk in her anger. "Kill Claudio," she tells Benedick, adding, "O God, that I were a man! I would eat his heart in the market place!" (IV.i.288, 305–6) Her sudden spitefulness taints Benedick's choice almost as badly as Don Pedro's mistake taints Claudio's. If Benedick is seen as the central character of the play, it shapes itself into a version of tragedy, not into comedy. Of course, it is a much softer version of the tragic pattern. Benedick makes his impossible choice early and easily; he makes it, moreover, in the scene after Dogberry and Verges make their first attempt to explain the whole situation to Leonato, and this attempt on their part is our promise of a happy ending. Shakespeare can allow Benedick to agree, after only thirty lines of discussion, to fight his best friend because we all know it will never come to that: the world of this play is simply too safe. But Benedick's most important gesture as *an individual* has been to make a choice; and choice itself belongs to the tragic world of realism. It is only as the male half of Beatrice-and-Benedick that Benedick is a comic figure. Beatrice, of course, never faces the kind of choice that compromises Benedick's comic freedom. Like Emilia in *Othello,* she acts out of absolute belief in the woman's innocence. She is guided by the truth, whereas the men must make choices in the absence of certainty.

The avoidance of choice is at the heart of Shakespearean comedy; the very genre can be defined in these terms. Shakespearean comedy avoids not only the choice between the philosophical options within the plays; it avoids the fundamental dramatic choice between realism and convention, between moral fiction and pure pattern-making. Fully to understand the importance of the feminine Other in comedy we must understand that her prerogatives here are those of the playwright himself. I want to define Shakespearean comedy in terms of the choice it avoids between serious meaning and frivolousness; and then I shall offer a reading of "The Owl and the Cuckoo" as an epitome of the gesture of avoidance the playwright makes in all these plays.

Literary critics tend to write about the comedies as if they were realistic fiction in which moral truths emerge from conflict. And so they do. But although the emergence of truth from conflict may be a primary process in the tragedies, it never is in the comedies. This is clear if we compare, for instance, *Twelfth Night* to *Hamlet*. *Hamlet* can be seen as a competition between equally valid principles and its resolution as the resolution of the struggle. We may define these principles as consciousness versus activity, or inner life versus public honor, or however we wish. In *Twelfth Night,* by contrast, the competition between "pleasure" and "reality" does not define the architecture of the play. At the end of the play the right relationship is established between the two principles; the limits of indulgence have been reached, Sir Toby is beaten, and a priest introduces some institutional order into the general flux of romantic emotions. Furthermore, the conflict is resolved between Malvolio and everyone else. The final order arises *from* the merrymaking and lovemaking instead of *in opposition to* it. But this resolution is by no means the resolution to the play as a whole. For the play as a whole is only loosely identified with its central conflict. The ending of *Twelfth Night* depends at least as much upon the completion of ritual and the removal of disguise as it does on moral cadences like the chastening of Sir Toby and the expulsion of Malvolio. There are resolutions to moral-realistic problems in Shakespearean comedy, but to make these resolutions and the process of arriving at them the primary point of the comedies is to attach too great an importance to the conflicts that make them necessary. Conflict in Shakespearean comedy is often simply dismissed, as it is in the song that closes *Twelfth Night*. This song tells a sad story of life's difficulties and losses but ends with a lighthearted refusal of responsibility:

> A great while ago the world begun,
>   Hey, ho, the wind and the rain;
> But that's all one, our play is done,
>   And we'll strive to please you every day.

(V.i.406–9)

Whatever conflicts are at issue here are flicked away by the insouciant singer, who refuses to take things seriously and warns us not to either.

In *A Natural Perspective,* Northrop Frye advises us not to look for moral realism in the comedies. Only tragedy, he says, will satisfy those who believe that "literature's essential function is to illuminate something about life, or reality, or experience, or whatever we call the immediate world outside literature." These people "tend . . . to think of literature, taken as a whole, as a vast imaginative allegory, the end of which is a deeper understanding of the nonliterary center of experience." Comedy, on the other hand, attracts critics like himself: "In comedy and romance the story seeks its own end instead of holding the mirror up to nature. Consequently comedy and romance are so obviously conventionalized that a serious interest in them soon leads to an interest in convention itself."[5]

An emphasis on convention is certainly a logical consequence of the comic vision: the conventional plot emphasizes the ease with which the author will bring about the happy ending. The relationship between convention and comedy holds true even at the level of *theatrical* convention; in realistic drama theatrical conventions are used to save space, whereas in the comedies they are valued for themselves. For instance, eavesdropping in realistic drama may be a way for the characters to learn what the play requires them to know; in comedies like *Love's Labour's Lost* and *Much Ado About Nothing* the eavesdropping scenes are elegantly patterned and enjoyable for their own sakes. Because the dramatist has the power and will to make all things "Atone together" (*As You Like It*, V.iv.110), we have a great deal of energy to devote to questions of technique—energy that would otherwise be claimed by moral anxieties.

But the comedies are not merely conventional. They do *include* moral and realistic conflicts. It is excessively sophisticated to try to deal with them entirely in terms of convention and technique, as Frye seems to do. What the comedies offer to "the world outside literature" is an alternative to seriousness that is yet not frivolous; it is a way of "placing" serious concerns that depends upon our taking things seriously in the first place. What is offered is a *relationship* between the moral mode and the conventional mode, between the mode in which we face our conflicts squarely and the mode in which all dualities—moral, aesthetic, and intellectual—may be blithely dismissed.*

In the tragedies this relationship is sequential: the sense of conflict intensifies as the plays go along, but yields in a great rush at the end

---

*Its duplicity of modes may be what makes Shakespearean comedy appeal so strongly to the modern sensibility. Our late prophet of modernism, Roland Barthes, argues that the modern work must "always have two edges": "The subversive edge may seem privileged because it is the edge of violence; but it is not violence which affects pleasure, nor is it destruction which interests it; what pleasure wants is the site of a loss, the seam, the cut, the deflation, the *dissolve* which seizes the subject in the midst of bliss." (Roland Barthes, *The Pleasure of the Text*, trans. Richard Miller [New York: Hill and Wang, 1975], p. 7.)

to a sense of resolution. Hamlet's personality seems to be pulled apart by the choice he must make, but at the end his personality seems coherent and he dismisses the very conflicts that have troubled him. Throughout the plays the hero struggles—and we struggle along with him—to imagine a solution to the moral problems of opposing truths, of duality. At his lowest moment the hero despairs of finding a solution and gives in to the impulse to rail against his mistress and his world. Finally our sense of struggle is rewarded: all our moral tension is released at the end of the plays by the simultaneous death, self-achievement, and achievement-in-love of the heroes. The sense of conflict yields in a great rush to a sense of resolution. There is a climax to the experience.

The comedies reach no such climax, release no such tension. They are an exercise in sustained poise. Pattern and convention triumph in these plays not so much by having the last word as by coexisting with the moral problems and thus neutralizing them. Rather than being a stunning achievement costing and exacting the ultimate price, the unity of the comic world is simple, natural, continuously available. Shakespearean comedy is a kind of balancing act: every time a moral issue is put on one side of the scale, something goes on the other side that mocks the very process of moral analysis. We are constantly recalled by jokes, songs, games, feasts, plays; when we see Jessica and Lorenzo teasing each other in the moonlight, for instance, we must let go of our efforts to analyze the relationship between justice and mercy. The quality of the comic counterweight is exactly reflected in a passage of *The Rainbow* by D. H. Lawrence where Ursula imagines that Noah's Flood only seemed cataclysmic to Noah. Probably, she decides, it was a local and unimportant affair:

It pleased Ursula to think of the naiads in Asia Minor meeting the nereids at the mouth of the streams, where the sea washed against the fresh, sweet tide, and calling to their sisters the news of Noah's Flood. They would tell amusing accounts of Noah in his ark. Some nymphs would relate how they had hung on the side of the ark, peeped in, and heard Noah and Shem and Ham and Japeth, sitting in their place under the rain, saying, how they four were the only men on earth now, because the Lord had drowned all the rest, so that they four would have everything to themselves, and be masters of everything, sub-tenants under the great Proprietor.

Ursula wished she had been a nymph. She would have laughed through the window of the ark, and flicked drops of the flood at Noah, before she drifted away to people who were less important in their Proprietor and their Flood.[6]

There is a point of view from which the great issues of tragedy are mostly a vehicle for the hero's fantasies of self-importance, and in Shakespearean comedy we must always be ready to see things from this point of view.

Evil itself may be dismissed in the comedies if only we choose to do so. Dogberry's warning to the Watch against excessive moral vigilance is one we should all take to heart:

> *Dogberry* If you meet a thief, you may suspect him, by virtue of
>   your office, to be no true man; and for such kind of man, the
>   less you meddle or make with them, why, the more is for
>   your honesty.
> *Watch* If we know him to be a thief, shall we not lay hands on him?
> *Dogberry* Truly, by your office you may; but I think they that
>   touch pitch will be defiled. The most peaceable way for you,
>   if you do take a thief, is to let him show himself what he is,
>   and steal out of your company.
>   (*Much Ado About Nothing*, III.iii.49–59)

In the tragedies, of course, we have no choice but to touch pitch and be defiled. Goneril and Iago are facts of life in tragedy. But in comedy we have another option, and the challenge is to take it up. Shakespearean comedy challenges our flexibility; it forces us to clear out the passageway that ordinarily blocks off serious moral activity from fantasy, self-assertion, social pleasure. We must be ready at a moment's notice to attend to our problems and at a moment's notice to forget them. The plays are perfectly poised between "It matters" and "It doesn't matter." And this poise itself is a triumph over the tragic necessity to choose, to be deeply serious, continuously responsible.

Obviously, then, the plays cannot resolve by releasing moral or philosophical tension: they have been dissipating this tension all along the way. The final gesture is always to sweep away the moral issue; "that's all one, our play is done" is the message not just of Feste's song but of the multiple marriages, the neat solutions to the intrigue, the final dance or masque or play. And yet such is the modesty of these plays that the final gesture is not a definitive victory for Ursula's mode. If the ending of a Shakespearean tragedy is like a prolonged symphonic finale, a Shakespearean comedy ends like a piano prelude that tosses off the expected final chord at the moment it stops developing its themes. The endings are too unassertive to end the dialectic. To contemplate one of the comedies after it is over is to start up again the alternation that was arrested by the ending: by turns the odd and even circles made by a stone in the water claim the whole pond for their own. Nothing is settled; the problems will recur. But when they do, we will always have the option we have exercised in these plays, of stealing quietly out of their company.

The lyric that ends *Love's Labour's Lost* demonstrates the poise Shakespeare maintains in comedy between moral-realistic meanings and pure convention. It is a good place, then, to continue the investigation of genre.

Spring   When daisies pied and violets blue
        And lady-smocks all silver-white
And cuckoo-buds of yellow hue
        Do paint the meadows with delight,
The cuckoo then, on every tree,
Mocks married men; for thus sings he, "Cuckoo!
Cuckoo, cuckoo!" O word of fear,
Unpleasing to a married ear!

When shepherds pipe on oaten straws,
        And merry larks are ploughmen's clocks,
When turtles tread, and rooks, and daws,
        And maidens bleach their summer smocks,
The cuckoo then, on every tree,
Mocks married men; for thus sings he, "Cuckoo!
Cuckoo, cuckoo!" O word of fear,
Unpleasing to a married ear!

Winter   When icicles hang by the wall,
        And Dick the shepherd blows his nail,
And Tom bears logs into the hall,
        And milk comes frozen home in pail,
When blood is nipped, and ways be foul,
Then nightly sings the staring owl, "Tu-whit,
Tu-who!" a merry note,
While greasy Joan doth keel the pot.

When all aloud the wind doth blow,
        And coughing drowns the parson's saw,
And birds sit brooding in the snow,
        And Marian's nose looks red and raw,

> When roasted crabs hiss in the bowl,
> Then nightly sings the staring owl, "Tu-whit,
> Tu-who!" a merry note,
> While greasy Joan doth keel the pot.
>
> (V.ii.892–923)

This "debate," of course, is a non-debate. There is no conflict between winter and spring, for one implies the other. The contrasts between the two seasons, furthermore, are contained within the form of the lyric, tamed by the emphasis on symmetry and repetition. This is a universe in which things are predictable; there is Winter and there is Spring, each with its bird that sounds its note in the sixth and seventh lines of the stanza. What matters is not the contrast, but that the poem can triumph over the contrast. Both seasons are bound to self-repetition; the second and fourth stanzas can only repeat what has been said in the first and third stanzas. But the poem as a whole has the freedom to move casually from one season to the other; so casually that it does not bother to find a new verse form as it does so. Winter and Spring each claims to be the central fact in its own world, but both in fact are shaped by the conventions of the song itself.

On the one hand, then, this poem minimizes conflict and even contrast. But inside its imperturbable shape, its contrasts provide a great deal of liveliness. The effect is not of detailed and committed analysis but of quicksilver play of mind. Every time we think we understand what the categories are, we are surprised by a variation or inversion. In the first four lines we are led to expect a simple pastoral celebration of Spring. But when the bird sounds his note it is a word of fear, "Cuckoo." Then we understand that Spring has its defects as well as its virtues; if we are to enjoy the flowered meadows, we have to take the risk of adultery that follows from the joys of spring. The next stanza is a reprise; then we are ready to hear from Winter, and we know what to expect. First a landscape with skaters, their voices ringing out through the clear, frosty night; then a bird's note that warns of the price to be paid for these pleasures. These expectations are thwarted on all levels. First, we have switched from pastoral to genre painting; the mode appropriate to Winter is grubby realism. Second, the bird's cry is not the kind of contrast we have been led to expect. If Winter is a rotten thing while Spring is a glorious pleasure, the bird should remind us of some compensation instead of some price to be paid. But the owl's song is traditionally associated with the idea of death. The final surprise is that this memento mori is called "a merry note." To account for this we have to make yet another distinction between Winter and Spring. Winter may be bad and Spring good, but Winter is only bad in a workaday way. If it were bad in the way that Spring is good, it would annihilate us. But in fact it is bearable, and that is why the owl's note sounds merry. When it reminds us of death it reminds us that we are surviving, not dying. There are worse things than being cold, bored, or greasy. We could be dead, like a tragic hero.

Our expectations of the poem are for parallelism: we expect Winter to be the obverse of Spring. Insofar as the poem fulfills these expectations, it is a formal pleasure, an aesthetic object. But insofar as it thwarts these expectations and makes distinctions, it makes a statement. The individual comedies are similarly balanced between making a statement and refusing to do any such thing. The comedies hold lightly to their meanings; this lightness of grip is at least half the point.

The comic heroine, like the poem, is both meaningful and hostile to meaning itself as an enterprise. She is a kind of paradigm for the author, herself producing entertainments that both mean something and refuse to do just that. Portia's ring trick is a good example. At one level the trick has serious meaning, for Bassanio and for us; through it we learn to mistrust the absolute division between our public and private lives that Bassanio has assumed. The joke on Bassanio, then, recapitulates the action of the play and emphasizes the same values. And yet what we see is Portia teasing her husband in a fairly unelevated way. The joke itself is unsophisticated and depends quite simply on a discrepancy of awareness. It is folkloric rather than inventive, and although it is elegantly acted out, there is a Dagwood-and-Blondie aspect to it all. Portia's performance does not alter the truth, but it alters our attitude toward the truth. The problems of justice and mercy, public and private, love and law shrink to the size of a foible of Bassanio's. We respond to the reduction with a surprised, slightly affronted laugh, followed by a sense of liberation. The comic heroine plays Ursula to our Noah and flicks water at us for taking things so seriously.

Why does Shakespeare associate the feminine with the most basic privilege of the genre? There can be no satisfactory answer to this question—which leads us, moreover, to a consideration of other male writers who have and have not privileged the feminine in their comedies. The authors of Restoration comedy do; Cervantes and Fielding do not; Henry James does. The issue can be discussed at the level of cultural psychology or individual psychology or both. But perhaps one explanation is that the feminine Other does not require of her male creator the fatal seriousness he summons up when dealing with the male Self. The Other can be contained within the boundaries of her type: like the other comic types— braggart, friend, priest, gull—the comic heroine is generic as well as individual. She is the marriageable type, young, pretty, and available. For all her self-awareness she can always be absorbed back into the plot as the unmarried girl, Jill to the hero's Jack. At one level she is there simply to be shoved into a couple by the finale, to satisfy our unholy eagerness for marriages. As Charles Frey puts it, "So long as weddings and babies result, society cares almost nothing for the varieties and mix-ups of particular loves."[7] In Shakespeare's case, the Otherness of the feminine seems to free him from the sense of particularity he directs toward representatives of the masculine Self. The feminine Other need not be particularized by her history, by the choices she makes. The plot can pass through her and leave her the same. This is perhaps the appeal of the feminine in comedy—that to her author she remains a type no matter how particularly she is imagined, and that she therefore serves the crucial modesty of the form.

The comic heroine herself avoids choice, and in imagining her the author is spared the choice between moral-realistic and comic-conventional modes. There is a second feminine privilege in comedy, the avoidance of change and development. Many would argue that change, and not the avoidance of change, is what we value in comedy; but the important changes in the comedies are collective rather than individual. Critics who see discovery of identity in the comedies, as even Northrop Frye claims at times to do,[8] are perhaps displacing a process that takes place within the social unit onto the individual members of the society. Sherman Hawkins, following C. L. Barber and Northrop Frye, points out that the action of Shakespearean comedy opens up a society that was previously closed in on itself;[9] by the end of the story all the characters who matter to us enjoy more freedom than they did to begin with. But this is not because there have been, as Anne Barton claims, "self-discoveries, a deepening and development of personality."[10] The discoveries take place at the level of the plot, not at the level of individual psychology. In *Twelfth Night,* for instance, Viola and Sebastian discover each other's existence, Orsino and Olivia discover that Viola is a woman and not a man, Malvolio discovers that Olivia is not, after all, pursuing him. These discoveries and the confusions that precede them realign the whole society for the better; but they do not, as Frye puts it, "lead to a kind of self-knowledge which releases a character from the bondage of his humor."[11] They are of quite a different order from the discoveries of tragedy, which often *do* amount to self-discovery. No recognition in *Twelfth Night* bears comparison to, for instance, Lear's recognition that he is implicated in the suffering of others ("I have ta'en / Too little care of this": III.iv.32–33) or Hamlet's recognition that he cannot create himself through the exercise of will alone ("The readiness is all": V.ii.224).

It is worth examining *Twelfth Night* in some detail because this play is often discussed as a play of self-discovery. No one argues, of course, that Malvolio is "released from the bondage of his humor." Clearly Malvolio is hopeless; at the end of the play he is simply dismissed. Nor is Sir Toby thought to change profoundly, although he is handily brought under control. It is the lovers—Olivia, Orsino, Viola, and even Sebastian—who are seen in terms of self-discovery. Helene Moglen's "Disguise and Development: The Self and Society in *Twelfth Night*" may represent the self-discovery approach to these four characters.[12] For my part, I find nothing that could be called "a deepening and development of personality" in any of them, although I do see some change in one of the four. Not coincidentally, the character who changes is male.

Two kinds of development are discussed in *Twelfth Night* criticism: development of sexuality, and development of a sense of humor as Frey defines the term ("a sense of proportion and propitiation" related to "the ongoingness of life").[13] In the case of Viola and Sebastian, however, both sexuality and sense of humor seem fully developed from the beginning. Take, for instance, Viola's opening lines:

> *Viola*   My brother he is in Elysium.
>   Perchance he is not drowned. What think you, sailors?
> *Captain*   It is perchance that you yourself were saved.
> *Viola*   O my poor brother, and so perchance may he be.
>
> (I.ii.4–7)

What Viola exhibits here is not what we normally think of as a sense of humor, but in Frey's terms it is. She has a sense of proportion about even so painful a fact as the loss of her brother; she leaves the door open to the comic coincidence that will resolve the play. "Perchance he is not drowned," of course, is a non-sequitur; it does not follow from "My brother he is in Elysium." It is nonsequitur, precisely, that we depend on in comedy to make things come out right in the end; Viola speaks in the true illogical spirit of comedy when she goes straight from her brother's death to the hope for his life. In her first scene she is firm, forthright, confident, and even wealthy. She praises the Captain, pays him "bounteously," chooses her disguise, and matter-of-factly commits herself to time. It is difficult to see her as the uncertain quester that Helene Moglen, for instance, describes. Moglen says that Viola's disguise is "the adolescent confusion of identity made visible";[14] but in fact it is a consciously adopted role with which she entertains both herself and the audience. Neither does Viola's sexuality seem to develop gradually; she loves her man immediately and con-stantly and, given her situation, pursues him as best she can.

Sebastian, similarly, is perfectly sure of his desires from the beginning. Moglen argues that we see Sebastian turning gradually from a homosexual attachment to heterosexual love; but in his very first scene Sebastian decisively turns away from Antonio, absolutely refusing his service. Sebastian's prose here is almost too virile:

> My stars shine darkly over me; the malignancy of my fate might perhaps distemper yours. Therefore I crave of you your leave, that I may bear my evils alone. It were a bad recompense for your love to lay any of them on you. . . . If you will not undo what you have done, . . . desire it not. Fare ye well at once . . . I am bound to the Count Orsino's court. Farewell.
>
> (II.i.3–8, 37–39, 42–43)

Moglen says, "Having endured the loss of his sister, inviting a separation from Antonio, Sebastian seems in growing control of himself";[15] but since the control is there from the start, it is difficult to perceive the growth.

Orsino and Olivia are another story. At the beginning these two characters lack both a sense of proportion and a clarity of desire. Orsino wallows in his own emotions and Olivia has "abjured the sight / And company of men" (I.ii.40–41). She is as self-involved in her mourning as Orsino is in his loving. These two characters seem to fit the pattern Sherman Hawkins describes in "The Two Worlds of Shakespearean Comedy": "In the comedies of the alternate pattern [as opposed to those that fit the pattern of New Comedy, where the older generation represses the sexuality of the younger] the heroes and heroines themselves are imprisoned in their inhibitions and aggressions, isolated by fear or repugnance from the general life, cut off not merely from others whom they ought to love but even from themselves."[16] Olivia and Orsino are certainly isolated at the beginning of the play, and by their own actions. But let us look more closely at Olivia in her very first scene. Although she has been three times described as "abandoned to her sorrow" (I.iv.19) before we even see her, on her first appearance before us she is no such thing. Her first action is to allow Feste to fool her out of her mourning; her second is to fall madly in love with Cesario. Although Shakespeare may have intended to show development in Olivia, when he gets her onstage he immediately privileges her with perfect comic presence. Olivia explicitly claims both sense of humor and the love-ethic as her own. When Malvolio protests against the liberty of the fool, she says irritably,

> O, you are sick of self-love, Malvolio, and taste with a distempered appetite. To be generous, guiltless, and of free disposition, is to take those things for birdbolts that you deem cannon bullets.
>
> (I.v.90–93)

We can find no fault with Olivia's definition of comic freedom: "to take those things for birdbolts that you deem cannon bullets." Again, it is a matter of proportion. And when, in the same scene, she finds that she has fallen in love with Cesario, she concludes, "Fate, show thy force: ourselves we do not owe./What is decreed must be—and be this so!" (I.v.308–9). To be of a "free disposition" as a lover is to know, precisely, that "ourselves we do not owe." Before her first appearance Olivia is condemned of a willful attempt to "own" herself, to protect herself from love's uncertainties; but as soon as she appears before us we must withdraw the charges.

Olivia, then, does not seem to change in this play; she is perfectly attuned to comic values right from the start. The change seems to be in the author, not in the character. Shakespeare seems to have meant Olivia as a companion piece to Orsino, a female solipsist. But when he imagines her in action he abandons his plans and showers her with comic privileges. It is perhaps when he imagines her in conversation with Malvolio that he finds himself developing her differently from the way he may have meant to. In Shakespearean comedy the heroine is almost automatically the antithesis of the masculine blocking figure, and perhaps Malvolio's presence in Act I, scene v, is responsible for the change of heart about Olivia.

Orsino, however, is truly narcissistic and self-enclosed, truly in need of the challenge of comedy. Orsino does not seduce his author, as Olivia seems to, away from his intentions. And so Orsino does ultimately change. As Hawkins puts it, Orsino learns to allow the intruder into his world: "The force which knocks at the door is love."[17] But although he does answer the knocking, Orsino does not seem to discover himself in the process. He discovers that Viola / Cesario is really a woman and forthwith admits her into his world: "Give me thy hand, / And let me see thee in thy woman's weeds" (V.i.271–72) is all he has to say. Moglen argues that Orsino has developed through a "transitional relationship"[18] with Cesario, but the transition is surely dramatic rather than psychological. It is we who are prepared by their exchanges for Orsino to love Viola, not Orsino himself who is. Orsino's change of allegiance from Olivia to Viola is as daringly conventional, as arbitrary, as unmotivated as anything in the comedies. Since he has known Viola only as his page, the change to loving her as his "mistress" is unrealistically sudden and abrupt.

Orsino, then, changes from a figure of self-enclosure to a prospective bridegroom, and he changes from Olivia's lover to Viola's. Olivia, by contrast, is "of free disposition" from the first time we see her, and her emotions have a single object. When the Cesario she has married turns out to be Sebastian, there is no need for her to stop loving him on that account. In her case two errors of identity have cancelled each other out. The feminine Other is spared the necessity of change even as she is spared the necessity of choice. She is a constant element in comedy, even when, as in *Twelfth Night,* the scheme of the play suggests that she is there to be redeemed. The feminine is unregenerate in comedy just as she is in tragedy; but in comedy it is unregeneracy we aspire to.

SIX

1 Henry VI to Henry V:
Toward Tragedy

In the two tetralogies of English history plays, the feminine Other seems to change as we go along. From the beginning of the first tetralogy to the first play of the second, the desires and activities of women are differentiated more and more from those of the men. My series begins with Joan of Arc in 1 Henry VI and ends with Isabel in Richard II; Joan is in many ways similar to the masculine Self, whereas Isabel is very different. The masculine Self in the histories is always defined in terms of his place in the world of men. His central activity is the struggle to procure, maintain, or wield power, and his experience of what lies beyond this struggle is limited. At the beginning of the history cycles the woman is also defined in terms of her success or failure in the masculine-historical struggle for power. Joan of Arc fights and kills like a man, desires only victory for her party and power for herself. Isabel, at the other end of my series, embodies an idea of the feminine that is fully differentiated from the masculine Self. She is queen of an alternative realm, the realm of the garden where her major scene takes place. The world of men offers political and military adventure and a headlong struggle for power; Isabel's garden world is private, slow, full of a sorrow that cannot be released in action. In the histories the feminine develops from an almost undifferentiated participant in the masculine adventure into an emblem of what is left out in the masculine-historical mode. Initially similar to the masculine Self, the feminine changes into something essentially different.

Although Joan is the best example of a woman defined in terms of the masculine enterprise, the other characters in 1 Henry VI insist upon her femininity. Her enemies hate her for a witch and her allies call her "sweet virgin" (III.iii.16) in the middle of a policy session. But although her femininity makes her a particularly exciting ally or antagonist, it does not define her in terms other than her alliances and antagonism. Like the masculine history heroes, Joan is exclusively engaged by the world of military and political activities. Her encounter with young Talbot on the field near Bordeaux is illustrative:

> Once I encountered him, and thus I said:
> "Thou maiden youth, be vanquished by a maid."
> But, with a proud majestical high scorn,
> He answered thus: "Young Talbot was not born
> To be the pillage of a giglot wench."
> So, rushing in the bowels of the French,
> He left me proudly, as unworthy fight.   (IV.vii.37–43)

What is at issue here is not sex but caste. Talbot sees Joan as an inferior member of the warrior society he himself inhabits. The apparent point is Talbot's refusal to fight her, but from the perspective of the plays that follow, what is most notable here is the image of Joan armed and ready to fight the opposing army's best man. Joan is a fighting soldier as well as the chief strategist of her forces; no other woman in the histories plays such a central role in the central historical activity of war.

The character who comes closest to doing so is Margaret in *2* and *3 Henry VI.* Margaret is of course quite central to these plays, as power-hungry, cruel, and vengeful as any male character. Edward IV accuses her of being the instigator of the War of the Roses itself:

> For what hath broached this tumult but thy pride?
> Hadst thou been meek, our title still had slept;
> And we, in pity of the gentle king,
> Had slipped our claim until another age.
>
> (*3 Henry VI*, II.ii.159–62)

Certainly the beginnings of the succession wars are fueled by Margaret and an equally ambitious woman, the Duchess of Gloucester. Compared to the role of the other women in the histories, and compared to her own role in the next play, *Richard III,* Margaret's involvement in the wars is almost as thorough as a man's. In *Richard III* Margaret will be reduced to vigorous and lengthy curses; here she acts on her hatreds and ambitions. She is the "general" (I.ii.68) of the Lancastrian army, the ambassador to Lewis of France; she makes policy, cheers her demoralized troops, leads her son in his battle for the crown, and chases the King from the battle of Towton, alleging that she will do better without him. Above all, she is a full partner in the killing of Richard Plantagenet;

she not only tortures him with the paper crown and the blood-soaked handkerchief but also helps stab him to death. But several things distinguish her from Joan. First of all, she always has a male protector or conspirator: Suffolk in 2 Henry VI and Warwick in 3 Henry VI. These men do much of the fighting for her. She is not, in spite of the stabbing of Richard, a woman warrior like Joan. Furthermore, her ambitions have a motherly motivation. She is fighting for her son's right to succeed his father. The following speech in 3 Henry VI strikes the chord of motherhood in the major key:

> Hath he deserved to lose his birthright thus?
> Hadst thou but loved him half so well as I,
> Or felt that pain which I did for him once,
> Or nourished him as I did with my blood,
> Thou wouldst have left thy dearest heart-blood there,
> Rather than have made that savage duke thine heir
> And disinherited thine only son. (I.i.219–25)

Joan's motivation is patriotic rather than motherly, and therefore more similar than Margaret's to that of the men. But the most significant difference between Margaret and Joan is that Margaret is measured against a norm of female behavior and Joan is not. We are constantly reminded that Margaret's actions are unnatural because unwomanly. Margaret has "stol'n the breech from Lancaster" when she ought to have "worn the petticoat" (V.v.23–24). As a general of the French forces Joan threatens us politically, and the insults to her gender are a response to that threat. But Margaret is more than a political threat. In York's famous denunciation speech sexual horror overwhelms the political issues:

> She-wolf of France, but worse than wolves of France,
> Whose tongue more poisons than the adder's tooth!
> How ill-beseeming is it in thy sex
> To triumph like an Amazonian trull
> Upon their woes whom fortune captivates!
>   . . .
> 'Tis beauty that doth oft make women proud;
> But God he knows thy share thereof is small.
> 'Tis virtue that doth make them most admired;
> The contrary doth make thee wondered at.
> 'Tis government that makes them seem divine;
> The want thereof makes thee abominable.

Thou art as opposite to every good
As the Antipodes are unto us
Or as the South to the Septentrion.
O tiger's heart wrapped in a woman's hide!
How couldst thou drain the lifeblood of the child,
To bid the father wipe his eyes withal,
And yet be seen to bear a woman's face?
Women are soft, mild, pitiful, and flexible;
Thou stern, obdurate, flinty, rough, remorseless.

(I.iv.111–15, 128–42)

This speech defines a female norm against which Margaret is found wanting; in *1 Henry VI* no such norms exist. Joan is all the more hateful for being a woman, but she is not reproached with failure *as a woman*. Talbot calls her "Devil's dam," "highminded strumpet," and "hag of all despite";[1] but his primary objection to her is that she fights against his party. Margaret sins against an idea of the feminine; Joan only sins against England.

In *Richard III,* the fourth play in our series, the women have become embittered observers of the struggle for power rather than active participants in it. They are still quite fierce, but their curses have no power over events. Their grievances, moreover, are personal, not political; their attachment is to the husbands, sons, brothers, and cousins they have lost, not to the Yorkist or Lancastrian causes. The Duchess of York turns against her own party after King Richard's murder of his nephews, her grandsons:

My prayers on the adverse party fight!
And there the little souls of Edward's children
Whisper the spirits of thine enemies
And promise them success and victory!   (IV.iv.191–94)

In Act IV, scene iv, Margaret, Elizabeth, and the Duchess of York form a kind of female alliance against "that bottled spider, that foul bunch-backed toad" (IV.iv.81), King Richard, who represents everything wrong with the masculine-historical enterprise.

But the women do not represent an alternative to Richard's world. First of all, of course, there is no kindness among them to contrast with Richard's cruelty; second, they are themselves defined by their position in the world of men. Where the feminine Other is fully distinguished from the masculine Self, she is not part of the timely rising and falling in the political world. Cleopatra, for instance, is associated with timelessness, with the endless ebb and flow of the Nile. But Margaret correctly calls Elizabeth "one heaved a-high to be hurled down below" (IV.iv.86), and continues,

> Who sues and kneels and says, "God save the queen"?
> Where be the bending peers that flattered thee?
> Where be the thronging troops that followed thee?
> . . .
> Thus hath the course of justice whirled about
> And left thee but a very prey to time.
>
> (IV.iv.94–96, 105–6)

The women in *Richard III* are all the "prey" of time and fortune; when the feminine Other is fully differentiated from the masculine Self, the fall from power of the women characters is no longer insisted upon in just these terms.

The one female character in these plays who is defined by something beyond history is Queen Isabel in *Richard II*. Isabel's sense of loss is resonant with more than the fortunes of the political moment. Indeed, in Act II, scene ii, she grieves a loss that has not yet occurred:

> Some unborn sorrow ripe in Fortune's womb
> Is coming towards me; and my inward soul
> With nothing trembles—at something it grieves
> More than with parting from my lord the king.
>
> (II.ii.10–13)

The conversation in which this speech occurs is itself an anomaly in a history play—leisurely, philosophical, dealing with the nature of emotion. Furthermore, Isabel rejects Bushy's commonsense analysis and insists on the reality of her "inward soul" and its feelings. It is not merely Richard's departure that she grieves, as Bushy supposes, but something hidden, mysterious, ineffable. Isabel alone of the history women connects us to this intangible world.

With Isabel's crucial scenes we get a sense of stop-action, a quick descent into a different world. Time moves differently when we are with her; nothing happens. It is the garden scene that most strikingly illustrates the alternative Isabel represents. Here we are aware of natural time, not historical time; of the growth of plants rather than the movement of the wheel of Fortune. The Queen, of course, is not the one who talks of grafting, pruning, and binding the flowers. But it is she who supplies the emotion in this scene, and her emotion at the news of Richard's demise is what forges the bond between man and the natural things in the garden. As she leaves she says, "Gard'ner, for telling me these news of woe, / Pray God, the plants thou graft'st may never grow" (III.iv.100–101). He answers,

> Poor queen, so that thy state might be no worse,
> I would my skill were subject to thy curse.
> Here did she fall a tear; here in this place
> I'll set a bank of rue, sour herb of grace;
> Rue even for ruth here shortly shall be seen,
> In the remembrance of a weeping queen.   (III.iv.102–7)

The symbolic connection between the woman and the flower, even though it is unhappy, creates a sense of a female principle apart from history. Like Ophelia and Perdita distributing flowers, Isabel in the garden reminds us of our place in nature, which, unlike our place in society, is not subject to the wheel of time. Isabel's grief interrupts the momentum of the action; it surrounds Richard's downfall like a nimbus of sorrowful love.

With Isabel we arrive at an idea of the feminine similar to the one that operates in the tragedies. For the feminine in the tragedies is associated with unhistorical experience. From one point of view, of course, this is a pity. At one level, the progression I have been describing is nothing but a progression toward the cultural stereotype. Isabel is passive whereas the typical history hero is active; while she grieves, he fights. A feminine defined in terms of gardens, the ineffable, and natural cycles of time is certainly nothing new. What we are missing are images of women who *do* participate in history, and the progression I have been describing may seem to be a movement away from the feminine as an element in history. But the women in the early history plays do not participate in history *as women*. Joan is a kind of second-class man and Margaret is presented as a woman who has betrayed her own gender. Since such characters participate in history only as inferior versions of the masculine Self, or as failed versions of the feminine Other, they do not offer the kind of images we might profit from. The women characters in these plays who are involved in the events of history either betray their own femininity or simply mimic the men. Nothing is lost, then, in the progression from Joan to Isabel. And from the perspective of what is to follow the histories, something is gained. For in the tragedies, the woman as Other becomes a powerful dialectical force, and the progression toward Isabel is a progression toward feminine Otherness. The separation of Isabel from the world of men prefigures the dialectical opposition in the tragedies between the world of men and the woman as Other. Only as the Other are women in Shakespeare consistently the equals of men. Only in opposition to the hero and the world of men, only as representatives of alternative experience do the women characters matter to Shakespeare's drama as much as the men.

In the tragedies the women characters oppose the world of men in several ways. Sometimes they represent an antihistorical world; sometimes they directly threaten the hero's place in history; sometimes they simply elicit such powerful and chaotic emotions from the hero that he can no longer play his public role. Examples of these three possibilities are Cleopatra, Gertrude, and Desdemona. Cleopatra's Egypt, like Isabel's garden, is antihistorical; although "Nilus' slime" is a far cry from the neat British shrubs, Egypt is also a place where the historical struggle for power is crossed by natural forces. Whether or not Cleopatra's own actions threaten Antony's place in the world of men, her territory is an alternative to that world. Gertrude, on the other hand, rules no alternative space. But by her marriage to Claudius she legitimizes his usurpation and bars Hamlet from the throne. She offers, therefore, a direct threat to the hero's place in history. And Desdemona illustrates the third option, a feminine to whom the hero reacts so violently as to forget and therefore lose his role in the world of men.

The feminine in the tragedies is always something that cannot be possessed, controlled, conquered; it resists the colonizing impulse of the imperial male Self. The feminine Other may be won, as Othello wins Desdemona; but she may never be properly owned. Whether or not she consciously resists colonization, like Cleopatra, or offers herself body and soul, like Desdemona, the feminine remains separate from and Other to the male Self. The feminine is finally antihistorical because it represents a frontier beyond which the efforts of the masculine-historical Self will not take us. The purest example of the unconquerable Other is Cordelia, who offers no threat to her father's power except the distinction she makes between her own desires and his. Her literal territory, France, is not necessarily antihistorical, like Isabel's garden and Cleopatra's Egypt. But her own emotions constitute a separate kingdom from the one in which Lear comes first. And this is enough to send Lear off on the tragic, posthistorical journey that comes when the male Self senses the limits of his power.

But in *Richard II* the challenge of Isabel's Otherness is only latent. The feminine offers too powerful a challenge to the idea of history itself for Shakespeare to deal with it in the history plays. The Otherness of the feminine challenges the ethos of power and conquest through aggression; history as a genre must ultimately base itself on that ethos no matter how it also criticizes it. If we lose interest in the military-political adventure we have lost interest in history itself as a genre. The feminine is not the only challenge to the history ethos; the struggle for power in Shakespearean history is always as tawdry as it is glamorous, challenged by common sense, common decency, and a sense of the common good. But apparently there is something uncommon in the challenge offered by the feminine. The feminine Other is too explosive a figure for history; having arrived, with Isabel, at a feminine that is truly Other, Shakespeare seems to put her away for safekeeping until he is ready to abandon history for tragedy. Not until he is ready to abandon history altogether does the feminine return in force.

After Isabel, the women characters neither participate in history nor challenge it. They merely create a kind of contrast or background from which the hero rides off to his adventure. Hotspur's parting from his wife is illustrative. In *1 Henry IV* Lady Percy tries to get a declaration of love from Hotspur as he is leaving her for the wars; he replies,

> Come, wilt thou see me ride?
> And when I am a-horseback, I will swear
> I love thee infinitely.   (II.iii.99–101)

Shakespeare seems to have understood the implications of history-as-a-genre for relations with women, and here presents them in their starkest form. If women neither seriously challenge the values of the history world nor participate as women in the crucial activities of this world, then they are supernumeraries in a world of men. Relations with the feminine take place but do not much matter: "This is no world," as Hotspur puts it, "To play with mammets and to tilt with lips" (II.iii.90–91). If the woman is not a version of the Other, she is powerless to counteract the lure of the masculine-historical adventure. Hotspur, the true believer in history-as-an-

ethos, demonstrates the irrelevance of the feminine to those who
live up to this creed. Kate's response to Hotspur's rejection is
illuminating:

> Do you not love me? Do you not indeed?
> Well, do not then; for since you love me not,
> I will not love myself. Do you not love me?
> Nay, tell me if you speak in jest or no.   (II.iii.95–98)

Where the woman does not represent the Other, she is and perceives herself to be merely the adjunct of the man. She has no
kingdom of her own, and if he abandons her she loses everything.

Of course, Hotspur and Kate are only one version of relations
between men and women in the last three plays of the second
tetralogy. A more significant version, perhaps, is the one represented by Henry V and Katherine of France. For Hotspur only
represents history at its most unselfconscious, and therefore he
verges on self-parody. Henry V is the opposite of Hotspur; he is
thoroughly conscious of his own role as a history hero, as detached
as can be from his role. But even Henry V is not confronted by the
feminine Other. Katherine is no challenge to Henry's public role.

As one critic has put it, "Katherine is regarded by everybody
(including herself), and by Henry in the first place, as part of the
war spoils resulting from the Agincourt victory."[2] Henry may love
Katherine, as he says he does, but she is no more serious an issue for
him than Kate is for Hotspur. The greatest challenge to the hero's
historicity comes not from Katherine but from Falstaff; although I
shall return to Henry V and Katherine, it is worth digressing to
consider the differences between the challenge of the feminine and
the challenge offered by such a character as Falstaff. In *Shakespeare
and the Energies of Drama*, Michael Goldman tells us that Falstaff
represents "our sensuality and our impulse to anarchy";[3] as such he
is a threat to political organization per se, not just to the feudal
monarchy Hal inherits. Falstaff suggests a world beyond the dialectic of politics, just as the women do in the tragedies. But finally
Falstaff is rejected completely: "I know thee not, old man"
(V.v.47), says Hal on becoming king. Maturity in history implies
the brutal rejection of whatever is incompatible with the hero's
public role; Falstaff is a part of Hal that is removed with surgical
precision.

When, by contrast, the masculine-historical adventure is chal-

lenged by the Other as woman, the surgical solution is never
adopted. In the tragedies the opposing principle is a sexual one
rather than a general, asexual principle of pleasure; here Shakespeare never imagines so successful a rejection as Henry's of
Falstaff. The hero who comes closest to rejecting the feminine
outright is Othello; but of course he cannot long survive his murder
of Desdemona. Henry, by contrast, goes on to dominate another
whole play. In the tragedies the feminine cannot be dealt with as
Falstaff is dealt with in history, by excision. When it is Falstaff who
represents "the vulnerable body of our sensuality,"[4] it is possible to
put that body aside; but when sensuality is what connects us to the
other sex, we must simply come to terms with the constant threat it
offers to our public identity. Falstaff shows history up for what it is,
an enterprise that denies much of our experience; the feminine in
tragedy is analogous to whatever finally makes history impossible,
as a genre for Shakespeare and as an enterprise for his heroes.

Katherine of France, however, is no representative of the feminine that ends history. When women represent a significant challenge to the masculine-historical mode, the heroes are never so
good-humored as Henry is in his relations with Katherine. The
great final wooing scene in *Henry V* is the most sustained encounter
between a man and a woman in the histories, and it is worth
looking at in some detail.

The most notable feature of this scene is the complete absence of
anxiety with which this great hero of history approaches the feminine. Henry is relaxed and self-confident, animated by an enjoyment of his own performance. He begins with a little easy hyper-
bole: "An angel is like you Kate, and you are like an angel"
(V.ii.110–11). But things aren't going to be *that* easy. Katherine
protests against the obvious flattery by murmuring something
about language and deception; so Henry immediately switches to
the plain style:

> I know no ways to mince it in love, but directly to say, "I love
> you." Then, if you urge me farther than to say, "Do you swear in
> faith?" I wear out my suit. Give me your answer, i' faith, do; and so
> clap hands, and a bargain. How say you, lady?
>
> (V.ii.128–33)

If Kate wants plainness, Henry seems to say, how is "clap hands, and a bargain" for plainness? Obviously, a little too plain. Henry will not be trapped into sincerity, even though his love may be sincere. His bluffness is a role he plays to reveal and conceal himself simultaneously. He does want to win Katherine of France, but he also knows he has already won her—at Agincourt. The bluffness is a way of being true to both these facts:

> I speak to thee plain soldier: if thou canst love me for his, take me;
> if not, to say to thee that I shall die, is true—but for thy love, by
> the Lord, no; yet I love thee too.   (V.ii.152–55)

Henry's feelings are clear enough—to himself, to Katherine, and to us.

Michael Goldman emphasizes the element of performance in this scene, and the effort it costs Henry to put on *all* his performances. The wooing scene, says Goldman, is "the right note of mirth to cap the play" because it is "as much a performance as his speech on Crispin's Day." It is consistent because it continues to illustrate, says Goldman, "the effort of greatness."[5] But surely it illustrates just the opposite. The Crispin's Day speech *did* require a great deal of effort; it was produced for a demanding audience whose assent was not a foregone conclusion. Henry's troops might have refused to be stirred and therefore to fight. The wooing speeches, by contrast, have an audience with no desire but to be charmed. If the Crispin's Day speech is a full-dress performance in front of an important and demanding audience, the wooing of Katherine is a piece of good-natured guerrilla theater before an audience of one. Henry teases this audience with her own desire to be told stories; flirts with the possibility of breaking through the fiction and telling the bald truth; and amuses himself at her expense with his own doubleness. Henry's effort to speak French, for instance, is self-forgiving, exasperated at the need to make an effort at all, self-entertaining. It is reminiscent of Viola and Rosalind pretending to be men—delighted that they can pull it off at all, and certainly without the ambition to do it very well. The speech is preceded, moreover, by a quick insult to the listener, who must identify with the hypothetical "new-married wife" to which Henry compares his own French:

> I will tell thee in French, which I am sure will hang upon my
> tongue like a new-married wife about her husband's neck, hardly

to be shook off. Je quand sur le possession de France, et quand vous avez le possession de moi (let me see, what then? Saint Denis be my speed!), donc votre est France, et vous êtes mienne. It is as easy for me, Kate, to conquer the kingdom as to speak so much more French; I shall never move thee in French, unless it be to laugh at me.   (V.ii.180–89)

Henry's speeches go wittily on and on, turning corners, leaping fences, backing into antitheses—while Katherine confines herself to dimples and coyness. Of Henry's insolent French, for instance, she says primly and conventionally, "Sauf votre honneur, le francais que vous parlez, il est meilleur que l'anglais lequel je parle" (V.ii.190–91). A heroine with the substance to challenge male strengths—a Desdemona or a Cleopatra—would never meet Henry's provocation with so mild and straight a response.

"Strain" and "effort" are precisely what this scene is free of. Henry's power and desire is wholly unopposed by Katherine, who is a negligible presence in the scene. Henry has all the good lines. If this scene is the right one to "cap" the play, as Goldman says, it is because Henry at ease is as compelling as Henry at his real work, not because Henry works as hard to play the lover as he does to play the general. The opposition by the French troops was real and dangerous; Katherine's opposition is nonexistent.

Neither Hotspur's Kate nor Henry's Katherine offers any resistance to the exercise of masculine power. The one woman after Isabel who does challenge the masculine mode is the Duchess of York in *Richard II,* and her challenge is a comic one. In Act V, scene ii, York discovers that his son Aumerle is part of the Oxford conspiracy against the new king, Henry IV. York rides off to denounce Aumerle for a traitor; the Duchess follows to beg for the life of her son. York, of course, is behaving prudentially; but at one level he also represents masculine honor, patriotism, and fealty as opposed to pure mother-love on the Duchess's part. The Duchess asks her husband incredulously,

Why, York, what wilt thou do?
Wilt thou not hide the trespass of thine own?
Have we more sons? Or are we like to have?
Is not my teeming date drunk up with time?
And wilt thou pluck my fair son from mine age?
And rob me of a happy mother's name?
Is he not like thee? Is he not thine own?   (V.ii.88–94)

And York replies,

> Thou fond mad woman,
> Wilt thou conceal this dark conspiracy?
> A dozen of them here have ta'en the sacrament
> And interchangeably set down their hands
> To kill the king at Oxford.   (V.ii.95–99)

To York the king must be treated as an absolute even when he is guilty, like Henry IV, of usurpation. To the Duchess the idea of the king is meaningless. She follows her husband to Windsor to plead her cause; but when she is heard at the door Bolingbroke says, "Our scene is alt'red from a serious thing, / And now changed to 'The Beggar and the King' " (V.iii.78–79). The arrival of the woman turns the tense political situation into a family comedy. In fact the seriousness of the conflict is undermined in the previous scene where Aumerle and the Oxford conspiracy are treated as the occasion for a domestic dustup. When York calls for his boots, for instance, the Duchess tries to prevent his departure by driving off the servant who brings them. She shouts to Aumerle to strike the servant, but Aumerle is dazed and does not obey. The Duchess then attacks the servant herself, "Hence, villain, never more come in my sight"; but York bellows, "Give me my boots, I say" (V.ii.86–87), and rides off, furious. There can be no real question of Bolingbroke's verdict on Aumerle when it has been preceded by such family antics. The conflict between the Duke and the Duchess is obviously comic and will not have serious consequences. Aumerle is forgiven and the Duchess tells Bolingbroke extravagantly, "A god on earth thou art" (V.iii.135). The Duchess as Mother offers only a comic contrast to the seriousness of the world of men.

From Joan to Isabel, then, the feminine in history follows a progression away from second-class citizenship in the world of men and toward a separate identity; but as soon as Shakespeare establishes the separateness of the feminine, he shelves the feminine as an Other until he is ready to write tragedy. The challenge of the feminine would destroy the historical mode; or, to put it the other way around, when Shakespeare is finished with history and ready for tragedy, the challenge of the feminine, heretofore latent, suddenly becomes central to his drama.

The evolution of the feminine must therefore be seen as part of the larger movement toward tragedy. This movement involves not only a separation from the feminine but a separation of the male Self from his father and his father's values. As the histories approach tragedy, a distance opens up between the father and the son just as it does between the male Self and the female Other. The father, like the feminine, becomes an Other as the cycle proceeds. In the early plays, the father and son are passionate teammates who share the family name, honor, and power. But by *2 Henry IV* relations between the generations have become strained. In the relationship between Hal and Henry IV is prefigured the tragic necessity to break with the father that echoes from *Hamlet* all the way down to Ferdinand and Florizel in the romances. As we approach tragedy, masculine identity becomes more and more individualized, less and less taken for granted as a gift from father to son. Prince Hal's rebellion against the father, partial and recanted though it is, prefigures the exhaustive analysis of breaking away that comes with the beginning of tragedy in *Hamlet.*

The best representatives of the early phase are Talbot and his son John in *1 Henry VI.* We first meet John at his initiation into his father's world. Talbot tells his son, "I did send for thee to tutor thee in strategems of war"; but as it develops, John needs no tutoring in what is more essential than the strategems of war, and that is the game of honor. For although Talbot urges his son to leave a losing battle, John refuses in the name of honor and chooses to die rather than flee. Talbot repeatedly reminds John of his obligation to perpetuate the family name and avenge his father's death; John repeatedly argues,

> And if I fly, I am not Talbot's son.
> Then talk no more of flight, it is no boot;
> If son to Talbot, die at Talbot's foot.   (IV.vi.51–53)

Of course, the argument between them amounts to no more than a lover's quarrel, for Talbot's son is behaving as Talbot himself would want to behave. He glories in his son's manliness because it is patterned after his own; and he dies satisfied to hold John's corpse in his arms: "Soldiers, adieu! I have what I would have, / Now my old arms are young John Talbot's grave" (IV.vii.31–32). Shakespeare develops the theme of the father and son through two patterns of imagery: on the one hand, he associates this relationship with images of dazzling brightness; and on the other, he describes it through metaphors of flowers and trees. Describing his son's last battle Talbot orchestrates both motifs:

And in that sea of blood my boy did drench
His overmounting spirit and there died,
My Icarus, my blossom, in his pride.   (IV.vii.14–16)

Icarus, of course, flew too close to the sun; the relationship between
the son and the sun is very close in the history plays. The son is like
the rising sun, a figure of bright promise even when the promise
will ultimately be unfulfilled.

Talbot and his son are to the remaining plays an image of lost
perfection, an ideal from which we fall sadly off. The rest of the
first tetralogy seems to explore that falling off as the father-son
ideal is perverted and betrayed. In *3 Henry VI* both the ideal and its
failure are fully developed themes; this play may serve as a plotting
point as we chart the changing role of the father.

At the battle of Wakefield in *3 Henry VI* the father-son ideal is
again made actual. York's pride in his sons' behavior there equals
Talbot's pride in his son John:

My sons, God knows what hath bechancèd them:
But this I know, they have demeaned themselves
Like men born to renown by life or death.
Three times did Richard make a lane to me,
And thrice cried "Courage, father! fight it out!"
And full as oft came Edward to my side,
With purple falchion, painted to the hilt
In blood of those that had encountered him:
And when the hardiest warriors did retire,
Richard cried, "Charge! and give no foot of ground!"
And cried, "A crown, or else a glorious tomb!
A scepter, or an earthly sepulcher!"   (I.iv.6–17)

Although York's cause is lost he tells his murderers, "My ashes, as
the phoenix, may bring forth / A bird that will revenge upon you
all" (I.iv.35–36). Just as young Talbot is an Icarus, York's son
Richard is a fierce bright bird, a phoenix. The son who will rise in
flames is still a powerful myth in this play. But the same play
includes in its *dramatis personae* "A Son that has killed his father"
and "A Father that has killed his son." These characters measure the
distance we have come from the ideal.

One of the crucial events of this play is Clifford's murder of a
young child, York's son Rutland. When Clifford comes to kill him,
Rutland says, "I never did thee harm. Why wilt thou slay me?"
Clifford's brutal answer contains much of Shakespeare's criticism

of the father-son ideal: "Thy father slew my father. Therefore die.
[*Stabs him*]" (I.iii.38, 47). The father-son ideal includes the responsibility of the son to avenge the father's death, but the fulfillment of
that responsibility may be an act of baseness, not honor. Rutland's
protest, "But 'twas ere I was born" (I.iii.39), could be the epigraph
for the whole tetralogy. The wrongs to be avenged are always in
the past; the father-son ideal has become a machine for keeping
them alive. This is clear in the argument between Warwick and
Westmoreland over York's right to the throne. When the argument
degenerates into threats of force, Warwick tells Henry's supporters,
"You forget / That we are those which chased you from the field /
And slew your fathers" (I.i.89–91), and Westmoreland replies,

> Plantagenet, of thee and these thy sons,
> Thy kinsmen and thy friends, I'll have more lives
> Than drops of blood were in my father's veins.
>
> (I.i.95–97)

When many sons have the deaths of many fathers to avenge, the
father-son ideal provokes a transgenerational free-for-all from
which no one emerges with honor. Instead of passing on the glory
of his manhood, the father passes on the injuries it has sustained; the
sense of injury, at least, is what determines the action, writes the
script. Shakespeare's disillusionment seems to grow with every
scene he writes.

Even the imagery surrounding the theme of the father and son
becomes an occasion for irony in *3 Henry VI*. The sacred metaphor
of the family tree is defiled by its user, Richard, whose crucial act in
the next play will be the murder of his brother's sons. Richard
complains that Clifford was

> . . . not contented that he lopped the branch
> In hewing Rutland when his leaves put forth,
> But set his murdering knife unto the root
> From whence that tender spray did sweetly spring:
> I mean our princely father, Duke of York.   (II.vi.46–50)

Root, branch, leaves, and spray are familiar terms for the relationship between the princely father and his sweet sons; but they sound
very odd in Richard's mouth. At the end of the play Richard kisses
the brother whose sons he will murder and once again invokes the
father as the tree of life: "And, that I love the tree from whence
thou sprang'st, / Witness the loving kiss I give the fruit" (V.vii.31–

32). Richard is fully conscious that he is using sacred language and gestures blasphemously, for he turns aside and adds, "To say the truth, so Judas kissed his master, / And cried, 'All hail!' whenas he meant all harm" (V.vii.33–34). The imagery, like the ideal itself, is put to base uses after *1 Henry VI.*

In the second tetralogy the disillusionment is over and Shakespeare no longer takes the father-son ideal seriously. Here it is Hotspur and Northumberland who enact it, not Hal and Henry IV; the theme is displaced onto secondary characters. Having given up the ideal, Shakespeare is free to play with it; in *Richard II* he creates a father-son initiation scene that is at once stirring and nostalgic, exciting and delicate. Here Hotspur and his father encounter each other en route, in dangerous times; Hotspur neatly delivers himself of some important political news and Northumberland responds by introducing him, then and there, to the family cause:

> Northumberland Have you forgot the Duke of Hereford, boy?
> Percy No, my good lord, for that is not forgot
> Which ne'er I did remember. To my knowledge
> I never in my life did look on him.
> Northumberland Then learn to know him now—this is the duke.
> (II.iii.36–40)

We are free to respond to the glamor of this moment because Hotspur and Northumberland are not the father and son we take seriously. Our hopes for the relationship they represent are safely in the past.

Meanwhile, the father and son who are *current* in this play, by whom we explore actual possibility rather than fantasies of the past, are rarely seen together. Henry IV asks, "Can no man tell me of my unthrifty son?" and complains, "If any plague hang over us, 'tis he" (*Richard II,* V.iii.1,3). Far from helping his father in battle, Prince Hal is off disgracing the family name in taverns and brothels. The tension of this relationship, of course, climaxes in *2 Henry IV* when Prince Hal takes the crown from his dying father. The king wakes up, sees what has happened, and feels that his son is murdering him:

> For this the foolish overcareful fathers
> Have broke their sleep with thoughts,
> Their brains with care, their bones with industry.
> For this they have engrossèd and piled up
> The cank'red heaps of strange-achievèd gold;

For this they have been thoughtful to invest
Their sons with arts and martial exercises.
When, like the bee, culling from every flower
The virtuous sweets, our thighs packed with wax,
Our mouths with honey, we bring it to the hive,
And, like the bees, are murdered for our pains.

(IV.v.67–77)

Of course, the scene ends in complete reconciliation. The crown is transformed back into a gift from father to son. Ultimately Hal accepts it as such, with all the requisite sentiments:

My gracious liege,
You won it, wore it, kept it, gave it me.
Then plain and right must my possession be,
Which I with more than with a common pain
'Gainst all the world will rightfully maintain.

(IV.v.220–24)

And yet Hal's theft of the crown remains in our memory as an alternative ending to the relationship. The common interest of the father and the son in the "household name" is no longer the simple force for unity it was in the case of the Talbots. Here it is also the cause of bitter antagonism between generations.

Prince Hal / Henry V is an approach to the tragic hero: he becomes more of a man for having been less of a man. The simple code of manliness defines honor as the courage to fight one's enemies and the loyalty to avenge one's friends. It is the corollary to the father-son ideal because such manliness may be straightforwardly inherited and learned from the previous generation. The son inherits his friends and enemies from the father, and he learns how to behave toward both simply by imitating his father. But Prince Hal refuses this kind of manliness even as he refuses collaboration with his father. Prince Hal has other friends than his father's, and he defies his father's standards of manliness. Henry IV describes him as a "young wanton and effeminate boy" who has turned honor upside down by supporting "so dissolute a crew" (*Richard II,* V.iii.10–12) as Falstaff and company. Prince Hal comes to manhood by no such simple route as Hotspur or John Talbot. Just as he accepts the crown *and* steals it, so he fulfills *and* defies his father's hopes. By refusing the simple code of manliness he becomes more of a man than he would by accepting it.

The two progressions I have been describing are part of the same general movement toward tragedy. At the beginning of the English history plays, the hero is seen in the image of the father and women in the image of the hero. All three are measured against an ideal of manly honor. But as the plays go on, the feminine is more and more differentiated from the hero and the hero distances himself more and more from the father. We might say, then, that the histories are in the process of differentiating the Self from the Other, the Other being defined in terms of gender on the one hand and generation on the other. But such a statement obscures an important difference between two kinds of processes that are taking place in the history plays. On the one hand the *author* is discovering the feminine as Other. Between *1 Henry VI* and *Richard II* the plays themselves seem to become aware of the feminine as separate from the Self. On the other hand, the *heroes* are the ones who discover the father as Other. From *1 Henry VI* to *Richard III* the heroes move from naive reverence for and attachment to the father to conscious, self-serving perversion of the father-son ideal; and in the second tetralogy Prince Hal enacts perfect, almost studied consciousness of the separation between father and son. Hal seems to control his own plot, to move away from and toward his father with perfect awareness of the meaning of his actions. By the end of the second tetralogy the father as Other is no longer a problem.

The history plays, then, seem actually to resolve the problem of the father as Other; but they only pose and postpone the problem of the woman as Other. The problem of the woman as Other breaks out in *Hamlet,* the great transition between history and tragedy, and is a dominant issue throughout the tragic phase. *Hamlet* grandly recapitulates and lays to a kind of rest the problem of the father; it only introduces, with a bang, the unresolvable problem of the woman as Other. Hamlet is the end product of the two progressions of the history plays, suffering all at once differentiation from the father on the one hand and from the feminine on the other. The differentiation from the father comes about not because Hamlet's father is dead; it comes about because Hamlet finds himself unwilling, unable, to inherit his father's grievances. Hamlet had expected to identify his own interests with his father's and he finds that he does not; he had expected Gertrude and Ophelia to identify their interests with his and he finds they do not. But the problem of the father is resolved, whereas the problem of the woman is not.

Hamlet ultimately finds a way to make his father's grievances his own. Just as Hal ultimately joins his father and fights the family battles, so too does Hamlet. The resolution of the problem of the father is tragic in *Hamlet*: the process of finding a place for himself in the battle of the fathers is mortal to the hero. But by the end of the play he has done it, and it need not, in Shakespeare's later work, be done again. The problem of the feminine, however, is utterly unresolved, and the later tragedies return again and again to this theme.

For Shakespeare the issue of the feminine is much more problematic than the issue of the father. The father clarifies and directs our desires; the woman as Other muddies and thwarts them. The history hero is unambivalent. He wants what his father wants: power, honor, glory, the crown of England for himself or his party. This does not apply to Richard II, of course, who is a kind of anti-hero of history. And Prince Hal/Henry V, although unambivalent about his worldly desires, does have other desires as well. He is aware of the price to be paid for becoming and being King. But even this hero, for all his sophistication and consciousness, never imagines that he might be unable or unwilling to pay that price. Whatever its price, the history hero must grab for the brass ring. He goes after what he wants, secure in the knowledge that it is what all men want. In history the world of the fathers is the source not only of the things we desire but of our desires themselves.

In tragedy, by contrast, the world of the fathers is in the past. Antony, Othello, and Lear begin at the height of their political power and have other things on their minds besides maintaining or increasing it. The tragic hero has already proven himself in the world of men and has arrived at the point where it no longer defines his desire. He is defined by nothing prior to himself; his desire is his own to focus where he will. But to do so, of course, involves him in contradictions. Take, for example, sexual desire. Up to this point the hero's sexuality has been a function of his position in the world of men. The heroes make politic marriages to advance their careers, and, conversely, their power in the world of men gives them the power to marry whomever they wish. Henry V both commands Katherine's love by virtue of his military victories and channels his own sexuality toward her for political reasons. Sexual desire is never in conflict with desire for the brass ring of worldly power, the crown of England, manly honor. Either the one reinforces the other or the sexual component of the hero's desire is a kind of irrelevancy.

But when desire is no longer mediated by the father, its sexual component takes on an independent life. The difference between the history hero's sexuality and that of the tragic hero may be illustrated by a comparison between Henry V and Antony. Whereas Henry's sexuality is at the service of his military-political identity, Antony's is not. Married for political reasons to Octavia, he cannot stay away from Cleopatra. "I' th' East my pleasure lies," (II.iii.39) he says, and that is the end of Octavia, manly honor, and Empire.

When desire is mediated by the father, the object of desire is the world itself of the fathers. The heroes want to possess that world by dominating it. But in tragedy the desired world is something that Shakespeare associates with women rather than with men. The world is like a woman in tragedy because it is simultaneously utterly desirable and thoroughly loathsome. Like Gertrude, Desdemona, and Cleopatra, the world outside the Self provokes the hero to radically ambivalent responses. On the one hand the hero passionately desires the world and everything it has to offer: "honor, love, obedience, troops of friends" (*Macbeth,* V.iii.26). But he also hates, rejects, and makes as if to leave the world because it has betrayed him, might betray him, or otherwise isn't good enough for him. His ambivalence has the tragic end of all ambivalence; ultimately he is separated against his will from what he has been threatening all along to leave. Whereas the father is a force for clarity of desire and headlong activity in pursuit of its object, the woman as Other is Shakespeare's representative of a world the hero cannot unambivalently pursue.

It might be argued that the father is also an object of emotional ambivalence in Shakespeare. The relationship between Henry IV and Hal is not, after all, without its difficulties. But ambivalence toward the father in Shakespeare's history plays may be understood as a kind of pre-Oedipal or resolvable ambivalence. Hal *solves* the problem of his ambivalence by moving first away from and then toward his father. (Othello, by contrast, does *not* solve the problem of his ambivalence toward Desdemona.) It is a matter of timing. We (men) may (must!) rebel against the father on our way to becoming fathers ourselves. Although it is a tricky business, it doesn't kill us. As we have just seen, the problem of the father *does* kill the hero in *Hamlet,* the one tragedy where it is an issue. But ambivalence toward the woman as Other is always tragic.

In Shakespeare, tragic, fully Oedipal ambivalence toward the feminine begins where the problem of the father ends, in *Hamlet*. Freudians have long made the connection between *Hamlet* and the Oedipus complex, pointing out the sexual quality of Hamlet's responses to Gertrude. But it is not that Hamlet feels incestuous desire for his mother, as the Freudians would have it; it is that in *Hamlet* female sexuality is suddenly an independent force. No longer under the control of the fathers, it is suddenly capable of betraying the child. What we see in Hamlet is not the Oedipal drama itself but the unraveling of the resolution to the Oedipus complex. According to the psychoanalytic myth, the boy resolves his Oedipus complex by making an implicit bargain with his father. The father may have exclusive sexual rights to the mother if the boy may inherit what the neo-Freudian Jacques Lacan calls "the phallus." The phallus symbolizes the boy's right to the social and sexual position of the male, and will eventually make it possible for him to exercise in his turn exclusive sexual rights over a woman. The Oedipal crisis is over when the boy trades his mother for the promise of the phallus.* In other words, the resolution of the Oedipal crisis puts female sexuality into receivership. The world of the fathers comes between the young boy and the threat of his betrayal by the feminine. Since the boy cannot compete with his father for sexual rights to his mother, he renounces his mother in favor of an allegiance to his father's world, which promises him sexual dominance as a function of manly accomplishment. The feminine is no problem as long as the world of the fathers mediates between women's sexuality and the masculine Self.

But in *Hamlet,* the play that ends history, with the father's death and the mother's remarriage the Oedipal resolution comes undone. The world of the fathers is shown to be vulnerable and divided against itself. It cannot be relied upon indefinitely to control the sexuality of women, who may sooner or later make choices against the interest of the masculine Self. *Hamlet* takes place not during the Oedipal crisis itself, but at the moment when the Oedipal resolution fails us and we (men) are returned to what threatened us in the first place: a world in which we may be betrayed by what we love most. After this point we develop an ambivalence that can never be

---

*In Freudian terms, the boy gives up his mother in order to avoid castration by the father. I have chosen to tell the Lacanian version of the story because the Lacanian phallus is a symbol of social as well as sexual virility; it is less a part of the body than the Freudian penis, conferring cultural identity as well as bodily or personal potency.

resolved. Gertrude can neither be loved nor hated; in *Hamlet* desire for and aggression against the Other become simultaneous and therefore tragic. The Oedipus complex forges together our love and hate by activating our sexual anxieties. After our return, in *Hamlet*, to the Oedipal situation, we can no longer love (women *or* the world) without hating the object of our love for its capacity to refuse us our desire.

If I seem to have abandoned the history plays for a discussion of *Hamlet* and the tragedies, it is only because Shakespearean history, like the life of the tragic hero, is illuminated by what ends it. If the tragedies return us to the Oedipal crisis, the history plays take place before the resolution to the Oedipal crisis has come undone. They take place before our ambivalence has been tragically intensified by the return of our sexual anxieties. Desire and aggression are unchecked by one another; the complexities of the tragic hero's emotional life are unknown in history. The purity of both desire and aggression is one of the great glories of the history mode; it is a great pleasure to see the history hero unambivalently pursue his brass ring and unambivalently strike out at whatever keeps him from it. But it is worth repeating that this pleasure is only available when relations with women have been finessed. In Shakespearean history, relations with women are unconscious, regressively pre-Oedipal, and mediated by the father.

Let us begin with aggression. In the history mode we have always the hope and sometimes the satisfaction of witnessing a fair and glorious fight. We can look forward to confrontations such as Hotspur's with Prince Hal. No ambivalence restrains either combatant; they are fighting each other flat out for their lives and their place in history. In order that we may fully enjoy the antagonism between these two men, Shakespeare makes them contemporaries—although the historical Hotspur was in fact a generation older than Hal. Generational otherness creates ambivalence, in the audience if not in the hero; it is painful as well as satisfying to see Clifford kill York's young son or Richard III kill his nephews. But the confrontation between Hotspur and Hal is purely satisfying. Meeting before battle, the characters themselves discuss what makes it so satisfying: their equality as combatants and the absolute nature of the antagonism.

> *Hotspur* If I mistake not, thou art Harry Monmouth.
> *Prince* Thou speak'st as if I would deny my name.

Hotspur   My name is Harry Percy.
Prince   Why, then I see a very valiant rebel of the name.
  I am the Prince of Wales, and think not, Percy,
  To share with me in glory any more.
  Two stars keep not their motion in one sphere,
  Nor can one England brook a double reign
  Of Harry Percy and the Prince of Wales.
Hotspur   Nor shall it, Harry, for the hour is come
  To end the one of us; and would to God
  Thy name in arms were now as great as mine!
                              (*1 Henry IV,* V.iv.58–69)

Hotspur is only expressing the desire we all feel in the history mode
for a good fight, a match, equal teams. Just as Shakespeare makes
Hotspur younger than he was, Hotspur would have Hal more
famous than he is for the sake of equality between combatants. But
the two Harries are quite equal enough as it is. As they themselves
perceive, they are versions of each other; theirs is the battle that can
be unambivalently fought, the battle of the fathers played out in the
next generation.

In *Hamlet,* by contrast, it is the minor figures, Fortinbras and
Laertes, who inherit their father's grievances and unambivalently
recreate in their own generation the battle of the fathers. The
challenge that Fortinbras offers, the challenge of history and the
world of men, cannot arouse Hamlet's passion. It is his mother
who enrages him, not his opposite number in the world of men.
But the confrontation with the woman as Other ends history. The
history hero forges on and on, fighting battle after battle; the hero
of tragedy has arrived at a battle he is unwilling to fight. The
woman as Other provokes such a mixture of intense emotions that
the hero's forward momentum is stopped and he ceases to impose
himself on the outside world. His energy turns inward and he
becomes tragic rather than historical.

But in the histories aggression is still pure and boundless, other-
directed and unmixed with desire. It is at one level simply childish,
and Shakespeare parodies its childish simplicity in the comic sub-
plot of *Henry V:*

Fluellen   . . . I shall think you do not use me with that affability
  as in discretion you ought to use me, look you, being as good
  a man as yourself, both in the disciplines of war, and in the
  derivation of my birth, and in other particularities.

> *Macmorris*   I do not know you so good a man as myself; so Chrish
>   save me, I will cut off your head!   (III.ii.129–35)

Macmorris's answer to Fluellen is a comic version of what lies
behind all the exciting encounters in the histories: "I do not think
you are so good a man as myself, so Chrish save me, I will cut off
your head!" But limitless aggression can be exciting as well as
funny, and no matter how Shakespeare parodies its uses, he also
depends on us to be moved by it. The argument between Mowbray
and Bolingbroke in *Richard II*, for instance, is on the one hand a
scene of pointless name-calling between two equally culpable,
equally self-serving nobles. But on the other hand it is a display of
such boundless self-assertion by two egos so equally matched that
we are thrilled by a sense of extraordinary risk and possibility. If
pre-Oedipal aggression is childish, it has the energy of its unpun-
ished childishness. It is deeply satisfying to see two such elegant
phrasemakers identify as passionately as babies with their feelings
of hatred and rage:

> *Bolingbroke*   Now, Thomas Mowbray, do I turn to thee,
>   And mark my greeting well: for what I speak,
>   My body shall make good upon this earth,
>   Or my divine soul answer it in heaven.
>   Thou are a traitor and a miscreant,
>   Too good to be so, and too bad to live;
>   . . .
>   Once more, the more to aggravate the note,
>   With a foul traitor's name stuff I thy throat,
>   And wish—so please my sovereign—ere I move,
>   What my tongue speaks my right-drawn sword may
>   prove.
>   . . .
> *Mowbray*   First, the fair reverence of your Highness curbs me
>   From giving reins and spurs to my free speech,
>   Which else would post until it had returned
>   These terms of treason doubled down his throat.
>   Setting aside his high blood's royalty,
>   And let him be no kinsman to my liege,
>   I do defy him and I spit at him,
>   Call him a slanderous coward and a villain;
>   Which to maintain, I would allow him odds,
>   And meet him were I tied to run afoot
>   Even to the frozen ridges of the Alps,

> Or any other ground inhabitable,
> Where ever Englishman durst set his foot.
> Meanwhile, let this defend my loyalty:
> By all my hopes most falsely doth he lie.
> *Bolingbroke*   Pale trembling coward, there I throw my gage,
> Disclaiming here the kindred of the King,
> And lay aside my high blood's royalty,
> Which fear, not reverence, makes thee to except.
> If guilty dread have left thee so much strength
> As to take up mine honor's pawn, then stoop.
> By that, and all the rites of knighthood else,
> Will I make good against thee, arm to arm,
> What I have spoke, or thou canst worse devise.
>
> (I.i.35–46, 54–77)

And so on. When Mowbray hears what Bolingbroke accuses him of he cries,

> O! let my sovereign turn away his face,
> And bid his ears a little while be deaf,
> Till I have told this slander of his blood
> How God and good men hate so foul a liar.   (I.i.111–14)

Given permission to speak freely, Mowbray says promptly, "Then, Bolingbroke, as low as to thy heart, / Through the false passage of thy throat, thou liest" (I.i.124–25). Everything depends, of course, on the contrast between the passionate feelings and the elegant ceremony of the situation. The feelings are contained within the ritualized preliminaries to a duel, and the duel itself is forbidden. Constant reference is made to the king, in whose presence these nobles claim to be restraining themselves. This scene lends itself to very formal production; but at its heart is the wild and fearless anger of the two antagonists.

The scene to compare to this one is the closet scene in *Hamlet*. Hamlet is angry at his mother, not, like Mowbray and Bolingbroke, at his opponent in the world of men. His anger therefore cannot run rampant lest it destroy the object of his desire, the subject he hoped would desire *him,* his mother. Before he goes to see her he reminds himself of the limits to his aggression against her:

> Now could I drink hot blood
> And do such bitter business as the day
> Would quake to look on. Soft, now to my mother.

O heart, lose not thy nature; let not ever
The soul of Nero enter this firm bosom.
Let me be cruel, not unnatural;
I will speak daggers to her, but use none.   (III.ii.398–404)

Hamlet's rage is deflected onto a third party, onto something that rustles behind an arras; and of course the death of Polonius cannot satisfy him. Hamlet's rage at Gertrude is if anything greater than Mowbray's and Bolingbroke's at each other; but his rage is thwarted by affection, desire, duty, and the sheer aloofness of the Other from the Self. For Gertrude is in some sense *absent* from the closet scene. She does not answer Hamlet speech for speech, as Mowbray does Bolingbroke, but murmurs broken protests, acquiesces, disappears. The image of Hamlet thrusting at the arras is the perfect emblem for the battle with the Other: the antagonist he wants to kill simply isn't there.

The confrontation with the Other, I have said, ends history; but it would be equally true to say that when the masculine historical adventure loses its glamor, the hero becomes aware of the Other for the first time. Until then he is too busy to notice its presence in his life. So it is as true to say that Hamlet's preoccupations are a function of his apathy for the masculine-historical adventure as to say that his preoccupation with the Other distracts him from the world of men. By *Hamlet* we have lost interest in the adventure of history; we have lost desire for its rewards and prerogatives. This loss is symptomatic of a more general loss of desire for anything the world has to offer. In history there seems to be something outside the Self which is clearly and unequivocally desirable, the brass ring of power or victory or the crown itself of England; in *Hamlet* this desirable thing seems to disappear. The hero mourns its disappearance and feels an absence of desire altogether. After *Hamlet* nothing actual is ever again unequivocably desirable to the hero of tragedy. King Lear wants something that can never be, a mother's love from his daughters; Othello wants a wife less likely to betray him than Desdemona. Antony's desire for both Empire and Cleopatra is equivocal, and Macbeth is insatiable, desirous of he knows not what. After *Hamlet* desire becomes intransitive, like aggression, and leads, therefore, back to the Self. In history, the desire of the hero for power is world-transformative; in tragedy, at most desire transforms the hero himself. Object-related desires such as Richard III's to be King or Henry V's to beat the French are not central to the dynamic of tragedy; Hamlet's desire is for peace within, not for dominion in the world of men: "O God, I could be bounded in a nutshell and count myself a king of infinite space, were it not that I have bad dreams" (II.ii.258–60). Of course, we need not take Hamlet entirely at his rather melodramatic word. But clearly in this play "bad dreams" like Hamlet's are more important than unfulfilled political ambitions. In *Richard III*, by contrast, the hero's bad dreams are dramatically relevant only when they prophesy what happens in the world of political power. Richard's desire is for the brass ring, the crown; Hamlet cannot discover anything in the outside world worth wanting.

The unambivalent aggression of the history hero is a pleasure that need not be explained. All that is necessary is to notice that it *is* the aggression we are taking pleasure in. But the unambivalent desire of the history hero is another story. From one point of view what the history hero wants—what all the aggression is *about*—is meaningless to us. The world of the fathers is at one level simply depressing, a version of the world Macbeth lives in after his wife dies: "Tomorrow, and tomorrow, and tomorrow" (V.v.19). Jan Kott puts it this way: "Feudal history is like a great staircase on which there treads a constant procession of kings. . . . Every step brings the throne nearer. Another step and the crown will fall. From the highest step there is only a leap into the abyss."[6] The crown is almost never enjoyed in the history plays. It is no sooner got than lost; or, if it is retained, it seems to bring more cares than pleasure. Henry VI, Henry IV, and Henry V all complain of it as a burden. The crown as a motive for action is from one point of view a version of the Emperor's New Clothes. It is an arbitrary sign, culturally designated as enjoyable but never in fact enjoyed.

But if the crown itself is an inadequate object of desire for the individual, it nevertheless represents our hearts' desire insofar as we are members of a society. The crown as symbol holds out the hope for a society ruled by its One True King, for natural rather than arbitrary social arrangements, and it is by virtue of that fact worthy of all the battles fought on its behalf. The crown is something we can unambivalently desire if we put it in the context of historical mythology rather than in the context of political reality. Although at one level the English history plays are a chronicle of unsavory power plays, at another level they are a kind of male creation myth. This myth says that once upon a time there was a True King,

Edward III. He stands at the top of the diagram like the original Adam, the point toward which everyone aspires. He has, and also is, the brass ring. From his paternity have issued all the complicated families that stand for England, every member of which has some of Edward's blood in his veins. The society as a whole is animated by the royalty within it although no individual character is truly royal. Every member of these families is somehow implicated in the interruption of the succession: Richard II because he deserved to be deposed and everyone else because they profit somehow from Richard's deposition. Everyone betrays the myth somehow or other. But there is always the possibility in history that what was once incarnate in Edward III could return. We are never without hope that England will have a True King yet. In fact, the Tudor myth of history guarantees that it will.

Insofar as aspiration forward toward the crown, then, is a version of aspiration backward toward Edward III, and insofar as both are a form of participation in the myth of the King's Return, the desire of the history heroes is something we can understand. The world of the fathers is depressing only from one point of view. From another it is glamorous and full of the almost religious promise of right rule. The crown symbolizes rightful inheritance as well as rightful rule. The one is in fact a function of the other, as York insists when Richard II is about to confiscate Hereford's property:

> Take Hereford's rights away, and take from time
> His charters and his customary rights,
> Let not tomorrow then ensue today;
> Be not thyself. For how are thou a king
> But by fair sequence and succession?
>
> (*Richard II,* II.i.195–99)

In history the idea of rightful inheritance, like the idea of the True King, is numinous. It lends excitement and hope to the relentless forward movement of historical time, even though the hope is so often betrayed. The idea of natural, rightful inheritance sparkles in the background while in the foreground kings, princes, and dukes conspire and revenge and usurp. Only if we are attuned to the mythic background does the activity in the foreground make sense. The history hero's unambivalent desire for the crown has its roots in myth.

The myth of the history plays involves fathers and sons. It does not involve mothers, daughters, or wives. That is not to say, of course, that there are no mothers, daughters, or wives in the history plays; only that they are not part of the myth. The women make rightful inheritance possible by bearing men sons, but they themselves are not inheritors. They serve the myth without participating in it. Young Talbot's mother, for instance, is a kind of mascot to the relationship between father and son, rather than an independent entity. She is invoked by both of them as they debate the obligations of John's manliness:

> Talbot   Shall all thy mother's hopes lie in one tomb?
> John   Ay, rather than I'll shame my mother's womb.
>
> (IV.v.34–35)

The father invokes the mother's love to support his argument, the son out-trumps him with a reference to the mother's body. But the issue is between father and son. The mother is only the physical connection between the two, an undifferentiated element in the whole process of succession and inheritance. Her sexuality is scarcely her own; it belongs to her family tree. She is always already possessed. Even a woman like the Duchess of York in *Richard III* is essentially passive before the process of succession. Realizing that she has served to pervert the myth rather than to further it, she curses her own womb for having given birth to Richard (IV.iv.138). But the active agent, of course, is Richard himself. It is he who kills his brother and his nephews in order to come into their inheritance. The inheritance itself is out of the Duchess's hands. Once our inheritance of the world and all its blessings depends on our relations with women, the myth of history no longer directs our passions; while it does, the feminine is largely irrelevant.

The history plays, as Coppelia Kahn puts it, are "a continuous meditation on the role of the father in a man's self-definition."[7] They are also a celebration of the splendid and unambivalent passions of the world of men. Before the Oedipal resolution collapses, before the world of men is shown to be incapable of protecting us from the mortal injuries of Fortune and women, we may lay about ourselves with great abandon, wanting this, hating that, drunk with our own emotions. Consciousness of the feminine Other dawns slowly in the history plays; until it breaks out, in *Hamlet,* the hero lives in the clarity of his desire that the world of his fathers also be his.

The history hero's virtues as a character—his unambivalent desire and aggression—depend upon his lack of awareness of the
woman as Other. I must conclude with a brief consideration of the
apparent exception to this rule, Prince Hal/Henry V. Far from being abandoned to his own emotions Hal/Henry is a consummate
and self-controlled performer. Hal/Henry is an approach to Hamlet, as much a creature of consciousness as of instinct. But Hal/
Henry's consciousness, his control, and his performances are all related, no less than the passions of the other heroes, to suppression of
awareness of the woman as Other. What Hal/Henry performs so
brilliantly are the king's two bodies; what makes his performances
possible is that neither body is primarily sexual, vulnerable to the
choices women may make. The vulnerability of the sexual body in
Shakespeare cannot be performed but can only be endured. Hal/
Henry's detachment and control are, like the other heroes' lack of
ambivalence, a gift of the world of men. The issue is worth explor-
ing at some length.

From *Richard II* through *Henry V* we are always aware of the
dialectic between the king's two bodies. The king has a divine and
invulnerable body—his official body—but he is also mortal. The
classic statement is Richard II's:

> I live with bread, like you, feel want,
> Taste grief, need friends—subjected thus,
> How can you say to me I am a king?   (III.ii.175–77)

The issue underlies *Henry V,* Act IV, scene i, where Henry goes
among the troops in disguise and ends with his speech on ceremony:

> And what have kings that privates have not too,
> Save ceremony, save general ceremony?
>   . . .
>
>   O, be sick, great greatness,
> And bid thy ceremony give thee cure!
> Thinks thou the fiery fever will go out
> With titles blown from adulation?
> Will it give place to flexure and low bending?
> Canst thou, when thou command'st the beggar's knee,
> Command the health of it?   (IV.i.243–62)

One more example out of the many offered will suffice. In Act II,
scene ii, of *2 Henry IV* Prince Henry complains "Before God, I am

exceedingly weary" and Poins, alert as ever, replies, "Is't come to that? I had thought weariness durst not have attached one of so high blood" (II.ii.1–3). Poins is not very clever, but, as we have seen, the kings themselves are fascinated with their own powerlessness over the body.

The solution offered by Hal/Henry is, as I have said, performance. He performs both his bodily vulnerability and his political role and is finally identified with neither. Michael Goldman's analysis of Henry's performances is relevant here:

A king is not simply his role; his power and authority do not flow directly from his person, as Richard, tragically, tried to insist. Neither, however, is a king simply a man like other men, no matter how attractive and at times politically useful the pretense may be. The demands of office change a man. A king is not a man like other men—but he is a man, and his humanity consists in this: he must pay the price of his role.

The achievement of the play—the fact that with all its ironies it remains great patriotic drama—lies with its ability to project the glory of the ruler in a way that is true to—indeed depends upon—the price of his role. In the St. Crispin's Day address, for example, we are stirred, certainly, by the way Henry meets the challenge of the moment and rallies his men, but our sessions with the Chorus and the army have made us sensitive to the fact that his speech, like the rejection of Falstaff in *2 Henry IV,* is a performance and not a revelation of some previously unsounded self. It is in part an attempt to deal with the cynicism he has met in the night. . . . We respond to his success as we do when a political leader we admire makes a great campaign speech: we love him for his effectiveness. The King is speaking *ex officio,* and if he calls himself Harry, this is not because he is a man like other men, speaking merely out of personal conviction and desire. He is, rather, projecting an "image"—the hero as good fellow (like "Ike" or "Jack" or "Bobby"). It has been developed for a purpose, and the King must rely on his muse, must place a strain on his imagination, himself, and his hearers. . . .[8]

In the St. Crispin's Day speech, then, Henry is the more a king because he can make his own ordinariness serve his kingly purpose—just as, in *1* and *2 Henry IV,* Hal made his kingliness serve ordinary pleasures. Hal and Henry are in complete control of the dualisms that define their world.

The comparison with Hamlet is striking. Whereas Henry fully performs both sides of his nature, Hamlet "[has] that within which passes show" (I.ii.85). Whereas Henry's performances serve his conscious purposes, Hamlet enacts and produces performances designed to accomplish uncertain goals. Whereas Henry is always magnificently in control of himself and his listeners, Hamlet is out of control of both. What makes performance and control impossible in *Hamlet* is something that has not yet occurred in *Henry V:* confrontation with the Other, with the world of radical uncertainty that Shakespeare habitually associates with women. Henry is the most sophisticated and self-aware of all the history heroes, the one who shares our vision of history itself. But he is at the same time innocent, a resident of the unfallen world of men. Henry's world is still the world of the fathers; in *Henry V* the Oedipal resolution holds good one last great time. But with *Hamlet* the pleasures of history come to an end; we must leave the garden of England for the unpleasantness in Rome, Venice, and Denmark. In these foreign lands the myth of rightful rule does not hold things together and the problem of women can no longer be finessed.

SEVEN

After Tragedy: *The Tempest*

In Shakespearean romances the feminine Other is lost and found or dies and is reborn. Marina and Perdita are lost and found by Pericles and Leontes; Thaisa, Imogen, and Hermione die and are reborn. The motif of the Return of the Feminine is a basic structural element in *The Winter's Tale* and important to two of the other three romances, *Cymbeline* and *Pericles*. This motif endows women characters with symbolic values that are first lost to the world of the tale and then recovered. The feminine goes underground (like Persephone), falls asleep (like Sleeping Beauty), or is locked away (like Rapunzel). The lost-and-recovered women have been variously interpreted as principles of pleasure, beauty, and fertility, or as the powers of the unconscious that have become inaccessible to the rational, conscious mind. In the absence of these women, life is a barren wasteland; when they return, the landscape flowers. In *The Winter's Tale,* the separation of the male Self from the feminine Other and his recovery of his wife and daughter create the central situation of the play. The first movement of the play separates Leontes from Perdita and Hermione; the second movement climaxes with their return. When the feminine Other returns, the situation of the play as a whole is resolved.

In *The Tempest,* however, there is no Return of the Feminine. Prospero recovers neither his wife nor his daughter at the end of the play. His wife cannot be recovered because she is not a character in the *dramatis personae,* and Miranda has never been lost. Prospero has had his daughter with him all along. Of course, Miranda has been lost to Italy and she does return there at the end of the play. Like *The Winter's Tale, The Tempest* ends with the daughter grown up and about to be married, returning to her native land. But in *The Tempest* we just don't care. First of all, Miranda's return is more of a loss than a gain for the central male character. As Prospero puts it, "I/Have lost my daughter . . . In this last tempest" (V.i.147–48,

153). If there is no concomitant sexual renewal for the father, the marriage of the daughter is a mixed blessing at best. Second, Miranda's return takes place after the play is over and in a place we have never seen. It is not, like Perdita's return, a formal as well as thematic movement. Perdita's return takes us back to where we began, but Miranda's Italy is unknown territory to us.

In many myths and tales we find an association between the motif of the feminine return and the figure of the May Queen. Persephone is picking flowers when she is abducted by the god of the underworld; presumably she returns to this pastoral activity when she is periodically restored to life. It is notable that the daughter in *The Winter's Tale* is the most fully developed May Queen in the whole Shakespeare canon whereas the daughter in *The Tempest* scarcely plays this role at all. Perdita, dressed up to resemble Flora, presides over a pastoral scene of feasting, dancing, and courting. She is the hostess, the authority on flowers, the champion of nature as against the human arts, and the object of admiration and desire. The closest we come to pastoral in *The Tempest* is the scene in which Prospero produces a wedding masque; and here, of course, it is Prospero, not Miranda, who presides. The masque constellates images of flowers, harvest, rainbows, and marriage; Juno and Ceres bless the couple with a song of earth's abundance:

> Earth's increase, foison plenty,
> Barns and garners never empty,
> Vines with clust'ring bunches growing,
> Plants with goodly burden bowing.   (IV.i.110–13)

But this celebration of the mythically female Earth is the product of a man's imagination. These are "Spirits," Prospero tells Ferdinand,

>   which by mine art
> I have from their confines called to enact
> My present fancies.   (IV.i.120–22)

And when his fancies abruptly turn elsewhere the whole scene vanishes. Even when the subject is flowers and fertility, the scene belongs to Prospero and not Miranda. It is striking that even Ferdinand's admiration here is for his prospective father-in-law and not, like Florizel's, for his future wife. He interrupts the masque with these strange words of praise: "So rare a wond'red father and a wise/Makes this place Paradise" (IV.i.123–24). In *The Winter's Tale* the intrusion of the father figure interrupts the pastoral scene; here the father produces it. There is no need of a May Queen when even pastoral is the creation of the magus-father.

In *The Tempest*, then, we find no May Queen and no feminine return. Oddly enough, however, the prevailing critical assumption is that something like the Return of the Feminine *does* take place in *The Tempest*. In *A Natural Perspective*, for instance, Northrup Frye includes *The Tempest* among the romances he compares as follows to *The Comedy of Errors*. "In striking contrast to the usual New Comedy structure," he says, *The Comedy of Errors* emphasizes the reunion of the mother and father, not of the younger generation characters. Frye goes on,

Here . . . this early experimental comedy anticipates the techniques of the romances. . . . In *Pericles* the emphasis falls on the reunion of Thaisa and Pericles, and the marriage of Marina is subordinated to her return to Pericles. . . . In *The Winter's Tale* the central action is the mysterious return of Hermione to Leontes, to which again the story of the young lovers is subordinated, and of course everything is subordinated to the return of Prospero in *The Tempest*.[1]

But if the point is the sense of reunion and return enjoyed by representatives of the older generation, then it seems wrong to include *The Tempest* in such a list. Prospero's return to Italy does not reunite him with his wife or with the feminine in any form. Whereas the returns of the feminine provide the other romances with a triumphant conclusion, Prospero's return to Italy is equivocal and concludes the play on a muted note. If *The Winter's Tale* is the measure, *The Tempest* is always disappointing. Frye tells us further that the conception of rebirth "is so central in Shakespearean romance, as Thaisa revives from a 'block' and Hermione from a statue, that perhaps what really emerges in the recognition scenes of the romances is the primitive feeling, which is incorporated in Christianity, that it is *death* that is somehow unnatural [rather than rebirth]."[2] But the idea of rebirth is *not* central to *The Tempest*. In this play the death of the feminine is not a nightmare from which we may ultimately awaken. Prospero's dead wife stays dead.

What happens if we emphasize this fact instead of glossing over it? The absence of a wife for Prospero is perhaps a key to the vision of *The Tempest*. This play defines the feminine, the Other, the world outside the hero as something that not only *may* be utterly lost, as in the other romances, but actually *has* been lost. Miranda, of course, has not been lost. She is the slim thread by which Prospero will be returned to the world beyond his own island. But Miranda's limitations as a representative of the feminine Other are, as we shall see, acute; and Prospero's return through the agency of her marriage is not wholly joyful. Prospero is not restored, as Leontes is, to the perfect condition that was his before the calamity. The family remains radically incomplete.

If we take the absence of a wife for Prospero to be a central fact in the world of this play, Shakespearean romance appears to be a kind of post-holocaust literature. It deals with survivors, with people who continue to live after unbearable losses. The tragedies take place just as the worst is happening; in the romances the worst has happened and life goes on, creating a sense of free fall, of having stepped through the looking glass. In the tragedies the catastrophe comes at the end of the play; we are simultaneously fighting it and rushing toward it from beginning to end. We are *engaged* with the catastrophe throughout. In the romances the catastrophe comes earlier and is less absorbing. The hero does not die, as in the tragedies; he merely suffers such terrible losses that his world takes on a kind of posthumous quality. Once the loss has actually taken place, a sense of disengagement sets in; we feel detached from the flux of events. In *The Winter's Tale* the catastrophe comes in the middle of the play; our detachment is insured by our instant removal from all that has mattered to us so far. In "The Patience of *The Winter's Tale*," John Taylor says,

When the scene shifts to Bohemia, and we learn that Perdita has been saved and Antigonus killed, there is little to anticipate. Time tells us of Perdita and Florizel, a strong hint of things to come, but Perdita has appeared in the play only as an infant and Florizel not at all, and we can feel only a mild curiosity over this pairing. Hermione is apparently dead, and Leontes still too removed from sympathy for the expectation of a reunion with his daughter to rouse a sympathetic interest. Polixenes and Camillo left the play too early for us to care much about their fates when they appear.[3]

In the comedies we may take a vacation from the serious concerns of the play because everything is sure to work out anyway. But the change of scene in *The Winter's Tale* is no vacation. It is an abrupt and apparently permanent departure from everything familiar and important, similar to the departure of Prospero from Milan. After *such* a change we will not commit ourselves again quickly to an intense interest in the action. In fact, it takes a miracle, the resurrection of Hermione, to restore our interest to its previous levels.

The loss in *The Tempest* has taken place prior to the action of the play, which accounts for the dreamy detachment of the whole story. We are "away" the whole time and never "come back," although the return is planned. But what exactly is the catastrophe that precedes *The Tempest*? Apparently it is the loss of Prospero's dukedom, his exile from everything but his daughter and his books. He loses his place in the world of men. But clearly that loss is not commensurate with Leontes's loss of Hermione. Prospero does not long for or value the thing he lost, and when it is restored to him he does not seem particularly pleased. Auden has caught precisely the tone of the ending when he puts these words in Prospero's mouth in "The Sea and the Mirror":

> In all, things have turned out better
> Than I once expected or ever deserved;
> I am glad that I did not recover my dukedom till
> I do not want it.[4]

Prospero does want his dukedom back, but not in the same way that Leontes wants Hermione. It is not an unqualified good. The return of the women in *The Winter's Tale* is life-giving and restores our original intensity of involvement; at the end of *The Tempest*, we are still detached and Prospero is still talking about death. We continue to have a sense of sadness and loss in spite of Gonzalo's naively cheerful account of the situation:

> O, rejoice
> Beyond a common joy, and set it down
> With gold on lasting pillars. In one voyage
> Did Claribel her husband find at Tunis,
> And Ferdinand her brother found a wife
> Where he himself was lost; Prospero his dukedom
> In a poor isle; and all of us ourselves
> When no man was his own.   (V.i.206–13)

Like Gonzalo's Utopian fantasies in Act I, this is endearing but incomplete. The happy ending is neither thoroughly happy nor thoroughly an ending, despite the restoration of the apparent loss. Prospero clearly suffers from something more than the loss of Milan. We might say that he suffers from his own limitations or mortality itself. But we may also associate the absence of ordinary joy with the absence of Prospero's wife. Not that we should imagine he is in mourning for her; he gives no sign whatever of grief. The only specific reference to the missing woman is Prospero's answer to Miranda's question, "Sir, are not you my father?" He says, briefly and conventionally, "Thy mother was a piece of virtue, and/She said thou wast my daughter" (I.ii.55–57). Miranda's mother is not only dead; she has sunk without trace from the consciousness of the play. But if *The Tempest* resonates with a greater loss than Prospero's exile from Milan, the death of his wife may stand for these extrapolitical concerns.

The absence of the wife in *The Tempest* is both a gift and a deprivation to the world of the play. On the one hand it creates a very unhappy sexual atmosphere. On the other hand it gives Prospero a kind of freedom enjoyed by no other character in Shakespeare. If Prospero has little to hope for from the outside world, he also has little to fear. The Other can neither oppose him, as in the tragedies, nor disappear, as in *The Winter's Tale* and *Pericles*. The most important representative of the Other is already missing from Prospero's life; let us begin with the unhappiness this creates.

The world of *The Tempest* is one in which sexual possibility for the male Self has retreated beyond all chance of recovery, perhaps even beyond memory. The sexuality of the daughter does not renew the life of the previous generation, as it does in *The Winter's Tale*. Leontes is restored to his full human connectedness when Hermione comes back, but Prospero's connections remain imperfectly willed. Hermione can come back to life because she exists in the minds of the characters and the audience, but Prospero's wife has no dramatic existence. Prospero is not just celibate; he is a figure of total sexual isolation.

Miranda's limitations as the sole representative of the feminine must now be painfully obvious. Her sexuality is inaccessible to the male Self, offering Prospero the horrid choice between incest and sexual self-denial. The feminine is not a source of gifts in *The Tempest* but a challenge to self-possession and restraint. So the sexuality of the play is strained. There is, in any event, very little sexuality in *The Tempest;* and when the issue does come up, it is mostly a matter of prohibition. Even the wedding entertainment is minatory; it deals with the intentions of Venus and Cupid to trick the young couple into premarital sex. Prospero's warning to Ferdinand sets the repressive tone of the play:

If thou dost break her virgin-knot before
All sanctimonious ceremonies may
With full and holy rite be minist'red,
No sweet aspersion shall the heavens let fall
To make this contract grow; but barren hate,
Sour-eyed disdain, and discord shall bestrew
The union of your bed with weeds so loathly
That you shall hate it both.   (IV.i.15–22)

If we turned one of the romantic comedies inside out we would
have the sexual mood of *The Tempest*. In the comedies, the father
presents an obstacle to sexual freedom that may and will be overcome; in *The Tempest*, the sexuality of the father is dominant. This
is the only play in the Shakespeare canon of which this is true.
When the wife is missing, the father's daughter is a temptation to be
overcome rather than a force for sexual liberation. It is the terrible
possibility of incest that darkens and dampens the sexuality of *The
Tempest*.

The sexual situation in *The Tempest* should be seen in the context
of the other romances. All four of them contain images of sexual
bestiality such as threatens the incest taboo in *The Tempest*. The
beastly potentialities of sex, however, are not a problem requiring a
resolution, as they are in the tragedies. The romances merely *include*
sexual horror; they are not dominated by it. The issue is always
displaced or distanced somehow. In *Pericles*, for instance, the
father-daughter incest is displaced from Pericles and Marina to
Antiochus and his daughter; in *Cymbeline*, the necrophilic embrace
between Imogen and the dead, disgusting Cloten is a case of mistaken identity. The isolated image of Beauty lying with the Beast
both counts and does not count; we see the image and react to it,
yet we know the situation arises from a simple and understandable
mistake. Leontes is similarly mistaken in *The Winter's Tale* when he
most vilely imagines his wife's adultery. His mistake is more important than Imogen's, but it is surrounded by every possible
assurance of Hermione's innocence and is ultimately rectified by his
own penance and absolution. The play has no sympathy with
Leontes's sex nausea. His vision is simply erroneous, whereas Hamlet's, Antony's, and Lear's all have some plausibility. Sexual loathing is here a kind of curiosity, like a figure vomiting in a Brueghel
painting while the villagers dance. The disease is there; but it is
contained and cannot infect the play as a whole. Leontes's jealousy

creates the plot; it does not, like Othello's, create the mood of the play. The world of *The Winter's Tale* is calmly disposed toward sexual joy.

In *The Tempest*, the sexual bestiality of the hero is displaced onto Caliban, where it is both more and less serious than in *The Winter's Tale*. It is less serious because Caliban is not really a human being; but it is more serious because he is always with us. He cannot be abandoned, like Antiochus, or renounced, like the errors of Imogen and Leontes. He is, as many critics have noticed and as Prospero admits, a projection of Prospero's: "This thing of darkness I/Acknowledge mine" (V.i.275–76). As such, he is always a threat. Prospero's Calibanism has never "gotten out" and caused havoc, as Leontes's foul projections have; since Caliban's attempted rape of Miranda he has been harshly and securely controlled. But neither does Caliban disappear over time. What in *The Winter's Tale* can ultimately be forgiven by the resurrected wife finds no mercy in *The Tempest*. In the absence of the proper sexual partner, the sexuality of the male Self can *only* be bestial and must therefore be continuously repressed. This is obviously regrettable, and Shakespeare registers the price of the situation by giving Caliban some of the most moving and sympathetic speeches of the play. Caliban's human characteristics, like those of all fairy-tale Beasts, are the more poignant for being discovered beneath his beastliness. In speeches such as the following Caliban appeals to us from behind his hatefulness:

> Be not afeard; the isle is full of noises,
> Sounds and sweet airs that give delight and hurt not.
> Sometimes a thousand twangling instruments
> Will hum about mine ears; and sometime voices
> That, if I then had waked after long sleep,
> Will make me sleep again; and then, in dreaming,
> The clouds methought would open and show riches
> Ready to drop upon me, that, when I waked
> I cried to dream again.   (III.ii.138–46)

But the freedom of this sad creature would mean the rape of Miranda. So it cannot be.

There is only one moment in the play when Caliban is truly threatening to Prospero, but that moment evokes the strongest emotions Prospero ever feels. During the wedding entertainment

he suddenly remembers "that foul conspiracy / Of the beast Caliban
. . . Against my life" (IV.i.139–41). He is beside himself, and
dismisses the masquing spirits "to a strange, hollow, and confused
noise." Ferdinand says, "Your father's in some passion / That works
him strongly," and Miranda wonders at it: "Never till this day / Saw
I him touched with anger so distempered" (IV.i.143–45). Prospero
himself admits to being in turmoil: "Sir, I am vexed. . . . A turn or
two I'll walk / To still my beating mind" (IV.i.158, 162–63). What is
strange here is that until now Prospero has seemed handily in
control of all the conspiracies taking place on the island. Why does
Caliban present such a problem right now? Caliban has suddenly
become unmanageable because something is taking place outside
Prospero that arouses his beastliness and makes Caliban, the exter-
nalization of what is beastly within us, a serious threat.

What is taking place, of course, is the celebration of lawful
sexuality, something from which Prospero is permanently excluded.
The situation may be clarified by comparison with a similar situation
in *The Winter's Tale*. Confronted with the sexuality of his own
daughter, Perdita, Leontes has a moment of unmistakable sexual
envy. When Florizel reminds Leontes of his own youth, Leontes remembers it somewhat too well.

> *Florizel*   Remember since you owed no more to Time
>   Than I do now; with thought of such affections,
>   Step forth mine advocate; at your request
>   My father will grant precious things as trifles.
> *Leontes*   Would he do so, I'd beg your precious mistress,
>   Which he counts but a trifle.
> *Paulina*   Sir, my liege,
>   Your eye hath too much youth in't.   (V.i.219–25)

In Shakespeare's source for *The Winter's Tale*, the Leontes figure
actually tries to seduce his daughter; here Leontes has only a fleeting
fantasy of loving Perdita. But in the light of his fantasy we may
perhaps understand Prospero's rage against Caliban. Perhaps Prospero, like Leontes, remembers his youth too well as he watches the
wedding entertainment with Miranda and Ferdinand. Perhaps, as
Leslie Fiedler suggests, Prospero's own "residual lust" has sur-
faced, breaking the spell of the masque.[5] Prospero has no Paulina,
no female Other, to control the Caliban within; he must rouse
himself to fight the projected, embodied Caliban or lose everything

to him. The wedding entertainment makes him vulnerable to Caliban because it arouses his own archaic desires—and these, in the complete absence of a proper object, are vicious.

In *The Winter's Tale* both the mother and the daughter come and go over time; in *The Tempest* the daughter is continuously present whereas her mother is missing completely. The presence and absence of the feminine are simultaneous rather than sequential facts. The feminine is a principle of death as well as a principle of recurring life. Yet the absence of Prospero's wife should be understood positively as well as negatively. *The Tempest* and *The Winter's Tale* are alternative visions—religious visions, really—of a world redeemed from loss. In each play the nature of the loss dictates the nature of the redemption. In *The Tempest* the loss is absolute and irreversible, but it is also over and done with. It need no longer be mourned or resisted. In *The Tempest* both the audience and the protagonist are free from desire for the lost Other; in *The Winter's Tale* we endure the absolute frustration of desire and then enjoy its amazing fulfillment. The world of *The Tempest* is redeemed by its freedom from desire, even as the world of *The Winter's Tale* is redeemed by the satisfaction of desire. The permanent absence of Prospero's wife, like the disappearance and return of Leontes's wife, is a basic structural element of the play.

Prospero's freedom from desire is not absolute. Indeed, we have just seen a moment when he experiences a painful resurgence of desire. Perhaps it would be more accurate to say that redemption in *The Tempest* requires the suppression of desire, whereas redemption in *The Winter's Tale* requires desire to be kept alive beyond its natural life. Leontes continues to yearn uselessly for Hermione some sixteen years after her death. Both Prospero's and Leontes's options imply some unnaturalness, some perversity. Prospero's repression of his sexuality obviously goes against the grain, but Leontes, too, deals unnaturally with his desire. In Act V, scene i, Leontes is offered the option of allowing his painful desire for Hermione to die away. He may, if he chooses, listen to Cleomenes, who tells him,

> Sir, you have done enough, and have performed
> A saintlike sorrow. No fault could you make
> Which you have not redeemed; indeed paid down
> More penitence than done trespass. At the last,
> Do as the heavens have done; forget your evil;
> With them forgive yourself.   (V.i.1–6)

But Leontes chooses to listen instead to Paulina, who keeps open a wound that might have healed. And Paulina at this point is much less compelling than she is both earlier and later in the play. Her sharpness toward Leontes has become routine and her praises of Hermione are both tired and excessive:

> If one by one you wedded all the world,
> Or from the all that are took something good
> To make a perfect woman, she you killed
> Would be unparalleled.   (V.i.13–16)

The language here is quite conventional. Hermione's eyes are stars; to take treasure from her lips is to leave them "more rich for what they yielded" (V.i.54); she is a composite of all that is best in women. These threadbare Elizabethan conventions cannot move us to more than an automatic assent. There is some willfulness in Leontes's submission to Paulina here; she is no longer irresistible, as she used to be. Cleomenes speaks for mental health: surely the time for self-forgiveness has come. Paulina urges Leontes to hang on to his desire beyond all reason, and it is she who ultimately prevails in this scene.

Leontes's desire for his wife ultimately creates the miracle: it calls into life the image of Hermione. But it has been as painful for Leontes to endure as for Prospero to resist the life in his desires. The option Prospero offers requires us to abandon intense desire and the possibility of intense satisfaction. The option Leontes offers means enduring prolonged unfulfillment without abandoning desire.

These are the costs of each option. The benefits are more obvious and require less explanation. Leontes's desires are finally fulfilled, and Prospero's world is continuously graceful. In the absence of desire, Prospero is gifted with his Ariel, his own unanxious creativity. Ariel is the visible manifestation of the freedom we feel when we can (however briefly) escape our sense of unfulfillment. *The Tempest* does not imply that such escape can be permanent, or even that we would want it to be. Our time on the island is always surrounded by our knowledge that we will soon leave it. But that time, this play says, may be almost perfect. Caliban may from time to time disrupt the world of *The Tempest,* but for the rest the mood of the play is Ariel's mood. Ariel's songs of solace, detachment, and harmony set the tone for the play as a whole:

> Come unto these yellow sands,
>   And then take hands.

> Curtsied when you have and kissed
>   The wild waves whist,
> Foot it featly here and there;
> And, sweet sprites, the burden bear.   (I.ii.377–82)

Ariel reminds us of a world beyond our difficulties. Shakespeare's early comedies move toward sexual liberation; in *The Tempest* our sense of liberation is spiritual and *post*sexual. The absence of a wife for Prospero is a liberating feature of the world of the play even though it creates an unhappy sexual atmosphere. Prospero is not just bereft of the Other, he is also free of the Other. If the feminine in *The Winter's Tale* is ultimately life-renewing, it is also capable of betraying and deserting the male Self. Prospero has little to hope for from the passage of Time, but he also has little to fear. Having no wife, he is free from the danger of losing her. His island world is stable and free, whereas the world of *The Winter's Tale* is ruled by Time's changes. Prospero is liberated from the powerlessness of the hero to control either himself or the Other. If sexuality is no longer the central metaphor for the relationship between ourselves and the world outside us, what we lose in emotional intensity we gain in control. The comparison with *The Winter's Tale* is again illuminating: Leontes maintains his sexual involvement with the outside world, renounces control, obeys Paulina, and passively accepts what Time offers; Prospero renounces sexuality and takes control of everything.

In *The Winter's Tale* some alliance of Providence, Woman, Time, and Nature—all versions of the uncontrollable Other—moves the plot. By contrast, all of Prospero's schemes are successful. In *The Tempest* the male Self strikes an assertive posture toward the flow of events and successfully diverts it. In comparison to the characters in *The Winter's Tale*—and especially in comparison to Leontes—Prospero is a very god over events. He is active in his own behalf and his activity accomplishes his ends. In *The Winter's Tale,* as Taylor says, all human schemes are "ambiguous, reversed, or thwarted in outcome":

Camillo spirits Polixenes away, but that only confirms Leontes' suspicions, and helps to bring about the persecution of Hermione and the death of Mamillius. In Bohemia, Polixenes disguises himself to retrieve his wayward son, but the immediate effect of this is that he loses him entirely. Florizel decides to escape Bohemia by ship, but in Sicilia he and Perdita are arrested; the immediate effect, again, is disastrous. In any case, the shepherds have decided to reveal the tokens of Perdita's identity, and the flight would soon have become unnecessary.

Passivity, patience and submissiveness are more fruitful than action and control: "Apart from the designs of Paulina, the only deliberate acts that achieve their immediate ends are either expressions of great uncontrolled passion or acts of conscious self-submission, the deliberate abandonment of control."[6] Activity in this play is not awesome, powerful, and dignified, as it is when Prospero is its exemplar. It is represented by Autolycus, whose busyness is trivial and ineffective. Activity is beside the point; what is powerful in this play is patience, faith, and receptivity. There is nothing to be gained by trying to control events, as Prospero does. In *The Winter's Tale,* says Taylor, "things just happen and are received like gifts. A ship is wrecked off the coast of Bohemia, shepherds stumble upon a baby and some treasure, a prince's falcon flies across a shepherd's land, and a hodge-podge of misguided and thwarted human actions forms a series of . . . coincidences."[7] In *The Tempest,* Ferdinand is not led to Miranda, as Florizel is led to Perdita, by some random falcon. No natural or providential flight brings the two together. Ferdinand is led by Ariel, flying under orders from Prospero. In *The Winter's Tale* it is a woman's will (or, more frequently, no one's) that makes things happen, but in *The Tempest* events are controlled by the masculine Self.

Prospero's control is not, of course, absolute. He must threaten, cajole, and bargain with the two figures who represent elements within the Self, Ariel and Caliban; and he must deal most watchfully with Miranda, who represents the Other. Finally, he controls both Miranda and Ariel by promising and preparing to let them go; and of Caliban, as we have seen, he may never be completely sure. Miranda is the most interesting case. She is simultaneously a figure of sturdy independence from her father and the obedient actress in a little drama of Prospero's own creation. Take, for instance, the wooing scene. At one level Miranda appears to act entirely on her own behalf, steadily pursuing Ferdinand against what she knows of her father's wishes. When Ferdinand asks her, "What is your name?" she replies, "Miranda. O my father, / I have broken your hest to say so" (III.i.36–37). Miranda's rebellion against her father is a late and stylized but palpable version of the rebellions of other heroines against their fathers: Hermia, Juliet, Desdemona, and Jes-

sica. Like these characters, Miranda organizes her own marriage
with straightforward energy. "Do you love me?" she demands of
Ferdinand, who cannot match her simplicity and speechifies in
response:

> O heaven, O earth, bear witness to this sound,
> And crown what I profess with kind event
> If I speak true! If hollowly, invert
> What best is boded me to mischief! I,
> Beyond all limit of what else i' th' world,
> Do love, prize, honor you.   (III.i.68–73)

Miranda follows up smartly with "My husband, then?" As usual,
we are attracted to the clarity of the heroine's desires, manifested in
the daring clarity of her language.

But Miranda's desires have been if not created by Prospero then
at least anticipated by him. At some level Miranda cannot avoid her
father: he makes use of her desires to serve his own purposes. He
controls the Other by knowing and accepting it. Miranda's readiness for a husband is not a wholly agreeable fact to Prospero, but he
accepts what he cannot change about her and makes the best of it.
Although he cannot keep her from sexual maturity and the con-
sequent abandonment of himself, he can direct her to the husband
who will best serve his own purposes. Some match she must make,
and this match is best for Prospero. Now his grandchildren, as
Gonzalo wonderingly points out, will rule his enemies' land: "Was
Milan thrust from Milan that his issue / Should become kings of
Naples?" (V.i.205–6). Miranda's courtship of Ferdinand simultaneously displays her courageous independence of Prospero and her
complete encirclement by him. Throughout the wooing scene
Prospero stands "behind, unseen," commenting on the action like a
playwright watching his own show: "Poor worm, thou art in-
fected!," he says appreciatively, and "Fair encounter / Of two most
rare affections!" (III.i.31, 74–75). And when the scene is over, it is
Prospero's pronouncement, not the lovers' actions, that determines
our response to what we have seen: "So glad of this as they I cannot
be," he says drily, "But my rejoicing / At nothing can be more"
(III.i.92, 93–94). Our very pleasure in Miranda's success is under
Prospero's control.

Prospero's control of Miranda is comparable to his control of his
Fortune itself. He controls his own Fortune by working with it

instead of fighting it. At the beginning of the play he explains to
Miranda,

> By accident most strange, bountiful Fortune
> (Now my dear lady) hath mine enemies
> Brought to this shore; and by my prescience
> I find my zenith doth depend upon
> A most auspicious star, whose influence
> If now I court not, but omit, my fortunes
> Will ever after droop.   (I.ii.178–84)

Prospero treats his own Fortune as something external to himself,
something he cannot fully control, but of which he can take advantage at the right time. And so he treats Miranda. Prospero's control
of the Other is discreet and respectful. He is conscious of the
possibility that he might fail; he does not bully his daughter but
pays close attention to her responses. When Miranda first sees
Ferdinand, for instance, Prospero offers him to her a little apologet-
ically, as if doubting the adequacy of the young man he has produced. He says,

>   This gallant which thou see'st
> Was in the wrack; and, but he's something stained
> With grief (that's beauty's canker), thou mightst call him
> A goodly person. He hath lost his fellows
> And strays about to find 'em.   (I.ii.416–20)

But Prospero's sidelong glances are lost on Miranda, who declares
flatly, passionately, and in the meter,

>   I might call him
> A thing divine; for nothing natural
> I ever saw so noble.   (I.ii.420–22)

Prospero discovers, through this gentle probing, not so much as an
iamb's distance between his own plans for Miranda and her desires.
Therefore he proceeds.

Prospero's control of the feminine Other, respectful and accom-
modating as it is, diminishes her dramatic significance. In *The
Winter's Tale* the hero abandons control, and the Other, including
the feminine Other, moves more freely. Where the feminine is not
encircled by the consciousness and will of the masculine Self it is
more significant, more interesting, more capable of surprising us.
Miranda is perfect, but unsurprising. She does not create drama

through her comings and goings as Perdita and Hermione do. In this play we must rely for our drama on wholly masculine themes. The plot of *The Tempest* is determined not by the Return of the Feminine but by the masculine-historical question of "Who shall be king?" The story is framed by the power struggle between Prospero and his brother Antonio; within that frame are the political conspiracies that take place on the island. In *The Winter's Tale,* the conflicts are personal rather than political; they come from the tensions between the sexes and the generations rather than from territorial disputes. Leontes imagines that his "brother" has cuckolded him, not that Polixenes threatens his power to rule in Sicily. But in *The Tempest,* Antonio's aggression against Prospero is real and territorial, not imaginary and sexual. What little plot there is to *The Tempest,* both comic and serious, is always a version of the struggle for power. Stephano, Gonzalo, Sebastian, and Antonio are all usurpers or would-be usurpers of Prospero's power; and of course Prospero himself has usurped Caliban's position on the island. Caliban will not let us forget it:

> This island's mine, by Sycorax my mother,
> . . . I am all the subjects that you have,
> Which first was mine own king.   (I.ii.333, 343–44)

Even Ferdinand is seen as a usurper—as indeed he is, at the metaphorical level. As the representative of the next generation, he usurps the power of the fathers whether he means to or not. When Ferdinand claims to be King of Naples, Prospero tells him,

> Thou dost here usurp
> The name thou ow'st not, and hast put theyself
> Upon this island as a spy, to win it
> From me, the lord on't.   (I.ii.456–59)

Questions of power are behind almost every scene in the play.

Where Prospero takes control and fights for power, Leontes confesses his powerlessness over himself and the events of his life. In *The Tempest* our desirelessness makes us powerful; in *The Winter's Tale* our abandonment of ourselves *to* our desires ultimately brings us fulfillment. Major elements of these plays—Time, Space, and the image of Nature—determine and are determined by the alternatives each play offers. Where the desireless Self is in command, the unities of Time and Space are observed and Nature is neutral; when we abandon ourselves to our desire for the Other, Time moves erratically, Nature is kind and cruel by turns, and we are swept from one place to the other ready or not. Let us begin with the element of Time.

In *The Winter's Tale* our sense of time is acute, whereas in *The Tempest* it is negligible. In *The Tempest* time seems to pass smoothly, evenly; it slips by without our noticing. In *The Winter's Tale,* however, it moves fitfully—now fast, now slow. Our sense of time is mostly a matter of dramatic expectations. When our expectations are many and urgent, time moves quickly because we want to see if they are fulfilled. In the first three acts of *The Winter's Tale* we are chock full of expectations (of disaster). Then, abruptly, we lose them all. After Hermione's apparent death, everything seems irrelevant and time moves so slowly that we are in danger of becoming bored. Toward the end of the play our expectations speed time up once again as we anticipate first the reunion of Leontes and Perdita and then, during the statue scene, the reunion of Leontes with his wife. In *The Tempest* we have much more moderate and steady expectations. We never expect disaster or transcendent happiness; we merely expect to see Prospero's plans succeed. And we do, one after another. Prospero does not plan anything so risky and important as the death or resurrection of the feminine, so we need never feel intense anticipation. Prospero's constant attention to his schemes—his conferences with Ariel, his adjustments and responses to events—reveal the difficulty of imposing his will over the island. But the audience knows that he will overcome this difficulty, and so does he. The passage of time does not imply peaks and troughs of dramatic experience as it does in *The Winter's Tale.*

The suspenselessness of *The Tempest* makes time not only move more evenly, but matter less. Coleridge has compared the play to "a finished piece of music": "still preparing, still inviting, and still gratifying."[8] The important word here is "finished." Coleridge may merely have meant "polished" or "accomplished," but the word also means "ended," "over." *The Tempest* should be heard playing all at once in the mind. It is more of a spatial experience than a temporal one; its situations seem to occur simultaneously rather than in sequence. This is why the inadequately happy ending is in fact adequate; we have not really been waiting for the end. Our satisfaction has been steady and continuous; we have not been particularly eager for outcomes. We scan *The Tempest* like a painting, noticing what it includes rather than how it proceeds. It includes Caliban and Ariel, a dead wife and a blooming daughter. In *The Winter's Tale* we see such elements as Leontes's Calibanism, Hermione's death, and Perdita's triumph sequentially. *The Tempest* is like a great mandala in which loss and renewal, creation and destruction are all taking place at once. *The Winter's Tale,* by contrast, seems to fit the pattern of the Judeo-Christian myth: we lose paradise and then, after an unimaginably long wait and against the odds, we regain it.

Prospero is spared the long wait for the gifts of Time because he commands an alternative Space. When Leontes loses Hermione, he can only wait, passively and without expectations, for her return. He is dependent on time and the feminine, neither of which can be controlled. But when Prospero loses his dukedom, he is removed to a place outside time that *can* be controlled. If the space that Prospero rules is in some sense an interior space, it is nevertheless a place where power is actively seized and wielded. Prospero does not waste his time, as Leontes does, but always rules. In *The Winter's Tale,* the happy ending resolves the anxious wait for the fruits of time; in *The Tempest,* we are in a place where resolution follows resolution without preliminary anxiety. There is so little unfulfillment on the island that the happiness at the end seems quite unspectacular.

The limitations of Prospero's alternative are obvious: to the extent that the island is an interior landscape, Prospero's powerful autonomy approaches solipsism. But that autonomy, that self-rule, finally is strong enough to lure the outside world onto his own island. Prospero's command of his own body and spirit gives him magical powers over other people and events, and in the end he uses these powers to reestablish himself in a social context. We are glad that he does so, glad that he avoids permanent residence among projections and emanations of Self; but what *The Tempest* invites us to contemplate is the order and harmony that Prospero enjoys during his island reign. If the gift of Time is renewal, the gift of Space is detachment; in *The Tempest* our detachment from grief and desire frees up our responses to the world as it is.

Nature in *The Tempest* is an image of precisely this—of "the world as it is." It is not an agent by which our desires are frustrated or fulfilled; it is merely itself. In *The Winter's Tale,* Nature alternates between creative and destructive relationships to man; like the feminine, it is ultimately beneficent, however changeable along the way, however capable of seeming, at least, to betray us. It sends winter and spring, storms and sunshine. In *The Tempest,* Nature is constant and neutral, and what sense we have of its mutability is mostly an illusion perceived or created by men.

In *The Winter's Tale* we begin by being almost unconscious of Nature; we only know what season it is in Sicily because Mamillus tells his mother, "A sad tale's best for winter" (II.i.25). In Bohemia, however, we are acutely conscious of the season, which is summer. We are amazed by the serenity and abundance and beauty of Nature in Bohemia. But Bohemia is also the haunt of the appalling bear who rushes out of nowhere to eat Antigonus. Nature is full of changes here. In *The Tempest,* by contrast, Nature is everywhere the same. For one thing it is always the same mild season in this play; the island's geographical location is near Bermuda. Nor do we have the alternations that are found in Bohemia between creative Nature, associated with feasting and courting, and destructive Nature, the agent of death by bear and storm. In *The Tempest* such distinctions are either the illusion or the creation of the human mind. Nature per se, which we see when we look through Caliban's eyes, is a constant, unified presence, indifferent to man and highly particularized. Through Caliban we see a world in which Nature does not alter according to human desires or human nature. Nature parallels human life, never purposively thwarting or satisfying us. Caliban tells Prospero,

> When thou cam'st first,
> . . . [I] showed thee all the qualities o' th' isle,
> The fresh springs, brine pits, barren place and fertile.
>
> (I.ii.334, 339–40)

In *The Tempest* what matters are the inherent qualities of natural things, not their positive or negative charge. Brininess and barrenness are as noteworthy in this play as freshness and fertility. Nature is interesting whether or not it serves our purposes.

In contrast are the illusions of the court party shortly after their landing:

Adrian The air breathes upon us here most sweetly.
Sebastian As if it had lungs, and rotten ones.
Antonio Or as 'twere perfumed by a fen.
Gonzalo Here is everything advantageous to life.

> *Antonio*   True, save means to live.
> *Sebastian*   Of that there's none, or little.
> *Gonzalo*   How lush and lusty the grass looks! How green!
> *Antonio*   The ground indeed is tawny.   (II.i.49–56)

We cannot discover anything about the island from listening to *these* voices. It is green and sweet to the optimist, foul and barren to the cynics. The optimist is a little foolish; on the other hand, Antonio and Sebastian are clearly projecting their own disagreeableness onto the island.

Prospero, too, projects himself on the island, although with Prospero it is a matter not of what he sees but of what he creates. His most notable creations are the storm and the wedding masque, destructive and creative nature, just as in *The Winter's Tale*. But whereas the wedding masque is indeed a vision of fertility that corresponds to the harvest feast in *The Winter's Tale* and the storm can be compared to the one that sinks Antigonus's ship, these are not the manifestations of Nature itself in *The Tempest*. They are only Prospero's *versions* of Nature.

It is through Caliban that we feel Nature's real presence, a presence that is without reference to man:

> I prithee let me bring thee where crabs grow;
> And I with my long nails will dig thee pignuts,
> Show thee a jay's nest, and instruct thee how
> To snare the nimble marmoset. I'll bring thee
> To clust'ring filberts, and sometimes I'll get thee
> Young scamels from the rock. Wilt thou go with me?
>   (II.ii.169–74)

Of course we *will* go with him, seduced as thoroughly by his pignuts and crabapples as we ever are by Perdita's daffodils, violets, and lilies. The scamels and filberts, the jay and the marmoset are neither beautiful in themselves nor set in beautiful language. They are useful to man, but the excitement they generate is out of proportion to their utility. We have not, after all, been worrying over how the shipwrecked group will feed itself. *The Tempest* is not *Robinson Crusoe*. The items Caliban names are exciting because they imply a vast and varied number of nameable objects in nature, another world, something we can know but not possess.

This kind of nature is at least as important to *The Tempest* as the sunny-stormy kind of nature, the nature that alternately gives and takes away. Nothing in *The Tempest* either dies or is born; Nature neither gives nor takes away. Even in the wedding masque we get no sense of a "great creative Nature" that might shower us with gifts; Iris invokes the realm of the fertility goddess with references to things that are cold, hard, and sterile:

> Thy turfy mountains, where live nibbling sheep,
> And flat meads thatched with stover, them to keep;
> Thy banks with pionèd and twillèd brims,
> Which spongy April at thy hest betrims
> To make cold nymphs chaste crowns; and thy broom groves
> Whose shadow the dismissèd bachelor loves,
> Being lasslorn; thy pole-clipt vineyard;
> And thy sea-marge, sterile and rocky-hard.   (IV.i.62–69)

This Nature is one onto which we cannot project our emotional-spiritual states; but it is no less interesting and exciting for all its obduracy. In the absence of urgent desire we have time to be interested in a Nature that is external to our own affairs.

All the action of *The Tempest* takes place on the island, but of course everything that happens on the island refers backwards and forwards over time to life in Italy. Antonio's rebellion in the past and Miranda's marriage in the future define the boundaries of Prospero's control over events. These things are beyond him. The stability of the island is surrounded by a sea of mutability; and at the end of the play the entire cast is about to launch itself on that sea. This is generally seen either as a triumph for the life-force itself over a place of deathly stasis and order or as a defeat and loss for Prospero. Both views, to my mind, miss the mark. Prospero's renunciation of the island and of his power should seem neither bitter nor triumphant to us. It should seem impressive, like a wild wind or a tidal wave; it should seem large, *enormous,* but neither good nor bad. It should seem exciting, like Nature itself.

In "The Sea and the Mirror" Auden has his Prospero say, "Ariel, Ariel, How I shall miss you";[9] but we do not hear this sad note anywhere in Shakespeare's play. Prospero tells Ariel only "to the elements/ Be free, and fare thou well!" (V.i.318–19). Nor is there sadness in the famous renunciation speech:

> Ye elves of hills, brooks, standing lakes, and groves,
> And ye that on the sands with printless foot
> Do chase the ebbing Neptune, and do fly him
> When he comes back; you demi-puppets that
> By moonshine do the green sour ringlets make,
> Whereof the ewe not bites; and you whose pastime
> Is to make midnight mushrumps, that rejoice

To hear the solemn curfew; by whose aid
(Weak masters though ye be) I have bedimmed
The noontide sun, called forth the mutinous winds,
And 'twixt the green sea and the azured vault
Set roaring war; to the dread rattling thunder
Have I given fire and rifted Jove's stout oak
With his own bolt; the strong-based promontory
Have I made shake and by the spurs plucked up
The pine and cedar; graves at my command
Have waked their sleepers, oped, and let 'em forth
By my so potent art. But this rough magic
I here abjure; and when I have required
Some heavenly music (which even now I do)
To work mine end upon their senses that
This airy charm is for, I'll break my staff,
Bury it certain fathoms in the earth,
And deeper than did ever plummet sound
I'll drown my book.   (V.i.33–57)

This speech is a display not of emotion but of power. Prospero's renunciation of control is still a demonstration of control, perhaps the most impressive of the play. It begins as a formal invocation and turns into a series of boasts: "I have bedimmed / The noontide sun, . . . the strong-based promontory / Have I made shake and by the spurs plucked up / The pine and cedar." Then, without any transition or explanation, Prospero announces, "But this rough magic / I here abjure." Because the reason for Prospero's renunciation is hidden, the renunciation itself seems as huge an act of will as the shaking of the promontory or the dimming of the sun. Our sense of Prospero as the agent of his own Fortune is unchanged; he is not suffering his renunciation, he is *doing* it. "I'll break my staff," he says with the deliberate strength of an advancing battleship, "I'll drown my book." It is clearly an impertinence to focus on the pain Prospero may be feeling at this moment.

And yet the return to Milan is very moving to us. This is not, I think, because we imagine that Prospero is making the choice for life over death. As opposed to the small and manageable island, Milan certainly *represents* the flux of life; but the idea of Milan does not have much resonance for us. Milan has not been made to seem like life with a capital L. The return to Milan is moving neither as loss nor as recovery, although it contains elements of both. It is quite simply a very large change; what is moving perhaps is that Prospero can make such a change without being driven by pain or

attracted by pleasure. Prospero moves toward the transition for no
other reason than that it is coming toward him. He neither fears nor
desires it. Behind this speech is the great, inevitable transition we all
must undergo in death; Prospero both chooses and accepts his
return as we hope to choose and accept our own death.

In his own way, then, Prospero, like the characters in *The Winter's Tale,* triumphs over mutability. He chooses to leave his island
at the moment when he must leave it. Necessity and desire are one
and the same to him, as they are for all of us when we are in a state
of grace. The characters in *The Winter's Tale* submit to change and
loss willy-nilly, and finally their losses are made good; Prospero
chooses his loss, and the act of choice is itself redemptive.

In *The Winter's Tale,* the reunited family is a poignant image
of human happiness bounded on either side by death and heightened
by the sense of wasted time. In the recent past is Hermione's supposed death, and in the not-so-distant future is her real one. In *The
Tempest,* where there is no wife to die or come back to life, we have
no sense of death as a boundary. We are already living *with* death,
not in reprieve from it. It is a continuous fact—not, as in *The
Winter's Tale,* an enemy who is now triumphant, now in retreat.
Death in *The Tempest* is felt as a recurrent dissolution, as when Prospero's own imagination of harmony fades at the end of the wedding
masque. He explains,

> Our revels now are ended. These our actors,
> As I foretold you, were all spirits and
> Are melted into air, into thin air;
> And, like the baseless fabric of this vision,
> The cloud-capped towers, the gorgeous palaces,
> The solemn temples, the great globe itself,
> Yea, all which it inherit, shall dissolve,
> And, like this insubstantial pageant faded,
> Leave not a rack behind.   (IV.i.148–56)

Death is a kind of deliquescence in *The Tempest,* familiar as the
departure of a mood or an inspiration. The ending of *The Tempest,*
similarly, is not an emphatic finale but a resonant moment, orga-
nized and endured by a hero who knows his own death. Such a
figure appeared to Shakespeare in the image of a man who has lost
his wife forever.

Notes

Notes

Chapter One

1. Kate Millett, *Sexual Politics* (Garden City, N.Y.: Doubleday, 1970).

2. Juliet Dusinberre, *Shakespeare and the Nature of Women* (London: Macmillan, 1975).

3. Patricia Southard Gourlav. " 'O my most sacred lady': Female Metaphor in *The Winter's Tale*," *English Literary Renaissance* 5, no. 3, p. 378.

4. Coppelia Kahn, "*The Taming of the Shrew*: Shakespeare's Mirror of Marriage," *Modern Language Studies* 5 (1975), pp. 88–102.

5. Myra Glazer Schotz, "The Great Unwritten Story: Mothers and Daughters in Shakespeare," in C. N. Davison and E. M. Broner, eds., *The Lost Tradition: Mothers and Daughters in Literature* (New York: Ungar, 1980), pp. 44–54.

6. All quotations from Shakespeare's plays are taken from *The Complete Signet Classic Shakespeare*, Sylvan Barnet gen. ed. (New York: Harcourt Brace Jovanovich, 1972). Prose quotations do not always occupy the same number of lines in this book as in the *Signet Classic* edition.

7. Two examples are Edith Williams's "In Defense of Lady Macbeth" (*Shakespeare Quarterly* 24, no. 1 [1973], pp. 221–23), and Lynn Veach Sadler's "The Three Guises of Lady Macbeth" (*College Language Assoc. Journal* 19 [1975], pp. 10–19).

8. Leslie Fiedler, *The Stranger in Shakespeare* (New York: Stein and Day, 1973, p. 61).

9. Maynard Mack, "The Jacobean Shakespeare: Some Observations on the Construction of the Tragedies," reprinted in the Signet *Othello*, ed. Alvin Kernan (New York: New American Library, 1963), p. 226.

10. *Ibid.*, p. 234.

11. Simone de Beauvoir, *The Second Sex* (New York: Bantam, 1961), p. xvi.

12. *Ibid.*, p. xvii.

13. Linda Fitz, "Egyptian Queens and Male Reviewers: Sexist Attitudes in *Antony and Cleopatra* Criticism," *Shakespeare Quarterly* 28, no. 3 (1977), p. 313.

14. *Ibid.*, p. 314.

15. Carol Thomas Neely, "Women and Men in *Othello:* 'What should such a fool/Do with so good a woman?'," *Shakespeare Studies* 10 (1978) p. 134.

16. *Ibid.,* p. 154.

17. *Ibid.,* pp. 136, 145, 148.

18. Fiedler, *The Stranger in Shakespeare,* p. 44.

19. Mack, "The Jacobean Shakespeare," p. 235.

20. E. C. Mason, "Satire on Women and Sex in Elizabethan Tragedy," *English Studies* 31 (1950), p. 8.

21. Robert Heilbrun, "Manliness in the Tragedies: Dramatic Variations," in Edward A. Bloom, ed., *Shakespeare 1564–1964* (Providence, R.I.: Brown Univ. Press, 1964), p. 24.

22. Alfred Harbage, *As They Liked It* (New York: Macmillan, 1947), p. 169.

23. *Ibid.,* p. 170.

24. Fitz, "Egyptian Queens and Male Reviewers," p. 304–5.

25. Lauren J. Mills, *The Tragedies of Shakespeare's "Antony and Cleopatra"* (Bloomington, Ind.: Indiana Univ. Press, 1964) and Daniel Stempel, "The Transmigration of the Crocodile," *Shakespeare Quarterly* 7, no. 1 (1956), pp. 59–72.

26. Sigmund Freud, "Instincts and Their Vicissitudes," reprinted in John Rickman, ed., *A General Selection from the Works of Sigmund Freud* (New York: Doubleday, 1957), p. 73.

27. Fiedler, *The Stranger in Shakespeare,* p. 103.

28. David P. Young, *Something of Great Constancy* (New Haven, Conn.: Yale Univ. Press, 1966), p. 183.

29. Kahn, *"The Taming of the Shrew,"* p. 98.

30. *Ibid.,* p. 99.

31. *Ibid.,* p. 97.

32. C. L. Barber, *Shakespeare's Festive Comedy: A Study of Dramatic Form and Its Relation to Social Custom* (Princeton, N.J.: Princeton Univ. Press, 1959), p. 8.

33. Dusinberre, *Shakespeare and the Nature of Women,* p. 114.

34. J. Dennis Huston, " 'When I came to Man's Estate': *Twelfth Night* and Problems of Identity," *Modern Language Quarterly* 33, no. 3 (1972), p. 274.

35. Clara Claiborne Park, "As We Like It: How a Girl Can Be Smart and Still Popular," *The American Scholar* 42 (1973), pp. 268, 276.

36. Barber, *Shakespeare's Festive Comedy,* p. 231.

Chapter Two

1. John Danby, *Poets on Fortune's Hill* (London: Faber and Faber, 1952), p. 148.

2. *Ibid.*, p. 150.

3. *Ibid.*

4. Linda Fitz, "Egyptian Queens and Male Reviewers: Sexist Attitudes in *Antony and Cleopatra* Criticism," *Shakespeare Quarterly* 28, no. 3 (1977), pp. 314–15.

5. Carol Thomas Neely, "Women and Men in *Othello:* 'What should such a fool/Do with so good a woman?,'" *Shakespeare Studies* 10 (1978), p. 134.

6. A. C. Bradley, *Oxford Lectures on Poetry* (London: Macmillan, 1909), pp. 283–84.

7. Norman Mailer, *Advertisements for Myself* (New York: G. P. Putnam's Sons, 1966), p. 16.

8. Robert Garis, *The Dickens Theater* (London: Oxford Univ. Press, 1965), p. 23.

Chapter Three

1. Robert Ornstein, *The Moral Vision of Jacobean Drama* (Madison, Wisc.: Univ. of Wisconsin Press, 1960), p. 17.

2. Bridget Lyons, "The Iconography of Ophelia," *English Literary History* 44 (1977), p. 65.

3. G. F. Bradby, *The Problems of "Hamlet"* (New York: Haskell House, 1965), p. 21.

4. *Ibid.*, p. 22.

5. Leo Kirschbaum, "Hamlet and Ophelia," *Philological Quarterly* 35, no. 4 (1965), p. 388.

6. A. C. Bradley, *Shakespearean Tragedy* (London: Macmillan, 1929), p. 16.

7. Harley Granville-Barker, *Prefaces to Shakespeare* (London: Sidgwick and Jackson, 1939), p. 284.

8. Baldwin Maxwell, "Hamlet's Mother," *Shakespeare Quarterly* 15 (Spring 1964), p. 237.

9. Bradby, *The Problems of "Hamlet,"* p. 26.

10. Kirschbaum, "Hamlet and Ophelia," p. 378.

11. Bradby, *The Problems of "Hamlet,"* p. 20.

12. Ornstein, *The Moral Vision of Jacobean Drama,* p. 234.

13. Robert Heilbrun, "Manliness in the Tragedies: Dramatic Variations," in Edward A. Bloom, ed., *Shakespeare 1564–1964* (Providence, R.I.: Brown Univ. Press, 1964), p. 24.

14. Lionel Abel, *Metatheater: A New View of Dramatic Form* (New York: Hill and Wang, 1963), p. 112.

Chapter Four

1. Robert Heilbrun, "Manliness in the Tragedies: Dramatic Variations," in Edward A. Bloom, ed., *Shakespeare 1564–1964*, (Providence, R.I.: Brown Univ. Press, 1964), p. 24.

2. Stanley Cavell, "Epistemology and Tragedy: A Reading of *Othello*," *Daedalus* 108, no. 3 (1979), p. 40.

3. O. J. Campbell, *Shakespeare's Satire* (New York: Oxford Univ. Press, 1943), p. 211.

4. Jarold Ramsey, "The Perversion of Manliness in *Macbeth*," *Studies in English Literature 1500–1900* 13 (1973), p. 290.

5. Jan Kott, *Shakespeare Our Contemporary* (Garden City, N.Y.: Doubleday, 1964), pp. 206–7.

6. *Ibid.*, pp. 208–10.

7. John Hollander, *The Story of the Night: Studies in Shakespeare's Major Tragedies* (Lincoln, Neb.: Univ. of Nebraska Press, 1963), p. 66.

Chapter Five

1. Charles Frey, "The Sweetest Rose: *As You Like It* as Comedy of Reconciliation," *New York Literary Forum* 1 (1978), p. 167.

2. Leslie Fiedler, *The Stranger in Shakespeare* (New York: Stein and Day, 1973), p. 30.

3. *Ibid.*, p. 145.

4. Stanley Cavell, "Epistemology and Tragedy: A Reading of *Othello*," *Daedalus* 108, no. 3 (1979), p. 40.

5. Northrop Frye, *A Natural Perspective* (New York: Harcourt, Brace and World, 1965), p. 8.

6. D. H. Lawrence, *The Rainbow* (New York: Viking Press, 1961), p. 324.

7. Frey, "The Sweetest Rose," p. 174.

8. Frye, *A Natural Perspective*, p. 78.

9. Sherman Hawkins, "The Two Worlds of Shakespearean Comedy," *Shakespeare Studies* 3 (1967), p. 69.

10. Anne Barton, "*As You Like It* and *Twelfth Night:* Shakespeare's Sense of an Ending," in Malcolm Bradbury and David Palmer, eds., *Stratford-upon-Avon Studies 14: Shakespearean Comedy* (New York: Crane, Russak & Company, 1972), p. 169.

11. Frye, *A Natural Perspective*, p. 79.

12. Helene Moglen, "Disguise and Development: The Self and Society in *Twelfth Night*," *Literature and Psychology* 13 (1973).

13. Frey, "The Sweetest Rose," p. 167.

14. Moglen, "Disguise and Development," p. 15.

15. *Ibid.*, p. 17.

16. Hawkins, "The Two Worlds," p. 68.

17. *Ibid.*, p. 69.

18. Moglen, "Disguise and Development," p. 16.

Chapter Six

1. In *The Stranger in Shakespeare* (New York: Stein and Day, 1973), Leslie Fiedler lists these and other insults on p. 58.

2. Zdenek Stribrny, "*Henry V* and History," in Arnold Kettle, ed., *Shakespeare in a Changing World* (New York: International Publishers, 1964), p. 96.

3. Michael Goldman, *Shakespeare and the Energies of Drama* (Princeton, N.J.: Princeton Univ. Press, 1972), p. 57.

4. *Ibid.*

5. *Ibid.*, p. 73.

6. Jan Kott, *Shakespeare Our Contemporary* (New York: Doubleday, 1966), pp. 10–11.

7. Coppelia Kahn, *Man's Estate: Male Identity in Shakespeare* (Berkeley: Univ. of California Press, 1980), p. 47.

8. Goldman, *Shakespeare and the Energies of Drama*, pp. 70–71.

Chapter Seven

1. Northrop Frye, *A Natural Perspective* (New York: Harcourt, Brace and World, 1965), p. 87–88.

2. *Ibid.*, p. 122.

3. John Taylor, "The Patience of *The Winter's Tale*," *Essays in Criticism* 23, no. 4 (1973), p. 348.

4. W. H. Auden, "The Sea and the Mirror," in *Collected Poems* (New York: Random House, 1976), p. 312.

5. Leslie Fiedler, *The Stranger in Shakespeare* (New York: Stein and Day, 1973), p. 250.

6. Taylor, "The Patience of *The Winter's Tale*," pp. 345–46.

7. *Ibid.*, p. 346.

8. Thomas Middleton Rayser, ed., *Coleridge's Shakespearean Criticism* (Cambridge, Mass.: Harvard Univ. Press, 1930), vol. 2, p. 178.

9. Auden, "The Sea and the Mirror," in *Collected Poems*, p. 316.

Index

Index